THE STRANGLER FIG
AND OTHER TALES

THE STRANGLER FIG
AND OTHER TALES

Field Notes of a Conservationist

MARY A. HOOD

ALTAMIRA PRESS
A Division of Rowman & Littlefield Publishers, Inc.
Walnut Creek • Lanham • New York • Toronto • Oxford

ALTAMIRA PRESS
A division of Rowman & Littlefield Publishers, Inc.
1630 North Main Street, #367
Walnut Creek, California 94596
www.altamirapress.com

Rowman & Littlefield Publishers, Inc.
A wholly owned subsidiary of The Rowman & Littlefield Publishing Group, Inc.
4501 Forbes Boulevard, Suite 200
Lanham, Maryland 20706

PO Box 317
Oxford
OX2 9RU, UK

British Library Cataloguing in Publication Information Available

Library of Congress Cataloging-in-Publication Data

Hood, Mary A., 1944-
    The strangler fig and other tales : field notes of a
conservationist / Mary A. Hood.
        p. cm.
    Includes bibliographical references (p.   ).
    ISBN 0-7591-0676-2 (hardcover : alk. paper) — ISBN 0-7591-0677-0
(pbk. : alk. paper)
    1. Nature conservation. 2. Endangered ecosystems. 3. Human
ecology. 4. Hood, Mary A., 1944—Travel. I. Title.
    QH75.H659 2004
    333.95—dc22

2004003423
Printed in the United States of America

∞™ The paper used in this publication meets the minimum requirements of American National Standard for Information Sciences—Permanence of Paper for Printed Library Materials, ANSI/NISO Z39.48-1992.

CONTENTS

༄

Preface

T HE WRITINGS IN THIS TRAVEL MEMOIR are about places of great natural beauty and biological importance. These places have forests such as tropical and temperate rainforests, temperate deciduous forests, boreal forests and pine forests; deserts; wetlands like marshes, swamps, and bogs; and grasslands such as temperate prairies, steppe lands, and savannas. Like a journey, the book begins at home and ends at home. What better way of writing about places than through the format of journey, for the stories that define our lives have often been journeys. The oldest written stories were journeys: *Beowulf, The Odyssey, The History of Herodotus, The Travels of Marco Polo.* Some are elaborate tales of adventure, struggle, and conquest, some are quests, and some, just descriptions of peoples and places in the form of natural histories, but they are fundamentally travel stories and journeys. Our nation's early nature writings—the expeditions of Louis and Clark, the travels of William Bartram—took the form of journey. Clearly, journey is one of our most basic and powerful metaphors and the travel tale, an effective way of writing about nature and place.

To write a travel book, the element of place is essential. But *place* is so much more than a tangible thing. In a broader sense, it is what we know. It is the landscape of the internal, the rooms of feelings and delight, the halls of desire and fear, the closets of ego and selfishness, the porches of imagination, the kitchens of social connection. A sense of place probably starts with self. The youngest infant has an innate sense of self, a tiny terrain but nevertheless a place, and if this self develops normally, it becomes separate from mother and expands from self to other-than-self. Like a pebble in a lake, the ripples grow and a sense of place expands. Place broadens to home, to the bed we sleep in, the chair we sit in, the table we eat from, and to the creatures we share our immediate space with, those we recognize as living and having sensitivities, our sisters and brothers, our dog. These are our first connections.

In our modern industrial society we have almost lost the connection to animal species other than our own. Once place included large domesticated animals like cattle or goats or wild ones like deer, bear, or buffalo. Narrower today, our interactions with other animal species often mean only pets or pests. As we grow and our sense of place broadens, it extends to friends and village, to schoolmates and school, to coworkers and community, and finally includes the world. Perhaps the final evolution of place may be to move out of the center, to redefine the narrow self place in a different context, from a different position. Mystics, Buddhists, and some enlightened persons may even attain the ability to move themselves out of place completely.

David Abram in *The Spell of the Sensuous* (1996, 137) asks "How did Western civilization become so estranged from nonhuman nature, so oblivious to the presence of other animals and the earth that our current lifestyles and activities contribute daily to the destruction of whole ecosystems—whole forests, river valleys, oceans—and to the extinction of countless species?" He answers that we might recapture our connection to nature by moving out of the center and we might do this through language. Many nature writers, perhaps best illustrated by Linda Hogan's *Dwellings: A Spiritual History of the Living World* (1995), try to do this. They try to move us out of the egocentric world of self as the center to a broader place by exploration "in the landscape of language." For just as language is a tool of organizing not only the physical world but our thoughts and our abstractions, language is also the means of connecting. Language is one of the means by which we make place.

We often define ourselves on the basis of place. Place is home or where we came into being. We are Americans, Floridians, southerners, New Yorkers, identities that connect us to a geographical region as well as to a group of others from the same locale. How important such identifications are, for without them, we would be alien, refugee, homeless, rootless, detached, terms that reflect the horrors of not having place. For all the value we put on individuality and independence, we are creatures of connection, connected to our homes, to each other, and to place.

We conserve places in many ways. Memory is one means. Even when our most cherished places are gone, we can return to them. We can retreat to a childhood woods, attend a dance, meet a deceased friend, walk along a shore that is no longer there, all through memory. Memory is the river on which the fluidity of place may float. Memory can sometimes be flawed and for all my struggle for clarity and truth, memory is not always error free. I hope any errors are minor. These essays are, in part, an act of conservation, an attempt to preserve the places I have experienced and care about. Writing through memory, I try to preserve these places.

We can also conserve places in a practical way by setting them aside, making sure they are not destroyed. In this way, the next generations may have natural and beautiful places. The Nature Conservancy preserves wilderness lands and unique habitats, the U.S. National Wildlife Refuges (NWR) preserve certain lands for birds and other wildlife, historical societies preserve homes and buildings, botanical organizations preserve species of native and endangered plants, and the list goes on and on of the many organizations involved in preserving our biological and historical heritage. All over the world, preservation efforts are occurring because it is a universal human need to save and cherish what we value. E. O. Wilson (2002) in *The Future of Life* and through his work with numerous conservation organizations advocates the urgency of conserving places that need special protection because of human encroachment. Conservation is an intrinsic act of valuing. In the process of conserving, we give value to a place and help others recognize its worth.

Throughout the book, I use the term *we* to refer to my traveling companions. Sometimes the *we* refers to my best friend and traveling companion, Darleen Abbott. We have been traveling the world together for twelve years and for two old dames, we most definitely get around. Sometimes the *we* refers to a group of strangers on an ecotour, sometimes to a group of friends, sometimes to a group of fellow scientists, birders, plant lovers, or nature lovers. It is not my intention to ignore them or imply that they are not important as individuals but for the sake of simplicity, I refer to the folks in my traveling groups as a collective *we*.

Finally, I would suggest that the book is about a broader sense of place and that means connection, the kind of connection that implies a reverence and respect for other. I hope that as a poet and a scientist and using the language of both, I have made some of those vital connections.

I thank my friend and colleague, Mary Rogers, for her help and encouragement, and Rosalie Robertson. Thanks also go to all the members of the Florida Native Plant Society–Long Leaf Pine Chapter, the Francis M. Weston Audubon Society, and all the other Audubon chapters and bird clubs nationwide.

THE BEGINNINGS OF
AN ECOLOGICAL ETHICS

Freshwater Swamp with Bald Cypress (Taxodium distichum). *Artwork by Eric Hinote.*

Louisiana: The Barge

I

T HANKSGIVING WEEK IN SOUTHERN LOUISIANA signals the beginning of
deer hunting season, and some years ago my father had planned a hunting
trip along the Tangipahoa River. He was up before daybreak fixing breakfast for his hunter friends and their sons, and the smells of sausage, biscuits, and
coffee drifted through the house. As I awoke to those wonderful smells floating
into my room, I heard the voices of the men gathered around the kitchen table,
and recognized this as an ancient ritual, this gathering and telling of tales before
the hunt.

My father began his story of a duck hunt by describing a couple of double-
barreled shotguns he and my brother had taken with them on a hunting trip into
the swamps and marshes around Lake Maurepas. Lakes Maurepas and Pontchar-
train are connected by a bayou called Pass Manchac. Part of the huge wetlands
that stretch along the southeastern coast of Louisiana, it falls in the region known
as the Mississippi alluvial plains. South of the lakes, the Mississippi River snakes
its way through the urban lowlands of New Orleans and empties into the Gulf of
Mexico. West of the lakes, Bayou Lafouche and the Mississippi River form a triangle that encompasses a large expanse of swamps and marshes. In the northernmost part of the triangle are the freshwater swamps of Lac Des Allemands and
Lake Salvador. Then further south it becomes brackish marshes. Even farther
south the Barataria Bay system, with its thousands of acres of salt marsh, spreads
out towards the gulf like a giant golden meadow cut by meandering tidal creeks.

These lakes, bayous, rivers, swamps, and marshes are part of the Mississippi
River delta system, a lowland created by the giving hands of the silt-laden river
and the watery fingers of the tides. From a cycle of deposition and erosion, these
wetlands began as the slow accumulation of sediment from river overflow. As the

river changed course many times over thousands of years, it formed oxbow lakes, channels, and bayous. It is now a land dotted with waterways, a land influenced by the tidal saltwater of the gulf from the south and the flow of freshwater rivers from the north. An edge land where sea meets river, it is a place where huge flocks of migrating ducks and geese overwinter in the marshes and along the lakes. Pintails, widgeons, mallards, gadwalls, teal, and snow geese speckle the waterways, making it a favorite spot for hunters.

My father continued his story of the hunt. He and my brother, who was ten at the time, and his new dog, a golden retriever named Ginger, left early one cold winter morning, boat in tow, for Manchac. The town of Manchac, next to the pass, is in the middle of a freshwater swamp. The interstate connecting New Orleans to Hammond passes over Manchac, but the exit there goes straight down into town and dead-ends at the edge of a marsh. The interstate was built fifteen feet above ground and took ten years to complete. Steel pilings had to be driven hundreds of feet down through the soft marshy soil to reach hard ground in order to make the road stable. These were all bits of information that my father related, perhaps to remind everyone that the marsh was a place that did not accommodate roads or people very well.

He said that driving along the interstate from Hammond to New Orleans was a little like flying over the swamp in an airplane just at tree level. Out of the car window, the tops of cottonwood, willow, cypress, and tupelo gum flashed by like a pen-and-ink mural. Many of the branches were bare in winter, but in spring the canopy becomes lush and green again. Below the road, thick mats of water hyacinth covered the bayous, giving the waterways a grassy textured look. Farther off in the distance, on the top of the tallest tree, a great blue heron sat so still he could have been a wrought iron statue. White egrets traveling in big lazy Vs drifted across the sky. In dotted lines that slowly changed from Vs to Ls to Ns, they could have been sending cryptic messages in sky letters.

Although Manchac has one of the best seafood restaurants in south Louisiana (a place called Meddendourf's), it is scarcely a town. It has a gas station, a few shacks badly in need of paint, a couple of fish camps, and a boat launch. The boat launch next to Cecil's Fish Camp was where the two hunters put in. They backed the boat down the ramp, loaded their gear, and took off for the backwaters.

Morning on the backwaters and bayous of Louisiana can be magical. Dark brown tree trunks along the banks widen as they reach water, and from their branches Spanish moss hangs down like gray tapestry. The trees could be gypsies in long flowing skirts or whirling dervishes or women turned to stone by an evil witch, and at any moment they might break the spell, return to their former selves, and dance off into the swamp. When sunlight breaks through the branches and falls on the surface of the brown, nutrient-rich waters, the water sparkles like blinking lights. Bream and bluegill leap from the waters, making rippled circles, and fall back into the circles, making more circles, until the whole surface of the water is an undulating pool of circles. Like molasses, the waters are rich with the sweet thickness of decomposition. And the smell of the bayou is exhilarating. A mixture of rotting leaves and new green growth, there is always something dying but also something new and growing in the swamp. The blend of opposites is intoxicating.

The two hunters and their dog motored across Lake Maurepas toward the shore where the Tickfaw and Amite Rivers joined the lake. There were duck blinds and some protection from the wind, which often turned bitter on late December days. They set up camp, then located one of the duck blinds, and settled in. They were in the blind most of the morning without seeing much, so they decided to move farther out into the lake. Out on the lake, they noticed the sky—which had been overcast most of the day—begin to get a little grayer as a light fog rolled in. The boat had been drifting quietly when they felt the air turning colder. They decided it was time to get back to camp. Cranking the motor, nothing happened. They looked for the toolbox, but it was nowhere to be found. They cranked again and again, but the motor would not catch. Time and time again, the motor choked and died.

Had there been anyone else around, they could have hitched a ride back to shore, but there hadn't been anyone on the lake all day. They would have to paddle back toward the rivers. It was beginning to get colder and the fog thicker. Before long, the fog was so thick they could barely see the outline of the shore. Ginger became restless and agitated. Suddenly, she barked and frantically leaped forward. She bounded up to the front of the boat, jerking it from side to side. The boat rocked and tipped over. Everyone and everything slid overboard.

The water was freezing. They splashed around in the gray waters trying to retrieve what they could. Finally, they got the boat upright and climbed back in. Ginger had calmed down, but they were soaked. Their gear was gone. Thermos, compass, guns, everything but the paddles that they had somehow managed to hold on to, sunk. They could barely see a few yards in front of them now, the fog was so thick. Their breath was frosty with the dampness and they were ice-cold and wet.

Looking around to orient themselves, they found that the features of the river had disappeared in the fog. There were no familiar landmarks, nothing but cold, gray fog all around and cold, gray water lapping at the sides of the boat. They could be far out in the lake now, since they had lost all sense of direction. It was growing darker and the temperature was falling. As they rowed they could barely keep the paddles in their hands. Their fingers were numb and they were shaking from the cold. They continued to row as it grew darker. They must have gotten turned around because there was no sign of the shore, only fog. If it weren't so thick, they could have seen a few lights along the shore and known in what direction to head, but they could see nothing.

It seemed as if they had been rowing for hours. They both feared that they had gotten turned around and moved out farther into the lake. Before long the paddle slid from my brother's hands and slipped into the gray waters. My father kept rowing.

Suddenly, there was a whoosh. The boat had hit something. It was a large black wall with rubber tires hanging from a railing. It looked like the side of a barge. Above the tires, a dark figure emerged from the fog. He stood above them on the deck, and in the fog seemed almost to float before them. He was shrouded in a long black coat with a hood and black boots and his face was hidden in the shadows of his hood. He shouted down at them to come aboard and dropped a rope ladder for them to climb aboard.

The man carried a lantern and motioned them to come inside where a kerosene heater was going full blast, warming the small cabin. They stripped off their frozen clothes and wrapped themselves in army blankets. The man left them with tin cups, a steaming pot of coffee, and a bottle of brandy. They drank cup after cup of the thick black coffee spiked with brandy. All around the boat the fog blurred everything. There were no familiar shapes, no edges. The lights seemed not to illuminate but only to scatter. Even the boat's running lights were dim and appeared like the pictures in science books of distant galaxies. Everything was diffused and muted by the fog.

The man returned and they began to exchange stories. He spoke softly with an odd dialect, part Cajun and part Portuguese, but his face remained hidden in the folds of his dark hood. Mostly, the conversation was river talk, of places and towns along the river, where the ducks had been feeding, places each had hunted. Finally both hunters and the dog drifted off to sleep in the warm cabin.

When they awoke it was daybreak and the fog had lifted. Off in the distance they could see familiar shore. The radio tower was a familiar landmark; they knew where they were. The man was not about, but the outboard motor cranked right up. In the frosty air it started on the first try. They headed back to camp and then to Manchac.

When they arrived back at Manchac they walked over to Cecil's for bowls of seafood gumbo. They were ravenous. Between mouthfuls of Cecil's dark, rich, steaming gumbo, my father asked about the barge on the lake. Cecil looked puzzled and said there weren't any barges on the lake; hadn't been anything on the lake except a few fishermen for months, and they were damn lucky to have weathered the marsh overnight in this kind of winter. He said the news on the radio reported that a cold front had moved in suddenly and it had gotten way down below freezing during the night. It was one of the coldest nights he could ever remember. The fog was so bad there were lots of accidents up and down the intracoastal canal. A couple of fellows out fishing from around Pointe a la Hache were still missing.

My father paused at this point and there was a long silence. One of the younger boys at the table asked, "Well, Mr. Boyd, what about that barge? Who was the man on the barge?" Another long pause. In a hushed quiet tone that he used when he was about to say something important, he said, "I don't know, but I've heard some ol' Cajun fishermen tell stories of a phantom barge. I've heard that the barge was piloted by a man who drowned many years ago on the Mississippi River when an oil tanker hit his boat in the fog. The old fishermen say that his ghost patrols the backwaters and the bayous of the area and that he helps fishermen who get lost or in trouble."

There was another long silence. Then the scuffing of kitchen chairs and boots as the hunters shuffled away from the table and left the kitchen for the woods. My father was probably smiling at the other fathers with a twinkle in his eye, when he said, "Well, you never know, it could be just another one of those camp stories that get started."

I rose slowly from the warm quilts and wandered into the kitchen for coffee. Mom was at the sink washing the dishes left by the hunters. She had cleaned the table, swept the floor, and put on another pot of coffee. As I poured my cup of coffee and tasted that first bitter jolt, I wondered if I would have such adventures. It would be years before I understood that it is generally men who move about in the world, free to be hunters, free to have adventures, free to be travelers and heroes. It would be some time before I would formulate the questions, would I have adventures, would I have stories to tell, or would I be limited to telling only the stories of my mom at the kitchen sink.

SOME LAST GREAT PLACES II

Map of North and South America: The Yucatan, Costa Rica, Panama, the Atacama Desert, and Patagonia (the Lake District and Andean) (Magallanes and Torres del Paine). Artwork by Rachael Poston

South America: Introduction

O F THE THIRTEEN COUNTRIES THAT MAKE UP SOUTH AMERICA, most have national borders that (like so many borders) are artificial constructs created by human affairs and politics. What perhaps defines the continent more significantly is its land. If we imagine the continent in the shape of a human body, the Andean Cordillera might be a spine, the skeletal support that runs over four thousand miles from Colombia to Cape Horn. The shoulders might be Colombia and Ecuador; the pot belly fed by the mighty Amazon River, Brazil; the back, Peru; the waist, the Grande Norte of Chile and Bolivia; the knees, the lake district of Chile and Argentina; and the feet, the tip of the continent, the wild lands of Tierra del Fuego. The first story, written in classical travelogue form, is about the wild lands of Patagonia. It describes the watery land at the end of the continent known as the Magallanes and the steppe lands. Returning to Patagonia to the region known as the Lake District, the second story describes the alpine region of Andean Patagonia. The third is about the driest place on Earth, the Atacama Desert that borders Peru and Chile.

A Wilderness: Patagonia 2

December 9–10, 1999

THE FLIGHT TO MIAMI with a stop in Orlando, then an overnight flight to Santiago, was boring and tedious, but as Paul Theroux in *The Old Patagonian Express* (1979, 5) says, "There is not much to say about most airplane journeys. Anything remarkable must be disastrous, so you define a good flight by negatives: you didn't get hijacked, you didn't crash, you didn't throw up, you weren't late, you weren't nauseated by the food. So you were grateful." And so we were grateful to be arriving in the early morning in Santiago. But the next flight, down the spine of the Andes to the southernmost tip of South America, was anything but boring. From the plane window, the long mountain range of the Andes, which defines the country of Chile, was a black-and-white mural of ice fields, snow-covered peaks, and snow-filled valleys. Through the cloud cover, the rough, jagged peaks of these incredible mountains rose miles high and then plunged back down to the sea. Truly, these were the most dramatic mountains I had ever seen.

We arrived at Punta Arenas in the late afternoon and, after checking into our hotel, took a stroll around this windy city at the end of the world. The streets around the hotel were bustling but the stores were small and rather limitedly stocked. Punta Arenas—even with a population of around 110,000—is still a frontier town, and although once a large oil-producing area and a major sheep-processing center, the shopping district was only a few blocks long. The wind and the temperature fluctuated constantly. One minute it was cold and gusty, the next, warm and calm—a condition we were soon to discover was typically Patagonian. After a walk and a pot of tea, we went to bed with the sun still shining. Summer daylight lasts twenty hours and it never did get really dark. Even at midnight, the sky was only a light shade of gray.

December 11, 1999

Morning began with a more thorough exploration of Punta Arenas. The Plaza Muñoz Gamero where a bronze statue of Ferdinand Magellan, his ship, and native Indians stood among colorful flower beds of blue and yellow lupine was our first destination. Ancient cedars—their dark green branches spread wide with Christmas cheer, decorated with brightly wrapped Christmas boxes and colored lights—lined the square. Some of the local artisans displayed stone carvings of penguins, seals, and whales for the tourists to buy. The Municipal Cemetery, about a mile beyond the shopping district, was a pleasant walk. Passing a bakery, we bought warm, currant-speckled rolls just out of the oven and stuffed ourselves with the sweet bread as we walked along the brick sidewalks. The cemetery, surrounded by a white stucco wall, had an arched, red brick entrance and a central plaza with pebbled paths radiating out like spokes of a wheel. Many of the graves were adorned with gold-framed pictures of the dead, rosaries, and other religious relics. Resembling a botanical garden with religious statuaries, it was a mixture of the gaudy and the elegant. Wealthy families had erected elaborate shrines resembling a formal European garden. Middle-class families had honored their dead by planting flowers in the burial plots, creating the look of small flower gardens. In the back and along the edges, the graves of the poor were stacked one on top of the other like mailboxes in a post office. While some cemeteries offer a quiet comfort, this one with its obvious class structure bothered me. Death does not care about wealth; it strips away our pretensions and makes us all equal. The obvious hierarchy based on the wealth and status of the living seemed to go against the very nature and truth of a cemetery. But then, I suppose, cemeteries are more about the living than the dead.

Later in the afternoon as we sipped hot tea in a restaurant over looking Colón Avenue, crowds of people carrying signs and banners congregated on the square. Occasionally, someone would walk up to the platform, speak into the microphone, and the crowd would cheer and wave colorful flags. A group of musicians played loud music but we could not identify any of the tunes. It looked like a political rally. I knew little of current Chilean politics, but remembered that Salvador Allende (considered a socialist reformer) began to make many economic changes after being elected president in the 1970s. I had read that within the first few weeks after the election, he distributed to every child in the country a new pair of shoes and a sweater. Within three years, his government was overthrown in a military coup, and the dictator, Pinochet, supported by a right-wing military, arrested, tortured, and killed thousands of innocent people who resisted his repressive regime. These citizens, called the "disappeared," were artists, musicians, writers, and students whose deaths were never investigated. Pinochet was recently arrested in Great Britain for crimes against humanity, but with his lawyers arguing for the dismissal of his trial on the grounds of illness, who knows if he will ever have to face the responsibility of his past. Money and connections have a way of excusing the sins of anyone's past.

This pattern of military coups, dictators, and repressive regimes has been a common theme in Central and South America. In Honduras, Guatemala, Nicaragua, and El Salvador, the Contras were the right-wing military who fought the leftist Sandinistas. We probably will never know the real truth about U.S. involvement with these drug-connected, right-wing guerrilla groups. Dictators like Córdova in Honduras; Martinez and Cristiani in El Salvador; Somoza, Garcia, and Montt in Nicaragua; and the infamous Noriega in Panama have left a terrible legacy of brutality in Central America. The other unfortunate pattern is that the U.S. government in its fear of communism and its ties to corporate interests has consistently picked the bad guys to support. In Argentina, it was the dictator Videla who created his "dirty little war." After twenty years, the mothers of the young people who disappeared (Madres del Plaza de Mayo) still march in protest in Buenos Aires. In Peru, it was Fujimori as president with his shadowy intelligence chief, Montesinos. In Bolivia, Banzer, in Paraguay, Stroessner—the list of dictators goes on and on. While I think of myself as moderately informed, I did not know the current political climate in Chile, but I certainly wished that I did. As I watched the rally, I tried to ease my discomfort by telling myself that if the political situation was really dangerous or unstable, there would probably not be so many tourists. I found myself wondering how visitors to the United States might feel if they were to witness one of the many demonstrations, in say, Washington, D.C. Would they think, "Oh, those unstable Americans, always demonstrating?"

Finally, it was time to board the ship for our Magellanic voyage. The *Terra Australis*, a small ship, accommodating around sixty passengers, seemed well made and sturdy. Our cabin, a bit like a college dorm room, consisted of two bunks and a small bathroom. Four large common areas—the dining room, the Magellane lounge, a game room, and the Penguin lounge—were located on four different levels of the ship. After getting settled, we explored the boat, met the crew, went through a safety drill, and toasted our departure with great fanfare. We watched the city of Punta Arenas grow smaller as we sailed westward into the Strait of Magellan on our way to Ainsworth Bay. That night with only the stars for lights, we sailed the Admiralty Fjord.

December 12, 1999

We woke to dolphins riding the ship's wake and the sun lighting snow-capped mountains along the channel. These mountains, the Darwin Mountains, first described in the 1830s, are one of many landmarks in this part of the world named after early European naturalists and explorers. We were soon anchoring in the bay with the Marinelli Glacier directly ahead of us. In the gray waters, ice sculptures drifted all about the ship. Pieces of ice as big as freight trucks and as small as ice cubes floated out from the glacier into the more open waters. The crew launched several small, rubber outboard motorboats called Zodiacs and took us onto a small island near the glacial moraine. We were warned to stay away from the water's edge because if large sections of ice break from the glacier and fall into the channel, the resultant tidal wave might wash someone away. As we hiked inland toward the mountains, we saw elephant seals dozing on bare rock. They looked like huge smooth rocks, and they mostly ignored us. Occasionally, a couple of males would rear up, grunt, and bang into each other with huffy neck blows.

The island was distinctly zoned with species of marsh plants and bog grasses that I had never seen before. In the tidal zone, a rose-colored, star-shaped grass grew flat against the ground. It made the ground look like a garden of red starfish. Farther back and more inland, a thick covering of green and rust-colored Sphagnum moss was a springy plush carpet. As we stood looking out over the beaver ponds, we couldn't help but jiggle up and down, testing the stability of the spongy ground. A mixed forest of *Nothofagus* trees (*Nothofagus dombeyi* and *N. betuloides* [coigue], *N. pumilio* [lenga], and *N. antarctica* [nire]) rose at the base of the mountains. Over forty species of *Nothofagus* grow only in the southern hemisphere and this first sighting of these ancient austral forests was a green vision. Around the ponds, many of the trees were denuded and fallen. Although we did not see beavers, they had been actively building lodges and dams. On the dark surface of the pools, the image of the white-trunk leafless trees rippled in the cold breeze.

That afternoon the ship anchored in Brookes Bay, and the Zodiacs took us onshore to a site where another glacier flowed down from the mountain into the bay. The ice cracked and millions of ice chunks exploded off the peak and splattered into the waters. The terrain on either side of the glacier was rocky and sparsely vegetated. Giant kelp fronds (*Macrocystis integrifolia*) littered the shore. Their long green fronds dotted with thumb-sized air bladders draped over the boulders like banners. A thorny green shrub thick with red berries the size of cranberries (*Pernettya mucronata*), a ground cover that looked like pennywort or dollar weed, and a few grasses (probably *Festuca* sp.) were the only plants. The glacial ice was aquamarine and oddly shaped. If you let your imagination run free, you might see almost anything— a line of priests in long robes, a parade of bizarre animals marching in a percussion band, a group of warriors armed and ready for battle. And birds were everywhere. Oystercatchers with their thick, bright, orange-red beaks flashing and crested ducks glided in and out of the cove. A pair of kelp geese stood on the rocks like the yin and yang symbol, the male totally white and the female completely black.

The pebbled beach sparkled with glacial ice. Typical of glacial ice, the chunks were full of air bubbles. Glaciers in Patagonia are probably a million years old and like glaciers all over the world, they are melting at phenomenal rates. Glaciers form when accumulated snow compacts and turns to ice. This traps air. When the ice moves down the mountain, it flows like a slow river, averaging around a foot per year. That night, exhausted from our walks among the glaciers, I slept soundly, snug in the cradle of the ship. My last thoughts before I fell asleep were of those slow-moving glaciers inching their way back home to the sea.

December 13, 1999

Monday morning we woke to the groans of the ship moving over ice floes. The deep moaning was at first disturbing until we realized there was little danger of the ice ripping a hole in the ship's hull. We had traveled through the Keats Fjord during the night and were in the D'Agostini Fjord near the Serrano Glacier. After breakfast, the Zodiacs took us ashore and we walked right up to the glacier wall. That wall of ice rose a thousand feet high. Again, we heard ice explode off the ice wall and hit the water farther down. The rocky shore and the littoral zone were almost bare of plant vegetation, but the smooth, orange stones seemed to support lichens of every conceivable color. The fjord waters were full of ice floes of all shapes and sizes, and when the sun peeked out from behind the clouds, the mercury-colored waters turned into flashing lights.

Lunch was a delicious paella and we ate heartily. About two hours afterwards, the ship entered more open waters and the seas became rough. We lay on our bunks trying not to think of the paella, sipping soft drinks to fight the nausea. Supper consisted of dry crackers. Finally, the seas calmed as we entered more protected waters, and we went up on deck to watch the coming of evening. The sky and the rugged landscape were shades of a gray background against the Magdalena and Cockburn channels. As we sailed through the channels, we began to notice the albatrosses. Black-browed albatrosses with nine-foot wingspans were flying all about the ship! Under their wings, white zigzag steaks like flashes of lightening appeared. They flew as daredevils, up and down, skimming the surface of the ten-foot waves, their wings coming half an inch from the water. We saw brown albatrosses, southern giant petrels, and several species of shearwaters, all incredible aerial acrobats, gliding, swooping, and slipping over the sea. In *The Rarest of the Rare*, Diane Ackerman (1995) writes about the short-tailed albatross. She describes the albatross as using the physics of the wind to soar as many as six hundred miles, flapping its wings less frequently than a sparrow crossing a narrow street. Like giant kites, the birds can dip and soar up to seventy miles an hour if the wind is right. We watched the birds late into the night and their movement seemed more like a dream than real. A verse from the poem "Solitudes" by Pablo Neruda (1998, 38) seemed to capture the moment:

> The coast broken,
> By thunder,
> consumed
> by the teeth of every dawn,
> worn by great stirrings
> of weather and waves;
> slow birds circle,
> with iron-colored feathers
> and they know that here the world ends . . .

December 14, 1999

Dawn saw us sailing eastward through the Beagle Channel. At 5:00 a.m., we woke to watch the "Avenue of Glaciers" glide by. Six glaciers sloped down from ten-thousand-foot-high mountain peaks into the sea. The morning was gray but the heavy mist of the day before had disappeared, and we could see the complex architecture of each glacier clearly. Caves and crevasses, ridges and massive cracks in the ice, pillars and pedestals, spires and arches were all part of the glacial structure. The topography included so many textures ranging from smooth polished surfaces to deeply grooved etched regions. We stood with our coats and blazers over our pajamas on the top deck of the boat in the frosty air and watched the sun climb higher and the glaciers turn from gray to white to blue. With the shadows cast by the rising sun, even more intricate and elaborate patterns formed in the ice sheets. The albatrosses were flying around the ship, conducting their morning exercises, and it seemed as if my eyes were just not big enough to take in all that magnificent landscape.

The ship arrived in Yendegaia Bay later in the morning and we went ashore onto the island of Tierra del Fuego. Tierra del Fuego (which means *land of fire*) is one of the truly last pristine wild places on Earth. The ranch we visited was a primitive affair consisting of a few wooden buildings, several horse corrals, and a few thousand acres of rugged land. It had recently been purchased by a Chilean conservation group in order to preserve what is known as "Old Gowandian" forest. Gowandian forests are ancient forests found in Australia, South Africa, Chile, and Argentina. Earth's original landmass, Pangaea, began to split around 225 million years ago into a northern continent, Laurasia, and a southern continent, Gowanda. Forests of Australia, South Africa, and South America were once contiguous. A ranger and a couple of gauchos served as caretakers on what was now a nature preserve. Since our departure three days ago, we had seen no settlements, no houses, no one at all in this archipelago of islands, sea channels, fjords, bays, mountains, and glaciers. These men had a hardness about them. They did not give the impression that they read Neruda around the campfire, but who knows . . . maybe they did.

Hiking the hills around the ranch amidst hordes of mosquitoes that constantly buzzed around our eyes and ears, we saw wildflowers everywhere. The paradox of such delicate flowers growing in this harsh rugged land did not escape us. One of the most vivid flowers, the fire bush (*Embothrium coccineum*) had a deep red multi-tubular blossom, and its shrubby tree grew all along the slopes. White daisies, blue pea, and violets were different from the common North American species I was used to seeing. They seemed more vivid. Epiphytes hung from all the trees, giving the place the look of a Louisiana swamp, but instead of Spanish moss (*Tillandsia usneoides*) on oak trees, bright green old man's beard (another *Tillandsia* species) draped down from beech trees. One of the guides pointed out two other epiphytes on the trees and called them false mistletoe and Chinese lantern. With the insect repellent wearing off and the cold seeping into our bones, we left the ranch and returned to the ship.

In the afternoon we docked at Puerto Williams, a Chilean naval base on the Beagle Channel. The town's buildings consisted mostly of small wooden shacks or single-story structures covered with sheet-metal siding. The town square had a few shops with shabby little displays in the windows and an open dirt pit surrounded by wooden sidewalks. We saw neither cafe nor grocery store, but we did pass a school and a post office. As we walked the rocky path to the edge of town on route to the cemetery, it began to drizzle. By the time we reached the cemetery, it was hailing. Sharp pieces of ice stung our face and hands so we made a hasty retreat back to the ship. We were ravenous that evening, maybe because a town without a restaurant or grocery store evokes a hardy appetite. We devoured the pumpkin soup and rolls, the palm-heart salad, the sea bass, and potatoes as if we hadn't eaten for days.

December 15, 1999

The morning sun shone on a new country, Argentina. Ushuaia, the southernmost city in Argentina, was very different from Puerto Williams. Originally a penal colony, it is the closest Argentinean city to Antarctica (about two hundred miles south), and so it is the main gateway to that frozen continent. The city had a more European feel about it, with one long main street of cafes, restaurants, and shops selling cameras, hardware, clothing, appliances, and almost anything imaginable. The street was busy and full of jeeps and SUVs. In the background, the snow-capped peaks of Mount

Olivia rose majestically into the clouds. We discovered a small shop at the eastern-most end of the main street and purchased stone-carved penguins. After lunch, a visit to the maritime museum provided a look at the old prison. Placards on the walls of the ten-by-four-foot cells, where men had spent lives of solitary confinement, gave the gory details of the prisoners and their crimes. One man had hacked to pieces three people and spent forty years in that stone box for his crimes. While the place had a certain morbid fascination in the same way a tragic accident might, we could not linger long in that bleak and dreary fortress.

During the twelve hours in Ushuaia, the weather went from drizzling to sunny to rainy to clear to misty to partly cloudy to a sky filled with a complete rainbow. But always there was the wind. Before departing the city, tea and sweet rolls in one of many teahouses along the main street ended our day in Ushuaia. That night we left the Argentine city and sailed back towards our Chilean home port.

A short lecture and video on the ancient peoples of Patagonia provided an informative evening of cultural and natural history. The documentary and lecture (the guide referred to a collection of essays entitled *Patagonia: Natural History, Prehistory, and Ethnography at the Uttermost End of the Earth* [McEwan et al. 1997]) revealed that four indigenous tribes once lived in the region, two who hunted guanacos on the pampas and two maritime peoples who hunted seal and other aquatic mammals. All of them are gone now, killed by the weapons or the diseases of the colonial Dutch, Portuguese, Spanish, and English. The Yamana were the canoe people of the Beagle channel and the story of their destruction is as sad as any in the saga of annihilation of native cultures all over the Americas. Darwin wrote that they were "a greasy, dirty and violent people." For a man who left the greatest legacy of biological understanding with his theory of natural selection and the origins of the species, he missed the boat when it came to understanding the human animal. He and other European explorers, naturalists, and scientists might have learned much about the biology, the geography, the natural history of the region from the indigenous peoples, but instead they dismissed them as savages, and as a result, the world lost whole languages, belief systems, folk knowledge, and entire cultures with the eradication of these Americans.

In Ushuaia, we had walked past a shop along the main street whose sign read "Jemmy Buttons" and the name had intrigued me. Jemmy Buttons was a Yamana who, along with three others of his tribe, were taken to England by Captain Fitzroy on his first voyage. All of the others died except Jemmy Buttons. The story goes that he spent several years in England where he was educated and made into a proper Englishman. When he returned to Patagonia on Fitzroy's second voyage, the famous "Voyage of the Beagle" described by Darwin, he reverted to his tribal loyalties. Much to the dismay of the English, he spent the next ten years, the rest of his life, fighting the English and the other colonial powers that had tried to conquer and colonize his native land (to no avail, I might add.)

Dispelling the myth of the noble Patagonian savage, Rosalind Miles (1989, 49) in *The Women's History of the World* writes, "a chieftain of Tierra del Fuego told Darwin during the voyage of 'The Beagle' that to survive in a famine they would kill and eat their old women, but never their dogs." As a potential candidate for their meal, I was reminded that cultural differences can be hard to understand. I was just thankful not to have lived in either culture, Darwin's or the Yamanas'. Given the choice of being eaten in times of famine or being an invisible house-keeper in Darwin's household, neither one appealed.

December 16, 1999

We again woke early to view the Avenue of Glaciers as we sailed westward through the Beagle Channel on route back to Punta Arenas. The mountains were gray rippling curtains; the glaciers, solid rivers of ice. One after another, solid sheets of white flowed down from the gray peaks to the gray sea, each one more spectacular than the last. The landscape could have been a life-sized black-and-white photograph taken by Ansel Adams.

After breakfast, we went ashore again near the Garibaldi Glacier to explore a cold rainforest. Climbing into this cold jungle in our yellow rubber raingear took a certain bravado because there were no paths or trails. We climbed over huge tree roots the size of oil barrels covered with slick moss and lichens. With no firm footing, we maneuvered up the slippery slopes through the dense tangle of green. We must have looked like a line of awkward ducks waddling up a tree trunk. Slipping and sliding over trees and branches, we made our slow way through the roots and mud, progressing little more than a couple hundred feet in an hour. We finally arrived at a waterfall.

Sitting on a small flat rock, I looked around for the first time at something other than my next step and noticed many beech trees covered with what looked like galls or tumors, some the size of basketballs. Galls form in many ways; these were the result of a fungal infection. The fungus (*Cyttaria darwinii*), called llao llao or Indian bread, infects only southern beech trees (species of *Nothofagus*). When the tree tries to fight off the infection, a saplike material forms, which heals as a scar. It is the tree's continual attempt to seal off the fungi that result in galls. Like all highly successful parasites, the fungus is slow acting, and it takes a long time for it to really damage the tree. From some of the galls, round orange protrusions (the fruiting bodies) could be seen. One of the guides said the natives commonly collect them, fry them in butter (like sautéed mushrooms), and consider them a delicacy.

Wet, cold, and thoroughly splattered in green slime, we made our way back to the warmth of the ship. The feeling of green was overwhelming. "Verde, Verde, Verde, el mundo es Verde," I thought. My first line of poetry in Spanish. How intense the color green seemed in Spanish, how like the word for truth, and how sensual, like the entanglement of that foliage. I looked back from the ship's deck on the cold rainforest and thought of a line from Neruda (1991, 19) as he asks in childlike wonderment, "Do you know that in Patagonia / at midday, mist is green?" And I could answer, "Sí."

The weather turned rainy and the seas got rough again so we spent the afternoon lying in our bunks slipping soft drinks and waiting for smoother waters. As the ship made its way through the Tierra del Fuego archipelago back to the Strait of Magellan, we watched the misty landscape from the window of our cabin. By dinner time, the seas had calmed enough to eat, although some of our fellow travelers were still a bit "under the weather," and the dining room was only half full. One of the passengers, an older Swedish gentleman, related with great effort in English how he saved all year to travel during the holidays. His wife had died some fifteen years previously and he had no children, so he spent all his money on traveling. He shrugged and said, "Well, the last shirt has no pockets." Perhaps the weather, the rough seas, and the near end of our voyage were making us a bit melancholy.

December 17, 1999

The morning sky was blue, the sun was bright, and we were back in the Strait of Magellan ready to begin the last day of the voyage. Ft. Bulnes, the original settlement on the strait, was our first stop. The fort had been restored by the Chilean government and was now a historical site. I have never quite understood why people want to preserve forts, but luckily some have scenic views and the preservation efforts often save rare plants. Built on a bluff, the fort overlooked the strait and a spectacular meadow of wildflowers. The windswept hillside was covered with the yellow blossoms of the calafate (*Berberis buxifolia*), the purple sweet pea (*Lathyrus nervosus*), and many others. The meadow sloped down to touch the blue water, and the leafless branches of gnarled beech trees rose to touch the blue sky. It was a breathtaking vision of coast!

Inside the fortress walls, several coniferous trees called monkey puzzle trees or araucaria trees (*Araucaria araucana*) grew. Their dark green, needled branches curved slightly upward, stiff as bottle brushes. At the ends of the branches, a resinous material leaked from a spiky cactuslike flower. It takes five hundred years for these ancient trees to mature and many live to over a thousand years. Endemic to the southern Andes, there were once great forests of araucaria trees but logging has almost eradicated them. Now protected as an endangered species, they are seen only as the occasional one or two. The few remaining natural stands of araucaria trees in the world are in Chile's national parks.

Probably the highlight of the trip was Magdalena Island where a colony of close to a quarter million Magellanic penguins nested. The wind had picked up that afternoon, the seas had gotten rougher, and getting to the island was treacherous. But every swell and dip, every dump on that roller-coaster ride in the rubber Zodiacs, thinking any moment we might be thrown over into the sea, was worth it. As we gratefully climbed out of the Zodiacs onto shore, a strong wind blew sand and sea spray up in our faces, but not even the stinging grit could dampen the excitement of seeing those creatures. Penguins were everywhere, entering, leaving, defending their burrows, waddling along the shore, swimming the surf, rising from the water and diving porpoise-like, or just standing around in groups. We spent every minute taking pictures and watching them as they allowed us to get almost within touching distance.

These penguins (*Spheniscus magellanicus*) are one of among seventeen species of the world's penguins; they are about 71 cm (2 feet) tall and weigh about 4 kg (9 lbs.). Called jackass penguins because they bray like donkeys, they have several concentric white circles around their head, pink blotches around their eyes, and a pink stripe below the bill. Mary Roach (2001) writes about these birds and those who study them. Probably the foremost authority on the birds, Dee Boersma, professor of biology at the University of Washington, heads the Magellanic Penguin Project. One of longest running penguin studies (nineteen years) and largest population studies (19,000 birds have been banded), the project has collected considerable data on the penguin colonies of Punta Tombo (located on the Argentine coast several hundred miles north of Magdalena Island). Much about the biology of these penguins has come from her studies.

Magellanic penguins arrive to breed on the island rookeries in December. Their nests, basically holes in the ground, are defended with much drama. They mate (mating patterns vary; some mate for as long as sixteen years, others change partners every season), have two eggs (usually only one survives), and the chicks mature in a couple months. The birds molt and migrate back to the coastal waters of Brazil. Their migration pattern goes like this: December through April, they breed along the southern coast of South America. In April, they leave, head north traveling thousands of miles up the coast as far as Brazil in search of food. They stay in Brazilian waters May through November and return to breed again to continue the cycle. Like other birds (and even bacteria), they probably navigate in part by detecting the Earth's magnetic force with a cellular compass. This molecular compass consists of an iron compound called magnetite found in specialized cells. Particles of magnetite align with the Earth's magnetic field and changes in direction can be sensed by changes in the alignment of the magnetite. Visual clues such as the position of the sun or stars also serve as landmarks and directional guides.

The penguins feed on anchovy, fish, and squid and are in turn eaten by leopard seals and giant petrels called skua. Their wings are flippers, their bodies are covered with short scaly feathers, and they have blotchy pink-and-black webbed feet and stiff little tails. They live to be about thirty years old. Estimates put the number of birds at one to two million along the east and west coasts of South America. They die from oil pollution and they starve when climatic changes cause food shortages. With global warming, populations are declining.

In *The Moon by Whale Light* (1991), Diane Ackerman's lovely chapter entitled "White Lanterns" describes the penguins of the southern waters, not only the Magellanic penguins but the gentoos, Adelies, king, emperor, and macaroni penguins. Her adventures aboard the ship *World Discoverer* exploring the Antarctic are some of the most beautifully written pieces on penguins. She describes them as the most anthropomorphic of all animals, as little humanoids, and it was hard not to see them as little people standing in groups as if they might be discussing the latest gossip. After several hours of the most pleasurable bird watching, it was time to leave the island. The seas were getting rougher, the cold was beginning to penetrate our clothes, and the wind, as always, was blowing and getting stronger.

When the ship arrived back in Punta Arenas around 8:00 p.m., we docked for the night and had a final dinner shipboard. Few of our table companions spoke English, and I spoke almost no Spanish, German, or Swedish, so the effort to be gracious in our good-byes to our fellow travelers was difficult. Actually, table conversation had been rather trying throughout much of the voyage. In Ushuaia a group of Spanish journalists who were covering the Chilean elections had boarded and were seated at our table. Young, arrogant men, they talked only to each other. They managed a few words with the other passengers who spoke a little Spanish, but they would not acknowledge us. When I asked one of them if he spoke English, he brushed off my question with a curt negative nod. I had the feeling they did speak English, but they were certainly not going to make the effort for two American women. And I so much wanted to know what was happening on the political scene. How frustrating to be excluded because I could not speak the language. It was a poignant reminder of how powerful language can be as a force to either exclude or include. Whether the language is Spanish or Russian, the scientific language or a computer language, every language has the potential to isolate or connect.

December 18, 1999

Though we left ship early in the morning, we felt as if we were still on board. The world rocked and sloshed and every turn of the head brought on a sudden queasiness. Having been on enough scientific cruises to know it takes time to regain one's land legs, I did not expect the intense light-headedness. It would take several days to regain our equilibrium. Chicken soup and a nap helped the adjustment to terra firma and later in the afternoon, a walk helped clear the rolling feel of my cob-webbed vision. The wind in midsummer was bitter cold as we walked to a nearby grocery store to buy apples, fresh rolls, and cheese for supper. The apples came from the central valley near Santiago where most of the country's fruits and veg-etables are grown. Sweet, crispy, and juicy, they reminded me of my grandmother's summer pears.

December 19, 1999

The drive from Punta Arenas to the national park Torres del Paine began with a short stretch of road that ran along the Strait of Magellan. Only the metal tow-ers of an oil refinery marred the view. The road turned north into the pampas and became one dirt lane and one paved. For 250 miles, we rode through the flat windswept steppes of Patagonia. The landscape had few buildings, few trees, only brown bunch grasses, shrubs, sheep, and more sheep. The miles of brown pam-pas and open sky occasionally broken by clusters of trees brought to mind a New Mexico desert only bleaker, drier, and browner. The van stopped once to let a gaucho and his dogs drive a herd of sheep across the road. The man's face, so deeply furrowed and lined, was as worn as the dark leather clothing he wore. Like a dusty wave, the flock rippled across the road and we sped on. Small clusters of trees and low buildings far off the road were sheep farms. Bruce Chatwin's *In Patagonia* (1977) traces the history of these farms (called estancias) and describes the life of those who lived on them. Like the American cowboy, the gaucho has a certain romantic appeal but in reality, many sheepherders and farm laborers are often little more than migrant workers. The families who own the ranches might not agree with this observation, but just as Chatwin fails to mention the monot-ony, the drudgery, the isolation, and the exhausting work of the ranch wife, it is sometimes easy to overlook that while life is rugged for everyone on these ranches, there is a hierarchy of work. For some, life on the estancia is harder than for others.

Three hours into the drive, along an outcropping of rocks with high cliffs, someone cried, "Condors!" We looked out the windows to see the enormous black outstretched wings of a pair of condors gliding over the van. They soared over the road and back up into the cliffs carrying their huge shadows with them. More like vultures than eagles or hawks, condors are carrion birds. In the air, they seem to shed the repugnant image of "feeders on the dead" and become gliders on the clouds. We watched them fade into the distance, tiny black specks moving on the graceful curves of the thermals.

A lunch stop at Puerto Natales, a small resort town on the shores of the Ultima Esperanza Sound about seventy miles from the park entrance, was a welcome break. The quaint hotels along the bay, the snow-capped mountains, and the blue lakes looked like a postcard of a Swiss alpine village. Black-necked swans floated in the blue waters and cormorants perched on the pilings of an old pier, occasionally opening their wings like fans. These birds—no matter what continent—seem to like airing and sunning their feathers. Thirty minutes from Puerto Natales, the Cave of the Milodon, complete with a replica of the twenty-foot giant extinct sloth, a mammal that once roamed these grasslands, offered another break. A boardwalk made a loop through the shallow cave, passing the bearlike statue and back around to the entrance. With the spectacular landscape of blue-gray mountains, blue sky, and blue lakes, it was hard to get excited about a plaster-of-Paris, long-gone sloth.

The Explorer, our lodging in the park, overlooked Lake Pehoe. Deceptively primitive, it appeared at first sight rustic and diminutive, but inside the soft bleached shades of an all-wood interior revealed a decided luxury. Wind-sculptured branches and native pottery decorated the tables, and old black-and-white pictures of nineteenth-century expeditions lined the walls. Every room had huge windows with spectacular views. From our window, the granite pillars of the Torres del Paine and the Cuernos del Paine (the towers and horns of the Paine mountains) rose ten thousand feet above a glacial lake. Only once had I been so awed by a view. Only the Grand Canyon had affected me in such a profound way. Almost too spectacular to believe, the mountain faces changed from moment to moment as the light varied. Clouds would form and the colors of the rocks would deepen or turn a different shade. The shadows cast by the clouds created seemingly infinite variations in the texture of the rocks, giving them the appearance of silk one moment and marble the next. Like Monet's haystacks, the mountains were different every time we looked at them.

Exploring the walkways around the hotel, the terrain was scraggly and windswept. The trunks of the beech trees looked like bleached driftwood worn smooth not by water but by the ever-blowing wind. An old burn had left many trees charred and void of leaves. We could not stay long outdoors because the wind nearly blew us off the slopes. Several times gusts of fifty miles per hour pushed us off the path until finally we gave up and stumbled back to the lodge. That night the wind roared down from the eastern mountains off the glaciers like a train. Several times during the night, the noise was so fierce, it startled me awake. The windows rattled and whistled, and it seemed the whole lodge might have been fighting against the abrasive wind.

December 20, 1999

The first morning hike was to Lago (Lake) Gray. Part of the third-largest ice field on Earth, Glacier Gray originates here and empties ice melt and icebergs into the lake. The thirty-minute drive to the trailhead was full of wildlife. Along the gravel road, a mural of hares, red foxes, flamingos, upland geese, crested caracara, and a few rheas moved by. We slowed to more closely observe these strange ostrichlike birds. Like a herd of lumpy shag rugs, the rheas loped away as we approached. A bit farther down the road, a single rhea followed by a dozen tiny chicks scampered off across the horizon. The male rhea does most of the bird rearing and this dad was ensuring the safety of his brood.

Crossing the Rio Gray on a suspension bridge, we walked single file over the swinging wire bridge with the wild whitewaters of the Rio Gray swirling below. A short distance through a mature lenga (beech) forest brought us onto a pebbled beach where the wind whipped up dirt and sand and blew it in our faces. Spitting out sand, we walked and were pushed by the wind along the ice-speckled shore. The trail climbed up and around to several rocky vistas that overlooked the lake. From those vantage points, we could see enormous icebergs floating in the lake. They looked like mountain peaks and buttes rising from a metal sea. As if lit from within, the icebergs had the appearance of blue milk glass. Far in the distance, the feeder glacier sloped down to join the lake. The blue blossoms of the wild sweet pea and the fire bush added specks of color to the trail as we looped back around to the beach. The wind would die down for a few minutes, then pick up, die down, pick up. It sprinkled off and on, but the cold, the sand in the teeth, and the wind-blistered cheeks were worth it to see this gray lake filled with blue icebergs.

The afternoon hike to Lake Nordenskjold took us through typical Andes shrublands. The vegetation of these grasslands consisted of several species of *Festuca* and low-growing shrubs, the most common, a smooth, dense, yellow-flowering bush called the mata bush (*Mulinum spinosum*). This bush, like many on the Patagonia steppe, looks like a cushion. Such round dense growth suits plants that must tolerate cold, windy, and arid conditions. The trail was easy but several times we had to squat in order to avoid the strong winds. Once we reached the shores of the lake, we sat in a hollow out of the wind, relaxed, and munched on chocolate bars. Across the lake, the horns of the Paines rose straight up from nearly sea level to ten thousand feet into the cold white clouds of the Chilean sky. Powerful winds known as williwaws were common on the lake. Originating as part of the westerlies that encircle the southern hemisphere, they flow up and over the southern cordillera of the Andes and descend onto the pampas. When they cross these leeward lakes, they lift up the surface waters, creating huge clouds of spray. We had seen several on Lake Pehoe from our room the day before. Luckily, we did not encounter any williwaws that day, so we stayed dry, but our guide told us that just the week before, his hikers had gotten soaked from one that blew up suddenly.

December 21, 1999

Lake Sarmiento was another easy walk through shrubland with only one difficult climb over a section of steep, sharp ledges. The wind had calmed, the rain was gone, and the sky was cloudless and a palpable blue. With our guidebook *Torres del Paine: Flora and Mountains* (Garay and Guineo 1997), we identified some of the many wildflowers along the trail. The most exquisite was the porcelain orchid (*Chloraea magellania*) whose name fit its ceramic-like petals. The flower's appeal was not because of its color as with tropical orchids but because of the delicate pattern of its white petals lined with green veins. It seemed a perfect flower for the Patagonian steppes. Lady slippers (*Calceolaria uniflora* and *C. biflora*), violets (*Viola maculata* and *V. reichei*), anemones (*Anemone multifida*), tiny wild geraniums (*Geranium magellanicum*), and so many more turned the hike into a treasure hunt. Among the gorgeous colors, our boots seemed to move with a lighter step.

The waters of Lake Sarmiento, alkaline and containing high levels of calcium, are spring fed. Against the blue waters, the limestone deposits made a stark white crenulated shoreline. The limestone deposits had the texture of coral, and I wondered if the carbonates were of microbial origin. We rested for a while on the shore of the lake enjoying the sun, the blue waters, and the white chalky outcroppings before making the trek back over the rock ledges and through the grasslands.

December 22, 1999

The drive to the northern section of the park was to be a photo excursion with many stops and a barbeque at the end. As our van rounded a curve near Salto Grande, a logging truck blocked the road; one of its tires had fallen off. Its heavy load of trees took over an hour for a crew to move to one side so we could pass. It was a reminder that even in the most remote regions of the world, in so many of the world's great wildernesses, logging goes on. Forests are cut every day and even though it is illegal in many national parks, it continues. In Chile, estimates are that less than 10 percent of the old forests remain. As long as profits are to be made, there is probably little hope of stopping it. But the cutting of trees in this beautiful park seemed especially tragic. By the time we got around the truck, we had time for only one stop along the Rio Paine. This wild river, for which the park gets its name, had many waterfalls and grand views of the towers and horns. The wind-bleached trunks and limbs of the gnarled old beech trees bent over the river's edge, giving the riverside a desolate look. Even the patches of yellow and white daisies that bloomed among clumps of green grass were not enough to dispel the bleakness.

Herds of guanacos speckled the austere grasslands. Spring babies not much older than a few weeks in soft reddish coats leaped and played with wild abandon in the bright sunshine. Like most feral herbivores, guanacos graze the Patagonian steppes in social groups. Breeding groups of several females and one male are the general rule, and park rangers estimate fairly stable populations of several thousand. The guide pointed out a great horned owl nestled in a dead beech tree, almost totally camouflaged. A crested caracara fed on a small (already dead) rodent (they are carrion feeders), a pair of upland geese flew off to a less disturbed spot, and a pair of southern lapwings in their black collars, looking like large killdeer, scampered off over a knoll.

We arrived at the picnic just as the food was being served. Racks of lamb roasted over beds of coals, and the pavilion was warm and smoky. The cooks sliced huge slabs of meat and slapped them onto the plates of the diners. We ate sparingly (just green salad, pasta, and rolls) because our stomachs were a little unsettled from the ride. But the horseback riders were ravenous. Again and again, the boys from the trail ride returned to the fire to have their plates filled with the charred meat.

The campsite was in a grove of beech trees covered in what our guide called false mistletoe (probably *Tristerix* sp.). In various stages of its life cycle, some clusters were bright green, almost succulent looking, some were rust colored (dying), and some were flowering. In general, mistletoes (and there are probably at least a thousand different species of mistletoes) have long histories and complex mythologies associated with them, most likely because they remain evergreen in northern climates and because they produce many medicinal compounds. Compounds ranging from alkaloids that lower blood pressure to cytotoxic lectins that cause apoptosis (death) of cancer cells have been isolated from mistletoes. We marveled at the beauty of this mistletoe and I wondered if any biochemist had studied this species.

The campsite was also on a high plateau overlooking a vast red canyon. While the gauchos rounded up the horses to return them to the stables, we sat for a long time looking out over the rim of the canyon. The endless miles of brown where nothing grew, then steppe lands where some vegetation turned the land a multitude of subtle yellows and greens, was a mesmerizing landscape. The only comparison that came to mind was with the paintings of George Ingles (his later, more abstract work) but it seemed foolish to think of this landscape in the same context as a canvas.

December 23, 1999

The drive back to Punta Arenas was as magical as the ride to the park had been. The brown grasslands hypnotized us as we sped along the road, and I knew I would always remember its stark beauty. We stopped at a tiny cafe called the Rio Rubins

Cafe; it was a Patagonian diner complete with swivel stools and counter, tables covered in red-and-white checkered tablecloths, wooden chairs, and a friendly middle-aged waitress who brought us steaming cups of coffee. The grilled chicken sandwiches on square slices of homemade bread were delicious. How fitting that the last impression of this place would be one of old familiar comfort. Too soon we were at the airport and involved with travel connections.

On the flight home, I thought about this wild "nowhere" land, this land that almost defies definition by political borders but rather demands to be defined by its landscape. Of all its qualities, Patagonia seemed a place of immense contrast, the contrast of desert and wetlands, of mountains and flatlands, of grasslands and coast, of sparse vegetation and lush greenery, of grand vistas and small delicate flowers, of harsh extreme climates and passionately blue skies, of vivid colors and places shaded only in black and white. Unlike the more tropical countries of South America, this place had none of the terrible poverty of the north. There were no slums, no big cities, few people, and the natural landscape was magnificent. Perhaps that is why it is such an intriguing place; it is a land not dominated by humans. The essence of this place seemed to be the absence of humans.

December 24, 1999

Arriving back in the States, it was Christmas Eve. People were carrying brightly wrapped packages, rushing to catch flights, and looking like typical, on-the-go Americans. Around the Miami airport, the tinsel look of Christmas was evident—not my favorite holiday with its commercial hype. The decorations were annoyingly familiar and yet, as always, there was comfort in the familiar. My deep need for reunion with home always surprises me when it washes over me, the way an old song can evoke such longing. I had seen one of the great wildernesses of the world, done it relatively comfortably and without excessive risk, and I felt exhilarated by the experience. But coming home and the resolution it provides must somehow complete the cycle of journey, a cycle that once resolved can begin again.

Highlands: Patagonia Revisited

A YEAR PASSED AND I WAS BACK IN CHILE again. Waiting for my suitcase at the Santiago airport, a dough-faced young man stood next to me impatiently lighting one cigarette after another. He wore a large expensive watch that he kept checking, khaki slacks, a polo shirt labeled Ralph Lauren, and burgundy leather loafers. He pulled out a cell phone several times but never actually made a call. As the same luggage kept making the same loop and we waited for the next load, he asked, in that way people do when they really want to talk about themselves, "Are you here on business or pleasure?"

"I'm just visiting," I said.

He said, "I'm here consolidating my interests with my Chilean partner. We manage a timber business. Making six figures, doing almost nothing, cutting trees. What a streak of luck! Are you with a tour?" he asked.

"Not really. But we'll be doing some touristy things."

"How much did your trip cost?" he asked.

"Too much," I replied, annoyed at his impoliteness.

"I paid a bundle for my first-class seat but it's worth it. Someday I'll have my own plane so I won't have to travel with the peons. I'm working on this deal, and if it works out, I'll be making seven, maybe eight figures. Who would guess cutting trees could be so profitable."

He spied his luggage, stepped on his cigarette, reached in front of me, grabbed his leather travel bag, nearly knocking me over in his haste, and hurried off. I sighed in relief, glad this man on his way to millionairehood was gone.

The twenty-mile stretch of paved road from the Puerto Montt airport to the Los Alerce Mountain Lodge ran along the bay known as Seno de Reloncavi. A light rain grayed the sea and all the surroundings. Along the shore, smoke leaked from the tin chimney pipes atop the fishermen's hovels, and magenta hollyhocks speckled the yards. Such stately flowers for such humble yards, their ruffles dripped with raindrops. Turned on their sides, small beached fishing boats looked like half-moons with their yellow hulls peeking out of the mist. Men along the mud flats collected *cochayuyo*, a local seaweed used in stews and soups. Out in the bay, several small rock islands emerged from the gray waters and terns flew in and out from the ledges. Dolphins played in the waves, surfacing and diving back down, enjoying the rain like kids in puddles.

The turnoff into the mountains was hardly a road but more like a rock slide. We bounced and jostled up every foot of the steep eight-mile track. Enormous conifers, some wider than the jeep grew on the slopes. Sparsely vegetated, their thin furry limbs towered two hundred feet high and maybe even higher. Related to the giant sequoia, the alerce (*Fitzroya cupressoides*) are called *tata*, which means grandfather. One especially large tree near the lodge was almost four thousand years old. In its shaggy red bark, it stood in the mist like an old wizard in a tattered coat. With its massive roots buried deep in the cold forest soil and its dark evergreen branches lifted high into the Andean sky, it was a creature of both earth and sky. I thought, how could anyone cut such a majestic creature?

The lodge, nestled among the trees, lay on the back side of a dark green lagoon. To cross the lagoon, we pulled a rope-drawn raft and reached the other side after a slow portage. As we floated across the lagoon, the deep green shrubs along the shore reflected in the water, making a double image of green. The image seemed fitting for this high-temperate rainforest. From the shore's edge, an elevated wooden walkway to the lodge passed over a watery garden of ferns and lichens. Silver-speckled lizards sunned along the weather-blanched planks. Inside the lodge, the smell of a wood-burning fire and supper greeted us. A dark-haired woman with a radiant smile introduced herself as Annabel, welcomed us with glasses of fresh orange juice, and showed us to our room. We napped until dinner, ate delicious baked fish, and immediately went back to bed to sleep another nine hours. I woke the next morning with the lines of Edgar Allen Poe, "It was many and many a year ago in a kingdom by the sea / that a maiden there lived whom you may know by the name of Annabel Lee" running through my mind.

The morning sky was so cloudless and so vivid it seemed as solid as a painted ceiling. Such a day demanded a hike, so we joined a young German couple on their trek up the mountain. The mountain overlooked the Parque Nacional Alerce Andino and had great views of the park. The hike turned out to be a six-hour climb up and slide down a mile-high mountain on a trail that was literally a streambed. Parts of it were so steep, it required real climbing. If it hadn't been for the tough little cane that grew in clusters along the streambed, I would still be struggling on that mountain. Using them like ropes, I was able to pull myself up and catch myself going down, but even so, by the end of the day, I had fallen several times and would develop bruises that would make a tattoo artist green with envy. I would also develop a profound respect for coligue (*Chusquea culeou*). This cane, also called coligue cane or araucano, looks like bamboo but, unlike bamboo, it is solid inside. It thrives in wet climates (the annual rainfall around Puerto Montt is 136 inches), is found at altitudes as high as 3,600 feet, often grows in tall dense thickets, and is all over the region. As a young plant, it is as flexible as nylon rope. As it ages, it becomes so strong that the indigenous people of the area, the Mapuches, made twelve-foot spears from the older stalks.

The most enjoyable moments of the hike were the rest stops, those all-too-brief periods when we could look around and see things other than the next flat rock. On a ridge about thirty minutes from the top, we stopped in a grove of lenga trees (*Nothofagus pumilio*) and sat beneath the shade of their branches. More like tall bushes, the lenga trees were only about ten feet high. They grow to heights of ninety feet plus at lower altitudes but with higher and higher altitudes, they get shorter and shorter. Lenga leaves look like dime-size oak leaves (in fact, lenga is called white oak or Tierra del Fuego oak) and the yellow leaf litter that we sat on had the softness of a throw pillow. Beyond the green peaks, the snow-capped peaks of the higher Andes rose into the thin air. We were almost five thousand feet high, the air smelled of evergreen, and the cold was invigorating. Our guides handed out bottles of water and cheese sandwiches made with thick slices of freshly baked bread. It may have been the best sandwich I had ever eaten.

The climb down was quicker but still too strenuous to enjoy. When all attention and energy are focused on the next step, much of the sights that make up the beauty of a trail become blurred background. I have met hikers who always seem in a hurry, anxious to get to the next place, and almost competitive in their rolling off the miles. Some will say, "We did twenty miles today," as if bragging about a hefty bank account, and I wonder if they have seen the interesting bird, the oddly shaped rock, the unusual plant, or the mysterious fungi. Of course, any hike can be defined by distance and time, just as any place can be defined in terms of measurement, but it is so much more. Perhaps the measure of a hike is really the quality of joy that opens in the moments of discovery. For a hike, any hike, is always about discovery.

I soaked in hot water for hours after that hike and by the next morning I was ready to give it another try on less rugged terrain. But first we made a quick survey of the birds around the lodge using our abbreviated *The Birds of Chile: A Field Guide* (Chester 1995). A pair of house wrens nested in a nearby cypress, flying in and out of their nesting hole, hustling to feed their young. Green iridescent hummingbirds (green-backed firecrowns) hovered at the blossoms of the fire bush, feeding from the long-tube flowers. A Patagonian sierra-finch puffed out to the size of a robin with soft gray and yellow markings landed on the porch and entertained us with a hopscotch dance. A bird called a chiricoca gave several penetrating gravelly chirps, but we were never able to see it with any degree of clarity. Finches flitted from tree to tree, moving so quickly their markings were invisible, and black-and-white Chilean swallows zoomed in and around the trees. None of the leisurely perching or languorous preening of tropical rainforests birds, these birds were constantly on the move, which seemed a more suitable behavior in the cold rainforest.

The three-hour climb to a waterfall was straight down precipitous gullies, up steep cliffs, over fallen trees, and up slippery slopes covered in moss. So much for less difficult terrain. Every bit of space on that trail was filled with something green and wet. Lichens, ferns, mosses, bracket fungi, an entire encyclopedia of mushrooms grew on the surfaces of the fallen trees and rocks. There was simply no surface left ungreened or bare of life. Orange and yellow fungi (*Dacrymyces* sp.) looking like jelly-babies dotted the decaying tree trunks and limbs with glistening spots. A club moss similar in appearance to running pine was abundant. Ferns sprouting new fronds covered the upper surface of fallen limbs. A pendant lichen known as devil's beard (*Usnea* sp.) wrapped the branches of trees in patches of mint green fur. Another lichen speckled the rocks like brown polka dots. The trail was a garden of primitive plants, and I wondered how so many organisms could squeeze together in one space.

Ecologists use the rather lackluster terms *productivity* and *diversity* to describe the number of organisms and types of organisms in a particular environment. Long ago at a rodeo, I remember seeing twenty clowns climb out of a tiny Volkswagen bug, and it seemed a wonder that so many could cram into such a small space. Some were enormous clowns, some were tall thin clowns, some were short fat clowns, and there were all sizes in between. Was it a trick or was it the most extraordinary packing and arranging of body parts? Places of high productivity and rich diversity with so many different kinds of living things still hold the same fascination for me as that VW bug and those clowns.

Unlike the hot and gummy feel of a tropical rainforest, this temperate rainforest was cool and clammy and reminded me of the Pacific Northwest rainforests. In the shade, it was cold; in the direct sun, hot; and in the thin ozone, the sun was a cryptic touch of fire. Such contrasting temperatures kept the body's thermostat in hyperdrive. Finally reaching a waterfall and a rest stop, I sat on a rock and contemplated the botanical wonderland around me. I felt embraced by epiphytes. That plants could grow from the trunks and branches and crowns of other plants challenges my notion of typical plants. Plants should grow from the soil, right? But epiphytes grow on other plants. They do not parasitize or harm them; they simply use them as places of anchor, and their importance is just beginning to be understood (Benzing 1990). Not only do epiphytes serve as some of the most critical medicinal resources for indigenous tribes but canopy biologists are beginning to understand how crucial they are to the ecology of the entire rainforest. They capture water, keep humidity high during dry periods, produce considerable biomass, and cycle nutrients at rates comparable to the traditional soil-anchored species. In a study conducted in the Andean Columbian rainforest, researchers found that 12 percent of a tree's biomass was actually epiphyte biomass. In terms of nitrogen and phosphorus, the percent climbed to nearly 50 percent. Epiphytes also maintain complex symbiotic relationships with some forest insects like ants and provide a valuable food source and home for birds and other animals. Who could not be impressed with epiphytes.

Every rock and every surface was slick with moss. Some mosses stood upright, some were prostrate. Some looked like stars, some like umbrellas. Some sprouted tiny pine seedlings, some hunched like pincushions, some crept and interwove their stems to form dense mats, so many different mosses. Chile has eight hundred species of bryophytes (true mosses, liverworts, and hornworts) and while all eight hundred were not on these rocks, there seemed an infinite variety at the edge of that waterfall. The two most common mosses were a species that looked a little like Spanish moss (*Weymouthia mollis*) and one that had a creeping segmented stem (*Papillaria crocea*).

Epiphytes in the bromeliad family were also abundant. Most of the 2,700 known species of bromeliads come from the rain and cloud forests of tropical South American, but there are a goodly number indigenous to the temperate rainforest. The common one on the trees here was the same one I had seen on my first trip to Patagonia. Related to Spanish moss, this bromelid was one of eight hundred species in the enormous genus, *Tillandsia*. A drab gray-green, it grew in long thick trellises. Draping everything like kudzu in the southern U.S. landscape, it gave the trees and shrubs the appearance of being too small for their clothes.

Fern, lichen, and fungal epiphytes filled in the other spaces, and I was almost overwhelmed by their abundance. As I looked around in awe of this epiphytic paradise, I thought of Nancy Willard's poem "The Hardware Store as Proof of the Existence of God" in her collection, *Water Walker* (1989). I thought I would change it to "Epiphytes as Proof of the Existence of God" or maybe more simply "In Praise of Epiphytes" and it would go:

> I would praise the ferns whose sweaters cover
> limbs or hang discombobulated like socks that miss the hamper.
> I would praise the lichens, never alone but always with partners.
> In marriage they become a single dancer, composing a colorful tango.
> And like giant paint spills, they leave their mark.
> I would praise the fungi whose crusts patch the bare spots,
> whose stepladders climb the sky, whose doilies drape
> the couches in old forests' parlors.
> I would praise the mosses, heads in brush cuts, punk spikes,
> hair nets, who raise the question, "who is imitating whom?"
>
> In a world that does not believe in perfection only in being,
> let there be photosynthesizers, let there always be room for one more.
> In their green hands, they can work wonders.

The next morning, sunburned, bruises in full bloom, and muscles aching, I voted to skip the suggested hike. Instead, my companion and I strolled the main road at a leisurely pace. The stone road opened into a forest of evergreens, mixed broadleaf trees, and ferns. In addition to the stately alerce, there were the Chilean cedar (*Austrocedrus chilensis*), a cypress called ten (*Pilgerodendron uviferum*), yellow pine (*Podocarpus nubigenus*), hardwoods like coigue or southern beech (*Nothofagus dombeyi*) reaching many stories high, other species of *Nothofagus* (there are eight common ones in the region), the great honey tree (*Eucryphia cordifolia*), laurel (*Laureliopsis philippiana*), and a yew (*Saxegothaea conspicua*). Below the great green parasols of the conifers in the shaded understory, ferns (*Lophosoria quadripinnata* most commonly) sprouted new fronds. The new fronds were shaped like curled fetuses and cinnamon colored. The occasional patch of daisies added splashes of white and the fire bush provided another ornamental shade of red.

Some of the fallen alerces had been cut and stacked. It is illegal to cut a living alerce tree because they (like the araucaria) are endangered, and in Chile, they are considered national monuments. The wood pieces were stacked high in red piles along the road. So resistant to decay, the wood can be used as roof shingles, and that was what they were going to be used for, expensive shingles. The newly cut wood saturated with fresh recalcitrant phenols was red; the older weathered wood, gray. In the middle of the trunks of some fallen trees, it was hollow, a reminder that a living tree is actually a cylinder. The insides of all mature trees are dead, and only the last outside ring below the bark is really alive. When that rock band of degraders begins to break down the dead tissue, they bang out the melody of decay from inside. The phrase "rotten to the core" takes on a literal meaning with trees.

This temperate rainforest is part of the Valdivian rainforest that extends along Chile's coast. One of the most biologically rich ecoregions of the world, it is threatened (WWF 2001). More than half of the four hundred woody plants are unique to the region, and they are fast disappearing. Estimates suggest that by 2020, the old-growth forests will be gone. Only 5 percent of the original cypress remains, less than 1 percent of the alerce remains, and the araucaria are almost completely gone. Chile, the third largest wood-chip exporter of the world, has used these trees for pulp. Although an American-Chilean mill (the Boise Cascade Chip Mill) recently canceled plans to build the world's largest chip mill in the region, efforts to stop the destruction of the forest are negated by the construction of a coastal highway and poor replanting practices. Landowners cut the native trees for chips and instead of replanting native species, they replant fast-growing pine or eucalyptus, a process that changes the entire biology of the region.

As I looked at the beautiful trees, I thought again of the young man I had encountered at the airport. To be responsible for cutting these unique trees, to send these trees to chip mills to be converted to paper, something that usually ends up shredded and thrown away, I simply could not comprehend. The desires of men who so need a new car, a new house, a new something, that they would destroy a forest, a forest that does not even belong to them, seems to be the root of great folly. Like the Spanish conquistadores before him, the young man was following in the long tradition of colonial exploitation; he was just another link in a long chain of those who exploit the natural world without thinking of the consequences, without examining the broader results of their actions.

Back at the lodge, Annabel gave us clean socks since our luggage missed connections and was delayed a couple days. Her kindness reminded me of another incident on the flight from Santiago to Puerto Montt, where my seatmates were an elderly woman and a young man dressed all in black. Everything about the woman was worn; her faded dress, her threadbare sweater, even the plastic frames of her glasses looked worn. The fellow was lean and rangy with oily, slicked-back, black hair. I was surprised when he struck up a conversation with the old woman. They were strangers. He spoke to her in a deferential tone as if she were his grandmother and when the food was served, he gave her his sandwich, his crackers, fruit, and cheese, and then his bottle of water. She put everything, including her own food, in her ragged purse. Given a choice of who I would want to run the world, the man who cut trees or the one who gave his food away, the choice would not be a difficult one. Unfortunately, the world seems to be run by the tree cutters.

Puerto Varas, a city on Lake Llanquihue, could easily have been a German village with its alpine-style lakefront houses, its wooden wagons painted red and blue with Bavarian designs (souvenir kiosks), and its big steepled German church on the tallest hill. This was the starting point for an excursion that took us from coastal Chile across the Andes into Argentina. The lake crossing involved a bus ride, a boat ride, another bus ride, a border check, another boat ride, a short two-mile bus ride, a third boat ride, and a final bus ride into Barilouche. The seventy-five-mile passage—from the coast up through a six-thousand-foot pass and down the eastern slopes of the Andes onto the steppe lands—was a textbook illustration of zonation. We moved through six distinct biomes in a single day and watched a multitude of landscapes molded by rain and elevation unfold.

The first two zones on the wetter Pacific side of the Andes (from 0 to about 2,000 feet and 2,000 to 4,500 feet) were exceptionally diverse. *Nothofagus* forests of coigue (*N. dombeyi*) and nire (*N. antarctica*) covered the land at the lower elevations and lenga occurred higher up. Other species of *Nothofagus*, such as guindo (*N. betuloides*), rauli (*N. alpina*), and roble (*N. obliqua*) were also present, as were alerce, cypress, canelo (*Drimys winteri*), and numerous other plants typical of the wetter region. Patches of tall coligue cane filled in where there were gaps in the forest. The drier mid-Andean zone, 4,500 to 6,000 feet, was less diverse and included mostly evergreens such as cypress, ten, and radal (*Lomatia hirsuta*), although the three species of *Nothofagus* (*N.*

dombeyi, N. pumilio, and *N. antartica*) could be seen. The alpine zone, 6,000 feet and above, was barren of trees and had patches of snow and rocks, a few grasses, bushes in humid spots, peat bogs, reeds, and mosses. Down the drier eastern side of the Andes, coniferous forests appeared again, but there was less diversity. The slopes gave way to chaparral and finally to the steppe lands. We would see these final two transitional zones even more dramatically later in Nahuel Huapi National Park.

The lake crossing began in the morning with a bus drive along Lake Llanquihue and a stop at the water chutes of Salto del Petrohue where glacier melt spewed from the mountains and rumbled over volcanic rocks. The contrast of white water over black rocks was a photographer's dream and everyone was snapping pictures. At Petrohue the first boat took us across Lake Todos los Santos. With the snow-capped volcano Osorno rising from behind the deep green slopes, we glided across the alpine lake. From Peulla, the drive to Puerto Frias, where we boarded another boat to portage Lake Frias, took much of the early afternoon. A bus ride uphill to Puerto Blest to board yet another boat that motored us westward along one arm of Lake Nahuel Huapi, letting us off at the Llao Llao peninsula, took the remaining afternoon. The final leg of the crossing was the bus ride into Barilouche. With the sky turning crimson, the end of the day was a welcome relief. No arguing that the alpine lakes and the montane forests that covered the mountains were lovely but too many people spoiled the scenery. The herd effect of tourists getting on and off buses and boats, the waiting in lines at the borders' checkpoints, the noise of too many people slurping drinks, crunching snacks, chatting, bumping into one another took much of the pleasure out of the trip. That a company can take a spectacular landscape, herd large numbers of people through it, and call it a scenic journey strikes me as ludicrous. But there were hundreds of us who found ourselves part of the lunacy. Riding along the last stretch of highway lined with expensive hotels and shops into Barilouche, what I most craved was quiet and privacy. The weather had changed from misty to sunny, from fair to overcast, from crisp to cloudy. We had transferred seven times, traversed at least six different biological zones, and I felt I had lived a week.

Barilouche is a resort town, so the streets of its shopping district were full of restaurants and shops selling T-shirts, souvenirs, ski equipment, chocolate, and film. My only prior knowledge of this city had come from news articles that claimed it was a place where Nazis escaped after WWII and where an outbreak of *Hantavirus* had occurred. Old Nazis and microbes do not speak well for a place, but it turned out that Barilouche was actually rather pretty. Red and yellow poppies bloomed in gardens along the streets, and the blue lake with its surrounding rusty hills made for a pleasant landscape. The snow-filled valleys and the majestic peaks of Cathedral Mountain provided good skiing south of the city, so a lot of skiers roamed the town. One day of city was enough.

To explore the countryside we hired a car and driver and made a grand loop through Nahuel Huapi National Park. Like the lake crossing, our route passed through many zones of vegetation. The highway out of town began as a ribbon of flowers. The subtle pink of the rose blossoms, the purple thistle heads as big as baseballs, and the blue lupine provided a colorful start to the day. A few miles outside the city, the garden flowers gave way to typical Patagonian grasslands and native plants. The arid steppe lands, brown with tussock grasses (*Festuca* spp., *Stipa ichu*, and *Calamagrosis* spp.) and semidesert cushion plants, lasted only a few miles. Turning eastward, the road climbed through the short bushy vegetation of the chaparral. Plants like calafate (*Berberis barilochensis*), neneo, chacay, and juniper-like shrubs dotted the low rolling hills. A few miles farther and the land suddenly turned green, and we entered the alpine terrain of the eastern slopes of the Andes. The transition from steppe land to chaparral to alpine occurred so suddenly, there was no missing the importance of rain and elevation on plant life.

Beside one of the glacial streams that fed Lake Nahuel Huapi, we paused to enjoy a crystal-clear creek lined with maiten or Patagonian willows (*Maytenus boaria*). Smooth white stones of granite bordered the banks. As the steam bubbled its way to the lake, our guide scooped up a handful of the water and drank. He said it was pure glacier melt and safe to drink. So, we did. I could not remember when water tasted so refreshing.

A few miles beyond the stream, we stopped again, near a copse of arrayan trees (*Myrceugenella apiculata*). The only arrayan forest in the world grows in this park, and this small groove along the lake was tiny compared to the larger stands farther north. Related to the southern crepe myrtle, the tree is in the eucalyptus family. Its fawn-colored bark was smooth and cold to the touch. It was as if the tree had ice water in its veins, or rather in its xylem. Our guide seemed to attach great significance to the fact that this was where the Disney movie *Bambi* was filmed or, rather, where the background for the movie was filmed. He took pride in telling us that the arrayan forest was the forest of Bambi. I would have preferred to hear any Mapuches legends about the trees, but like so many in the tourist industry, guides seem to cater to U.S. icons. It made me sad that U.S. culture seems to dominate the whole world. To think that a corporate story from the United States, produced, marketed, and sold globally, had become more familiar than a story from the native people. It struck me as unhealthy. Although I doubt if any of the legends of the indigenous peoples had survived about the arrayan tree, it seems more appropriate to think of this place as the forest of the Mapuches.

After tea in a village cafe, we moved on to some of the small inlets and streams where fishermen tossed their lines for trout. The lakes have been stocked with rainbow, brown, and brook trout (nonnative species). As we stood on a bridge overlooking a stream that connected two lakes and watched the torpedo-sleek bodies of brown trout ripple just below the surface, I wondered if there was any place on Earth where humans had not altered the biology.

A bit farther on at a park and boat landing, we walked among a grove of beech trees (*Nothofagus dombeyi*). The trees were full of galls, galls similar to the ones I had seen in Tierra del Fuego. The gall-producing fungus was a different species (*Cyttaria hariotii*) but it was also called lloa lloa. One of the mysteries of this genus of fungi (*Cyttaria*) is that it only infects the southern beech trees (*Nothofagus* spp.) (Minter et al. 1987). Biologists refer to such a relationship as *narrow host specificity* and suggest that it offers clues about phylogenetic and evolutionary phenomena. The fungi and the ancient austral trees have coevolved. They have been together for hundreds of thousands of years. That their complex host-parasite relationship has evolved into an almost benign one suggests that connection over time results in accommodations. It is one of those wonderfully appealing ideas in evolutionary biology.

For lunch we ate some of those nonnative rainbow trout covered in thin slivers of almonds at a tiny restaurant near a popular campground. They were delicious! Continuing our tour we drove on, stopping at a few overlooks to marvel at the lake and the mountains and by midafternoon, we entered an area known as the Enchanted Valley. Unusual rocks formations, the result of ancient erosion by water and ice, bordered the road. Beyond the cliffs, condors soared on the thermals. They glided in wide lazy circles in the sky above the rusty, strangely shaped rocks. The last leg of the drive, the road followed the Rio Limay with its fast-moving waters rushing to Lake Nahuel Huapi. By dusk we had completed our circle and were back in the city.

From Bariloche we flew to Buenos Aires where we stayed only as long as it took to make flight connections. This huge delta city is where the Rio de la Plata and the Rio Parana (rivers that come from the vast swamplands to the north called the Pantanal) empty into the Atlantic Ocean. It is supposedly one of South America's most famous and vibrant cities, but I was glad we were just passing through. Approaching the city from the air, the plane passed over the empty steppe lands; the brown steppe land gave way to green river land; the green river lands became spotted with the occasional hacienda and then small clusters of houses. The closer to the city, the more numerous the houses and the less green until finally there was only the urban gray of one concrete building after another. Where the Rio Plata-Parana flowed into the Atlantic, an enormous brown plume darkened the blue ocean waters.

The travel company's car picked us up and drove us via the freeway around Buenos Aires from the domestic airport to the international terminal. It took forty minutes to travel the concrete beltway around the concrete city. The final image of the city was of cars parked along the freeway and families using the shoulder as a park. Some were sitting in folded chairs, some were picnicking, some played volleyball but most just sat on the grass trying to catch a little cool. A few trees offered limited shade and the only escape from the concrete city, the city whose name means "good air."

Drylands: The Atacama Desert — 4

ᔆᕽᕽ

THERE ARE MANY WAYS OF KNOWING A PLACE. Facts are only one form of knowledge but certainly the fact that the Atacama Desert is one of the driest places on Earth creates a doorway to understanding this land. In some parts of the desert, it never rains, and these rainless regions, called absolute desert, have no vegetation whatsoever. Other spots experience less than half an inch of rain a year and only the hardiest scrubs survive. It rains occasionally in inch pulses and a phenomenon called the blooming desert occurs. Along the coast, a mist referred to as *camanchaca* forms in the winter and blankets the desert. These fog zones (called *lomas*) support the richest biota of the desert, but by rainforest comparison, the biota is not rich. To know the desert is to understand the importance of rain.

What makes this land a desert involves the cold, stable offshore Peruvian (Humboldt) current, the westward winds that blow away from land, and the mountain ranges that prevent the accumulation of rain clouds. Not just one mountain range but many rise like barricades, blocking clouds from getting over and delivering rain. The coastal mountains that run right along the edge of the coast of Chile, Peru, and Ecuador are the most seaward mountains and they rise one to five thousand feet high. Just behind them lie the first of the high, dry desert plains. Beyond them, the foothills of the Andes rise slowly, and the high plateaus known as the altiplano give rise to peaks and volcanoes, many as high as twenty-three thousand feet. Flying to the Grande Norte from Santiago to Calama, it was easy to see why land right next to the ocean was desert. The position of the massive cordilleras of mountains clearly blocked the rain clouds.

But a land is so much more than its landscape, more than facts, and no writer has captured the spirit of this land quite like Lake Sagaris in *Bone and Dream*

(2000). An ingenious weave of fact and myth, history and present-day events, travelogue and subtle political commentary, her story is one of the most ingenious written on the region. She creates the tapestry of her tale using the quest for a mythical Inca princess. Hers is not a romantic or sentimental journey but an insightful one that explores the struggle of a native American woman in the days of the Spanish conquistadors.

Leaving Calama, the circular green piles of waste from the world's largest open-pit copper mine, Chuquicamata, were the first landmarks we noted. Smoke from the smelters cast a haze over the area, and as we drove passed this mining town, I thought of all the terrible things humans do to their environment for wealth. People have been coming to this place for the minerals for thousands of years. The whole history of the region is scarred with the tracks of foreigners looking for rich minerals. Although some used trade and diplomacy, many used brute force. Pre-Columbian traders came looking for salt. The Incas came for gold. The Spanish conquistadors in the sixteenth century came for gold and later, silver. Copper was mined extensively in the seventeenth and eighteenth centuries by Europeans, nitrates in the nineteenth and twentieth centuries for fertilizer and explosives by Americans and Canadians, and now the mines are owned by huge international conglomerates that dig up the earth for lithium, iodine, and molybdenum as well as copper and nitrates.

Because of this history, the mines of the region have been places of violent struggle. I remember the story a friend told of her family's escape from the nearby Potosi region of Bolivia in the 1950s. Her father took a job as a manager for an American mining company and they moved to the region. He was a kind man, befriended the native mineworkers, and learned their language, Quechua. They warned him to have an escape plan because a revolution was coming. As a child of five, my friend had to sleep nights wrapped in a coat with her shoes on. One night she was rousted from sleep and quickly hustled onto a plane. The mine had been blown up, her father had narrowly escaped the explosion, and her family was barely able to escape with their lives.

Today, the Chilean mine workers have a better life and are paid better wages but, like workers throughout the world, the struggle has been a long one and still continues. The massacre of Santa Maria de Iquique symbolized the early twentieth-century struggle of Chile's mine workers. In 1907, the miners initiated a strike for better pay and safer work conditions only to be massacred on the school grounds and plaza where they had gathered. Reports vary but probably two hundred workers were killed and four hundred wounded by army soldiers controlled by the mine owners. This means of suppression using military-government forces continued throughout the twentieth century (and was mastered by Pinochet and his gang of generals in the 1970s). The struggles between the foreign powers, generally rich nations (Europeans initially, and American and Canadians later) who owned the mines, and the indigenous peoples and the imported poor who worked the mines, left a brutal legacy of injustices.

We left the smog and garbage of Calama and sped towards the village of San Pedro de Atacama. For thirty miles through the Plain of Patience, there was nothing but rock and sand, without a sign of even the smallest plant. This was clearly absolute desert. There was nothing alive, nothing but raw stones. As we neared San Pedro de Atacama, a few dusty plants appeared and the road climbed up and through the Domeyko Mountains. The Domeyko Mountains are an inland mountain chain and a second barrier to rain clouds. Continuing east, the road climbed through yet another chain of mountains, the Cordillera de la Sal (the Salt Mountains), where the rock formations along the roadside resembled the scaly back of a dinosaur. Not surprisingly, the pass was called Dinosaur Valley. The road crested the highest point in the Salt Mountains, and the vast salt flats of Salar de Atacama stretched out like a field of snow. The road sloped down out of the mountains, and we descended into the green oasis of the red adobe village of San Pedro de Atacama. This village would be our home for the holidays.

The fact that humans have been in the Americas for many thousands of years as hunters and gatherers is probably common knowledge, but to realize that stable organized cities existed here as far back as five thousand years ago was a surprise. The archeological site of Tulor dating back to around 800 B.C.E. was not quite as old as some of the ruins further north, and while not on the scale of the grand ghost cities of Mesopotamia and Egypt, the artifacts exhibited in the small museum in San Pedro, the Museo Arqueológico Gustavo Le Paige, reflected a viable, advanced civilization. The people of the San Pedro culture produced beautiful metal ornaments and tools, rust-colored and black pottery, huge vessels for storing grain, flutes, and most interesting, mummies. Mummies predating those of Egypt had been discovered all over the region, but unlike Egyptian mummies preserved with chemicals and herbs, the mummies here were preserved by the natural desiccation of the desert air.

In the museum, I found myself fascinated by the remains of a woman seated in a clay burial pot. Knees bent to her chin, her hair was in long black braids. She was surrounded by her meager possessions: a wooden comb, a string of blue beads, a small faded herb pouch, part of a woven basket, a cactus needle with a thread of yarn attached. With the skin on her skull weathered and shrunken, the details of her face were gone but her feet and toenails were so intact, it looked as if she might rise up and walk off. What a strange sensation to stand staring at this three-thousand-year-old woman—even stranger when the light hit the glass exhibit case and reflected back my own image. My image was superimposed over hers. My eyes fit into her eyes; my lips became her lips; my checks, her checks; my shoulders, hers. I stood immobilized and mesmerized by that moment of clarity, that moment of absolute truth.

To get to the excavated site of Tulor, we drove through Coyo, one of fifteen *ayllus* or subdivisions of the village (perhaps large, extended family farms might also describe these units). Canals provided water for growing dry-tolerant crops like hay, corn, and alfalfa. I noticed a small tractor under a shed but leaning against the fence was a wooden plow. A long-eared gray mule grazed in the field. Beyond the road, small adobe huts built low to the ground had open doors, and the small fields were bordered with short adobe walls. The walls marked each property and acted as container walls for the water when the fields were flooded. The contrast of driving from brown desert with almost no vegetation to entering a green lane of trees surrounded by green fields made the concept of oasis very real. The boundaries of watered land and waterless land were as distinct as night and day. Moving from one to the other was an instantaneous transition. One moment it was brown, the next it was green. Truly, this was a place where water was the transforming element.

At Tulor, we climbed inside one of the round reconstructed huts. Cool, comfortable, and out of the blowing sand, the adobe walls were a foot thick at the base and thinned as they rose seven feet to a straw ceiling. Wooden beams held in place with strips of llama hide radiated from the center. Overlaying the beams, layers of grass and over that adobe on the outside provided the roof. The huts did not differ much from the present-day village houses, so the design must have been well suited for the desert. A boardwalk stood above the excavated half-walls of the buried village, and off in the distance, a line of treetops peeked over the dunes, marking the banks of the Rio San Pedro. The village was once closer to the river but with time, the river had changed course, leaving the village high and dry in a graveyard of sand dunes. Against the cloudless cobalt sky, the vibrant green treetops seemed to be losing the battle to the shifting sands. Sand seemed bent on covering everything in its path. In this rainless land, desert certainly trumped river.

The bone-woman had been found here at Tulor by the priest—amateur archeologist who had established the museum. Our guide said that some of the locals resented that she had been taken from her resting place and put on display in the museum. I was reminded of Alison Deming's essay "Inside the Wolf" from *Temporary Homelands* (1994, 58) where she contemplates death as a real place in nature. She writes about a Tohono O'oohdam elder who refers to death as a place in the desert and points to an actual physical spot. She writes, "Death is our home— where we all go at the end, a place we all share in common, and therefore a place we must not defile."

At Quitor, another *ayllus* to the north, we crawled up a seven-hundred-year-old pre-Columbian fortress for a bird's-eye view of the village and surrounding *ayllus*.

Strategically located on the highest spot overlooking the river valley, it was built by a people from Bolivia, probably the Diaguitas who were overseers for the Aymaras (the Andean people who originated from Lake Titicaca). With control of the river, they imposed a tax for water rights on the local Atacamenians. Huffing and puffing up the steep trail, we stopped momentarily as our guide pointed to a stone wall with tiny window holes. He related a gory tale about the wall. The last stronghold of this early empire, the fortress fell to the Spanish conquistador, Pedro de Valdivia. Overtaking it in a short few hours, he executed every warrior and hung their bloody heads on poles along this wall. Ah, the glorious past, I thought, as I struggled to catch my breath in the thin air. Finally reaching the top and a most welcome resting point, the view was a patchwork quilt of smooth sepias and mahoganies (desert soil), plots of textured green (the agricultural fields), and the lighter brown streaks and whirls of disturbed earth (the ubiquitous mines).

Large groves of salt-tolerant tamarugo trees planted as part of an agriculture project in the 1950s grew along the road to Laguna Chaxa. The trees shaded a tiny village of families who had been relocated after a volcano eruption destroyed their homes to the north. The people were herders and their flocks of llamas and goats grazed among makeshift huts and thorny trees. Along the way to the lagoon, the white village of Toconao lay in sharp contrast to the red abode of San Pedro de Atacama. About a fourth of the population of San Pedro (San Pedro has about two thousand people), Toconao's buildings were constructed of white porous lava rock called liparite. Averaging five to ten blocks a day, village artisans carve each stone by hand. Unlike the usually heavy, mineral-laden rivers that come from the mountains, Toconao's river had few minerals and provided clean potable water. Trees and plants unable to grow in the salt-saturated and mineral-laden soils of the area flourished here, and the landscape had a healthier look. Poplar trees, trees that looked like sycamores, fruit and nut trees, and even small vineyards appeared around the village.

After a quick walk through the square and the church, we ended up at an artisan shop where we purchased soft alpaca scarves and a llama wool rug. The family who lived behind the shop invited us back. In the open-air courtyard, an old man and his grandson sat at a small wooden table putting together a jigsaw puzzle. In one corner, the women's spinning wheel and loom sat ready for the next project, and beyond them, several llamas munched hay in a wooden pen and nuzzled each other. What a successful business this mother and daughter had created. Amazed at the resourcefulness of these women and the complexity of the processes they carried out, I offered a heartfelt "gracias" as we left and a silent homage of praise to their industriousness. How many women would be capable of that repertoire of skills: to care for animals, to shear their wool and make yarn, from the yarn to weave materials of great beauty and functionality, and to sell them to support their families. And yet, is this not what women all over the world have been doing since the beginning of family?

A few miles south of Toconao, the salt flats of Laguna Chaxa stretched for miles across the greater plain of the Salar de Atacama. Like a plowed field of salt, the white lava stones were encrusted with salt. Everywhere, white salt deposits like frost lined the edges of upturned soil and stones. Walking the road among the lava chips, our feet made music, like the notes of wind chimes. When some of the boys in our group discovered that the lava rocks made music, they began to beat out tunes on the rocks. The flamingos, Andea avocets, and puna plovers that fed in the lagoon seemed not to mind their xylophone melodies at all. Half a dozen flamingos fed on *Artemia,* a small crustacean called fairy or brine shrimp. The shallows were so full of brine shrimp, the water appeared gray.

Of the world's six species of flamingos, three species are found here: the Andean or puna flamingo, the James, and the Chilean. A lighter pink with different markings than the Caribbean flamingo or the lesser and greater flamingos of Africa, these birds migrate between Chile, Bolivia, and Peru. In the 1950s, the James flamingo was thought extinct, but a 1997 survey of one hundred lakes in the Andean wetlands revealed over thirty thousand birds. Other bird counts have estimated that while there may be as many as a hundred thousand South American flamingos totally, overall populations are in decline. The Andean flamingo may be declining because of habitat disturbance due to borax extraction. The mining and processing of borates releases products which affect the waters and the organisms upon which the birds feed.

In the salty waters of Chaxa, only the puna and the Andean flamingos were present. On long stilted legs, long necks bowed in the waters, they never fail to evoke the idea that nature has a sense of humor, and when I think of the ease with which Alice in Wonderland used them as croquet mallets, I cannot help but smile. As the sun dropped below the mountains and the landscape turned a hundred shades of pinks, the flamingos rose from the roseate waters. Only the black tips of their wings and beaks distinguished them from sky as they faded into the coralline horizon.

To watch the geysers of Tatio erupt, we left San Pedro two hours before sunrise and drove through the mountains in the dark. As the sky lightened, we crested a hill and below us a flat steaming field stretched out like a grill. Some geysers were wide boiling pools, some no bigger than a volleyball, with white ribbons of steam rising from them in the cold morning air. Some were minivolcanoes with high yellow cones of mineral deposits; some opened like rock flowers. They sputtered, gurgled, and spewed steam and boiling water, but while their eruptions were small, not more than a few meters at best, the vast number (probably a hundred in all) of bizarre shapes gave the landscape an otherworldly feel.

We stumbled in and out of the steam, disappearing and appearing like creatures of the mist. It was warm in the steam clouds and our glasses kept fogging up. Within less than an hour of our arrival, the eruptions quieted and we began exploring the surrounding terrain. Small streams flowed from the geyser holes and they were full of interesting things. Strands of green and red algae attached to the banks floated on the current like frayed rope. Black minnows and black frogs no bigger than quarters drifted in and out of the algae strands. In the cold, thin altiplano air at an elevation of fourteen thousand feet, I was surprised to see fish and amphibians. Yes, we spotted vizcachas, those chinchilla-like rodents, hopping in the rocks and vicuñas grazing on the sparse grass, but these mammals had fur to protect them. The frogs had nothing. They lived within a small temperature gradient, not too close to the geysers to burn, yet not too far away that they would freeze in the high cold nights. On what an amazing temperature tightrope these creatures lived.

On the way back to San Pedro, we noticed the change in vegetation with declining elevations. Much of the unique vegetation has been described by botanists (Rundel et al. 1991). At fourteen thousand feet, only grasses grew. The grass (our guide called it "pajas bravas" which translates as "brave little hay") grew in circles. Also known as coiron, puna grass on ichu, severals species (*Stipa ichu, S. frigida*, and *Festuca chrysophyllum*) made up the flora of the high meadows. The circles were like fairy rings, the result of the live tufted grass growing at the outer edge. Over time, the center dies and is blown away, leaving the outer ring of grass. Sometimes, the clumps of grass had crescent shapes, the side toward the wind dying off, leaving half-moons. What lovely circumferential patterns these grass circles and crescents etched on the landscape.

Covering the occasional rock outcroppings near water, a deep green lichen called llareta made its home. These algal-fungal symbionts grow only one centimeter per year and are believed to live for several thousand years. I wondered if the merging of two organisms to create a new one that could survive these harsh conditions was an example for the old adage "two heads (in this case, bodies) are better than one." The endosymbiont theory of cellular evolution, which suggests that merging makes more adaptable life-forms, is certainly based on this premise. And this Methuselah lichen was certainly a good illustration of the principle.

At twelve thousand feet, other grasses appeared and at about eleven thousand feet, shrubs and cactus speckled the landscape. Of the forty species of *Copiapoa* (cactus) in the Atacama, the most abundant ones here were ground huggers. Many were fat pincushions. Some looked like little furry stuffed animals but how deceiving, for what looked like soft fur was actually sharp barbed needles. One tall species similar to the Sonora desert saguaros raised its arms like the victim of bandits. Almost all of these candelabra cactuses were scraggly, diseased, or damaged, and I thought, in a land of few trees, overharvesting of the little available wood might quickly lead to this plant's demise. It turned out this was the case. In an effort to protect them, the Chilean government has passed laws making it illegal to cut or damage these cactuses. But, of course, such laws are about as effective as the laws against logging in national forests.

Down a steep rocky road, we descended into a narrow lush canyon where the hot waters of the Rio Puritama had been partially dammed to make thermal pools. Termas de Puritama was a welcome stop. Tall Juncus reeds bordered the pools and turquoise dragonflies perched on the tips of the reeds. A rufous-collared sparrow sang a melodious tune as we soaked in the warm waters. Like the little frogs, we floated in a narrow temperature range. Too far upstream and the waters would scald us, too far down and the waters would freeze.

As we descended from ten thousand to seven thousand feet and back to San Pedro, the landscape remained fairly desolate, with vegetation consisting mostly of small thorny shrubs and no sign of trees. Although a few woody species appeared (probably belonging to the genus *Polylepis*), these creosote-like plants were hardly trees. Certainly, this land was striking in its stark minimalism but a place without trees feels lonely. Back in the village, many trees welcomed us. There were algarroba (carob) trees with their long leathery pods of chocolate seeds, chanar trees with their smooth olive-size nuts, various mesquite and acacia-like trees (*Prosopis* spp.). Belonging to the mimosa family with their community of root microbes to provide nitrogen, their small fernlike leaves are capable of closing to prevent water loss. With their green lacy shade, the *Prosopis* trees were the most enchanting.

To end the day, we traveled through the Cordillera de la Sal (the Salt Mountains) and up onto a high mesa to watch the sunset. Stretching fifty miles north–south, this narrow mountain chain completely devoid of vegetation presented the most haunting landscape of the region. The scenic highway first crossed the cordillera, then ran north paralleling it, crossed the mountains again, and looped back around to San Pedro. Part of the Los Flamingos National Reserve, it was a popular spot for tourists who frequented the pull-offs and the roadsides where the scenery was the most spectacular. But there were not so many people as to be a Grande Canyon or a Yellowstone, where summer tourists have turned the parks into traffic jams and crowded tangles of gawkers, where winter tourists in their snowmobiles have turned the parks into noisy, exhaust-filled freeways. Here, the landscape was not marred by too many people.

The Salt Mountains, younger than the sixty-million-year-old Andes, were formed about ten millions of years ago as a fold in the Earth's crust. Once a great salt lake, the evaporated lake bottom was pushed up by the collision and pressure of two tectonic plates. The action of the wind and water sculptured bizarre monuments in the rock. Composed of gypsum (a sulfate of calcium or crystalline chalk), clay (aluminum oxide or bauxite), and salt (sodium chloride or table salt), the landscape was the color of these minerals, shades of rust and white. The rock formations went by names like "The Three Marys" or "The Monk"—undoubtedly named, like the village and most of the surroundings, by the Catholic priests. With the look of tormented souls forever tortured by the relentless wind, I wished they had been named after local folks but, of course, like most indigenous cultures, the histories of their heroes rarely survive and are even more rarely honored.

Massive sand dunes formed buttresses against the red cliffs, and what appeared to be the intricate facades of columned temples perched high on the cliffs. Along the roadside the surface of the clay had dried to form gigantic floor tiles. Jumping from one tile to the other, we played a game of avoiding the cracks. A few hardy plants grew in the spaces between the tiles like weeds between sidewalk cracks. One scrub often seen along the roadbeds producing a deep maroon flower grew dwarfed and nearly colorless in the dry clay.

From atop the mesa, the landscape spread out like a museum map: to the east, the green oasis of San Pedro de Atacama; stretching south, the huge salt flat of the Salar de Atacama; behind the village, the spectacular peaks of the snow-capped mountains and the volcanoes (Licancabur, Juriques, Sairecabur); and to the west, below the mesa, the rusty salt-encrusted ridges of the Valle de la Luna, like the spine of a half-buried vertebrate. As the sun cast its last rays on the mountain and volcano peaks, I stood in profound awe of the red land. As it turned a graying auburn, I was struck by the color. It was the last color I remembered of my mother's hair and I understood the phrase, Pachamama, Mother Earth, that place from which we come and to which we return, that place which sustains and nurtures us, that place which gives us meaning.

The next morning we returned to the mesa and hiked down into and across the Valley of the Moon. A sand dune buttressed against the mesa wall provided the trail down. As we bounced down the dune, I imagined myself an astronaut, the first human walking the surface of the moon. It was like on a trampoline, nearly gravity free. The trail crossed a salt flat where gypsum crystals sparkled in the sun. Like a snowfield or a meadow of ice or a pasture of glass, the field flashed with reflected light. Reaching the high walled canyon, we entered an ancient streambed and made our way along the narrow passageway. To get through, we had to bend over and crawl on all fours in some spots. Twice we entered dark tunnels but they were not long and the only difficulty we had was with our eyes adjusting from the bright sunlight to the darkness and back again. Stopping for short rests, we noticed salt everywhere. Like frosting on a coconut cake, it lay in whirls on the ground and in every nook and cranny of the canyon walls. Among the salt deposits, gypsum crystals protruded from the rock like shards of glass. There were no trees, no brush, no grass, no vegetation whatsoever, not even a rugged lichen in this land of salt and rock. Truly, it was a land of "negative possessions."

Just as caravans traveled from Europe to China, ancient traders (known as the Changos) loaded llamas and carried goods up and down the coast, and traveled back and forth from the mountains to the coast, down the eastern side of the Andes, and into the jungle. An entire network of caravan routes that predated the Inca trail once existed in northern Chile, Bolivia, and Peru. We rode north of the Calama highway to where two rivers joined to form the Rio San Pedro. The ancient trail ran along a shallow trickle of the stream. Instead of the Silk Road, this one might have been known as the Salt Road. The petroglyphs carved in the rocks might have been the graffiti of the ancient traders: primitive llamas; turtles; a monkey; birds; serpents; a flute-playing hunchback resembling the native American deity Kokopelli; stick figures in elaborate headdresses; figures with bows, arrows, and shields; and even a few crosses the Spanish priests had later added to mark their presence. Unlike organic artifacts, rock carvings are difficult to date but our guide said archeologists estimated them to have been carved about three thousand years ago. The slippery river rocks, the biting flies, the heat, and the difficult-to-walk-on, loose stones evoked a sense of the hardship these traders must have endured to make a living transporting salt. Yet traditional peoples still make these trips. Victor Englebert (2000) writes of a Bolivian highlander who still practices the life of the caravan merchant. Englebert traveled with this trader (a man who made his living by collecting salt, transporting it by llamas, and bartering it for grain) and from his description, it was exhausting trip, a trip probably much like those made thousands of years ago.

A day in the high lagoons began along the Salar de Atacama, a thirty-five-mile stretch of desolate land of salt flats. The smoke plume of a lithium mine in the distance gave way to gently rising slopes as we turned eastward into the mountains toward the village of Socaire. Agricultural terraces, some no more than a few yards wide, hugged the slopes like plaited corn rows near the village. The narrow canals that brought water from the mountains to the small diked plots had turned the land green with crops. Few vegetables survive the cold dry climate, so arid-tolerant cereals like corn, wheat, and an Andean grain called quinoa were grown in the gardens. Folks working in the fields pulled weeds by hand and tilled with long hoes. In the heart of the village, a fifteenth-century church, a tiny red-rock chapel braced with thick stone buttresses and covered by a thatched roof had been replaced with a newer, larger, and less interesting building. Nearby under a three-sided tin-roof shed, a family was busy preparing Christmas dinner. An old woman in a pink sweater with a pink wool hat and a long, purple, flowered skirt with most of her front teeth missing sat on a wooden bench peeling potatoes with her bare thumb. She had arthritis and couldn't hold a knife, she told us. Men washed radishes and vegetable greens in the irrigation ditch. Through our guide, we learned they had made a special trip to the lowlands to get greens for the Christmas feast. Kids played with balloons and sucked on hard candy. One kid had a ball on a string-paddle, mastering the game with great seriousness.

Leaving the village, the road climbed higher through a section of blooming desert. Although this phenomenon is more pronounced in the southern coastal regions of the Atacama, small areas of the blooming desert occur here. This is how it happens. Every two to five years, if it rains enough (pulses close to one inch are needed), about a month afterwards, short-lived annuals and geophytes (perennials whose buds or bulbs live underground during dormancy), germinate and flower. Dormant shrubs also bloom, and the desert is transformed into a sequential flowering garden. Along this section of road, a scraggly little woody shrub covered with miniature marigold-like flowers had transformed the landscape into a chartreuse meadow. Another bristly shrub far less abundant produced a violet flower and still another, a maroon blossom. With a little rain, these straw-colored shrubs had painted the desert. That these shrubs awaken to life after so many years of dormancy, live in splendid color for a brief few weeks, and return to a dry sleep seems a remarkable cycle and, yet, is that not what life is, an ever-so-brief time of color, of awareness?

The road climbed to twelve thousand feet and the vegetation narrowed to a monoculture of puna grass. Tufts of puna grass leaning away from the wind dotted the landscape and from a distance transformed the land into golden fields. The sun glistened off the high patches of snow, and the sulfur turned the mountain slopes the color of butterscotch pudding. On one mountain, the outline of a black serpent appeared as a natural geoglyph. At every bend in the road, the landscape became an ever more intriging mural, a confluence of oxides, burnt sienna, rust, and ocher. Against this canvas of earth paints, the lagoons were vivid splashes of primary colors. Some mirrored the sky and were deep blue, like Lagunas Miniques and Miscanti. Some were lighter blue, some were mint green, and some, milky white. Some mirrored the land and were the charcoal of nearby mountains. What gives these lagoons their intense color involves not only what is reflected but also the high concentrations of minerals. High levels of sodium chloride give water an opal color; borax, a blue tint; and copper, a greenish hue.

The ecology of these high wetland lagoons is fairly simple. The few studies on them report a small number of phytoplankton species, a scarcity of diatoms, and a single genus of fish (*Orestia* sp.). In short, very little grows in the waters. The surrounding vegetation consisted of a hardy collection of plants able to withstand not only the stresses of high altitude, cold, and extreme aridity but also high concentrations of salt. Although some of the lagoons had no vegetation around their shore at all, others had grassy shorelines. What a surprise to see in the high desert, a hundred miles from the sea, a salt marsh! Familiar grasses that I remembered from my Gulf Coast salt marshes days (*Distichlis* sp., *Scirpus* sp., *Festuca* sp., and others, but no *Spartina*) grew in the cooked oatmeal-textured soil around Laguna Aguas Calientes. A green cushion plant (probably *Oxychole andina*) was also common around the shoreline and a submerged seaweed (*Rupia* sp.) clogged the edge-pools with its boa-like strands of brown and green.

Exploring the plains called *cienegos* that surrounded the high lagoons, we walked slowly and at an easy pace to avoid altitude sickness. Off in the distance, clusters of vicuña grazed on the grassy slopes. Of the four species of South American camelids, the vicuña and the guanaco are wild; the alpaca and llama, domesticated. The estimated twenty-six thousand vicuñas in northern Chile, like the guanacos, are protected, and they have much the same biology as the guanaco. Our avifaunal companions in the waters of Laguna Aguas Calientes included the three flamingo species, Andian geese, puna teal, and pintail while sierra-finches and miner birds feathered the shore. At Laguna Miscanti, horned coots had built nests like little brown volcanoes in the littoral zone of the lake. Several species of finch—the greenish yellow, the ash-breasted, and the common duica—inhabited the shores of Lagunas Miniques and Miscanti. One species of gray finch (which we could not find in our bird book) skittered along the salt-encrusted ruts of the shore so unaccustomed to humans that they nearly crawled into our hands. In the milky green waters of Laguna Tuyajto, perhaps a hundred flamingos sieved the waters for plankton.

Salar de Tara, a large salt flat fourteen thousand feet high, took four hours of climbing the Andean foothills to reach. The road snaked around the volcanoes Licancabur and Juriques, and I could understand why the people of San Pedro believed Licancabur to be a god. With its snowy concaved peak and massive ashen slopes, it looked very much a sacred place. When it rumbled, shook the ground, and belched stream, it must have been an even more awesome sight. Through portions of Los Flamingos National Reserve, the road ran along side the Rio Pujsa, one of the few rivers that flowed eastward into the Andes. Puna teal, cinnamon teal, and ruddy ducks speckled the narrow marsh of the slow-moving river. Overhead, blue-and-white swallows swooped up and down, slicing the azure sky like boomerangs. The higher we climbed, the less vegetation we saw. Passing through a type of scrubland called a tolar, which consists of several species of heathlike shrubs (probably *Parastrephia* spp.), we finally reached fourteen thousand feet where the only plant was puna grass.

When the road disappeared, we traveled for miles through a red plain where the rising heat rippled away the base of the distant mountains, making them appear to float. From the plain of the floating mountains, we entered a valley of wind-sculptured monoliths and rock formations. More striking than the finest gallery of modern art, the sculptures were immense, some five or six stories high, and they rose from a white pebbled floor. One green plant the size of a brussel sprout was the only plant life other than puna grass in that rock-art garden.

Arriving at Laguna Tara and a twelve-thousand-year-old archeological site, we paused for lunch. The ground was littered with shards of obsidian, the black glasslike stone used by ancient hunters to make skinning tools. University students used this site for workshops, reenacting the ways of the early Paleolithic hunters. The only other indications of human presence were vicuña skins that lay dried and curled across a stone wall and a tiny stone hut that provided a haven from the wind. On a hill behind the hut, a rock-walled encampment had been constructed as a lookout, and we climbed the rocks to get a better view of a herd of vicuña grazing on the distance shore.

On the opposite shore of the lagoon, the snow-capped mountain Cerro Quisquiro rose into the sky and doubled its image in the gunmetal gray waters. We dubbed the mountain the Three Corners Mountain because our guide mentioned that from the top, the countries of Bolivia, Chile, and Argentina could be seen. Comfortably seated in canvas fold-up chairs, we watched a flock of black siskins fly in and perch among the dark green branches of a Polylepis bush. Their yellow bellies glistened like butter. We watched a grayish miner flit in and gather crumbs. Wild burros came down from the hills to drink from the freshwater springs and roll in the waters. Rodents called *tuco tuco* peeked out from their burrows. In the noon sun, life around the lagoon was a procession of Andean creatures.

Back at the hotel, the staff prepared a special dinner in celebration of the holiday. The food served outdoors was good, but more exciting was the local band (*grupo de músico*) that played Andean folk music for us. Dressed in traditional Andean attire, long woolen ponchos of yellow and red stripes and high boots, with their coal-black hair braided in a single plait, their music filled the ramada. All the joy of their lives seemed to pour forth in their songs. It was difficult to sit still to the sounds of mandolin, guitars, panpipes, and a large drum, and soon the dance floor was full of kids (mostly the hotel staff) swinging and swaying. I asked what the songs were about and learned that some were dance tunes, some were odes to the land, some were about heroes, lovers, and important events. There was even a song that involved cleaning out the irrigation ditches.

The morning before we left the Atacama, we strolled around San Pedro, spent a little money buying things we did not really need—bottles of water, bananas, mints, postcards—and took a few photographs of the church, the craft market, and the central square. As I passed village women on their way to market, I wondered if they were descendants of the bone-woman in the museum. The lady behind the counter at one of the grocery stores had a polite but distant look and I remembered Lake Sagaris's interviews with Sandra Berna, the mayor of San Pedro, and Mirta Solis, the president of the town council. The women expressed the double-edged sword of progress. They described how outsiders had bought up their people's land, established businesses that employed only themselves, put heavy demands on the limited water supply, and filmed their town ceremonies with captions labeling the people "boy or woman of San Pedro," forgetting they had names. How I wished I could have told the lady behind the counter and the other villagers that I loved their land, that I honored it. I would have told them I was not like the Coca Cola or Ford companies who came to film advertisements, who photographed their land to make money. But then I remembered, I had stayed at a hotel owned by outsiders; I had bought Cokes and used a lot of water without thinking; and probably worse, I could not even speak their language, neither their original language, Cunza, nor Spanish. Yet without outsiders, I, an outsider, would not have been able to visit their homeland, to experience its beauty or to honor it by writing about it.

In spite of the paradoxes we live with and the duplicity we encounter trying to live both comfortably and in a way that respects others and the environment, there was no ambiguity in my appreciation for their land. It may be that in places with such sparseness, illusions are stripped away and what remains is a place where "the peace of cleanly seen truth" can be experienced. Not just facts but grand and important truths seemed clear in this land—truths about the necessity and power of water, the shortness of individual life but the continuum of all life, the wonder of life's adaptability, how few things humans really need to live and the way less can be more. As an outsider, I can only give thanks to the people of the Atacama for allowing me to be a visitor. In a broader sense, perhaps that is what we all are, just visitors.

Central America and
Mexico: Introduction

I F WE IMAGINE the shape of a horn of plenty—with its narrow end partially uncoiled and attached to South America and its mouth gaping open into the southwestern United States—that cornucopia is Central America. The seven countries of Guatemala, Belize, El Salvador, Honduras, Nicaragua, Costa Rica, and Panama that make up the land bridge connecting the North and South American continents share much in common. Some think of Mexico (and the Yucatan Peninsula) as Central America but it is actually part of North America, though clearly it has more in common with its Latin American cousins. Although these countries have their own unique characteristics, they share a similar geography of mountains, lowlands, and coasts, a common language, a culture whose roots lie in Spanish colonialism, and a tropical climate. The mountain range that runs through these countries stretches from the tip of Alaska to Cape Horn and goes by many names. In Canada and the United States, it is the Rockies; in Central America, the Sierra Madres; and in South America, the Andes. Because tectonic plates run through Central America, volcanoes and earthquakes heavily impact the region. Although Central American countries are sometimes thought of by North Americans as banana republics, Third World, and politically unstable countries, within their borders are some of the most complex and diverse biological ecosystems and intriguing archeological sites in the world. In the springs of 1994, 1997, and 2001, I traveled to Costa Rica, the Yucatan, and Panama.

Tropical Places: Costa Rica, the Yucatan, and Panama

5

❦

Costa Rica

THE CAPITAL CITY OF SAN JOSÉ, our starting point, was a city with a busy shopping district, squares, museums, government buildings, and parks but as with so many cities, the noise, the congestion, and the things that develop when humans live crowded together were generally uninspiring. A demonstration by the city's taxicab drivers had jammed the streets with thousands of little shiny red cars. In a starched white shirt, tie, and pressed trousers, Carlos leaned against his red taxi. When we asked, he replied in perfect English, "We are letting our president and government officials know we expect them to pass better wage protection laws." The "slow down" lasted only a few hours and soon the taxis were back on the streets, zooming here and there like little red bees. I never learned if their efforts were effective, but the incident illustrated the simple beauty of democracy—people letting their government know their wishes in a peaceful way. It also made me think of the paradoxes and complexities of the gasoline combustion engine. I wondered if the automobile would do to this country what it has done in the United States. Would there be gas-guzzling SUVs all over town, traffic jams, thick smog from automobile emissions, oil drilling and refineries polluting their environment, and an unhealthy economic dependency on oil? Would their citizenry realize that some technologies create as many problems as they solve?

A drive (yes, via a gasoline combustion engine) around the countryside within a fifty-mile radius of the city took us to the *meseta central* or central valley and the cultivated fields of coffee, banana, and sugar plantations. The sugar cane fields were typically monoculture, but I was glad to see many coffee plantations still in shade culture. Shade culture involves planting and growing companion trees like banana, nut, and other trees along with the coffee bushes. Ecologists, conservationists, and especially birders have suggested that such farming provides more habitats than single-species monoculture. Peter Stangel, director of the Southeast Regional Office of the National Fish and Wildlife Foundation, has been a vocal advocate of multiculture farming. He claims that declines in songbird populations are due to habitat destruction and monoculture coffee reduces habitats. Because monoculture is a bit more productive, many coffee-growing areas in Central and South America have converted to this type of agriculture. The results have been a reduction in habitats and reductions in certain populations of neotropical migrants. In other words, some of our beloved North American songbirds may be declining in part because of this practice.

While shade-grown coffee is gaining support from many well-meaning folks concerned with habitat preservation, I feel a little embarrassed criticizing other countries when my own has had such a terrible track record. The fact that most of the midwestern United States consists of corn and wheat fields—monoculture the size of some Central American countries—makes even the hint of criticism of monoculture practices in Latin American countries by a U. S. citizen seem hypocritical. "What has made the United States rich and productive," we might be accused of saying, "is not good for you," which is true, but we may not be the ones who need to say it. Sometimes the best we can do, we who live in the richest country in the world, we who live with the paradox of that wealth, is to reframe the issue. Perhaps the best we can do is economically support conservation efforts by buying shade-grown coffee (if we can afford it) and to try to convince U.S. coffee companies to do the same. As we made our way through the valley, I was glad to see shade-culture practices in the region still going strong, just as I have been hopeful when I read about patches of prairie lands being left between wheat and corn fields and tracts of farmland in the Plains states being restored to indigenous grasslands.

The green-jungle hills of the Braulio Carrillo National Park offered a hike and a trek through a Costa Rican rainforest. White clouds and patches of mist hung from the lush slopes of the cloud forest as we made our way along the Guapiles Highway to the park. A plant aptly named "poor man's umbrella" (*Gunnera* sp.) with its six-feet-broad leaves grew profusely along the roadside. At a rest stop, we stood under one of the leaves, imagined a hard rain, and all agreed it would make a fine umbrella.

The trail was full of leaf-cutter ants. Watching the ants cut chunks of leaves the size of dimes and carry them back to their nest, I resolved to read more about them when I returned home. And I did. *The Earth Dwellers* by Erich Hoyt (1996) provided an informative read on this group of social insects. I discovered that there are probably forty different species of leaf-cutting ants. Scaled to human dimensions, a forager ant cuts a section weighing about five hundred pounds and carries it thirty miles at a speed of four miles per minute when it brings its green parasol back to the nest. Leaf-cutter ants in general have castes and each caste performs different tasks. Patrollers and foragers are larger ants that move along trails marked with recognition chemicals (everything about ant communication involves chemicals and touch), while the nest maintenance ants, the processors, chewers, and gardening ants are smaller in size. This division of labor among worker ants makes for efficient gardening of the fungus upon which as many as ten million ants in a colony may feed.

Studies by Deborah Gordon (1999) have challenged some of the old biological determinant theories by showing that harvest ants have great flexibility in behavior. She and her colleagues have shown that ants of a particular caste can switch from one task to the other as the result of encounter patterns. In other words, social interactions act as the causative element in task and division of labor choices. Behavior is embedded in a social pattern, she states. It is only a small step forward to recognize that scientists in many disciplines are discovering that social interactions influence not only behavior but the essential biology of creatures—so the touching of antennae, the smelling, tasting, and intimate contact of these ants influence their being.

Not only having intricately complex social interactions, these leaf-cutter ants or fungus-growing ants use as much as 15 percent of the forest vegetation to sustain their gardens. To see pieces of green canopy bouncing across the dark forest floor and to realize that these diminutive insects move a substantial part of the jungle each day, borders on the superlative. As we sloshed along the muddy trail, that funny little tune about an ant moving a rubber tree plant kept running through my mind, but probably a more appropriate tune might be "no man (substitute 'ant') is an island."

A stop in Cartago and the Basilica de Nuestra Señora de los Angeles was a reminder of the omnipresent Catholicism in Central America. The old Byzantine structure, built over a spring, was the site of a healing miracle that took place hundreds of years ago. With the same appeal of Lourdes, people lined up with empty bottles to fill. They believed the waters that trickle from the small brown spout had healing powers. Hundreds of people also stood in line to view the Black Virgin. As we moved along in our antlike line, I noticed on the walls thousands of gold and silver reliquaries in the shapes of body parts. Those strange little metal charms created an oddly surrealist collage. Disconnected hands, arms, and legs were gifts to the Virgin Mary—so many ways people hope for miracles.

On our way back to the city, we stopped briefly on a bridge overlooking the convergence of two rivers. One originating from the fertile Orosi Valley was full of sediment and rust colored. The other was clear with a slight greenish tint and came from the mountains. For several hundred yards, the waters flowed side by side like Christmas ribbons, one green and the other red, remaining separate. Far downstream, the waters finally mixed into a rich creamy brown. It always intrigues me to see how ordinary colors when mixed can result in such lovely new hues.

A day trip to the volcano Poas was a several hour drive through rugged mountainous terrain. The temperature became cooler at the higher elevations, and coffee plantations gave way to small dairy farms and then potato fields. Groups of men covered with dirt carried burlap sacks and walked slowly along the road. Some sat in the shade, taking a rest from the backbreaking job of digging potatoes. Passing them, our guide and driver, two young men in their twenties, wrinkled their noses and remarked that potato diggers were a filthy lot. I was surprised by their blatant disregard for the working poor. Perhaps I had misunderstood their English, but a rest stop left the remark unclear.

Along the steep mountain slopes, trees covered with bromeliads, orchids, and other epiphytes gave way to bare limbs as we neared the top of the volcano. At the lookout point, the slopes were entirely stripped of vegetation and covered with ash. The air smelled sulfurous, a reminder that the volcano was still active, its most recent eruption in the late 1970s. The bleak landscape, the unpleasant smell, and the mocking comments about the potato diggers made that day one that weighed heavily in my memory.

The loveliest place in Costa Rica was a highland village in the cloud forest of the Tilaran Mountains about a hundred miles north of San José. The trip to Monteverde took several hours of steep winding travel on a road full of rocks and awful potholes. Sheer drop-offs with no shoulder whatsoever made the drive a nerve-racking experience. It was the dry season, and as we climbed, the terrain changed from dry forest to dry meadows. Except for the occasional patches of green along streambeds, the landscape was brown—brown rock and brown grass. The few small wooden-frame houses were covered in brown dust and surrounded in barbed wire. Some of the stick fence posts had leaves on them, and I wondered if they were actually still growing. Near the village, we pulled off the road next to a shed about the size of an old outhouse. It was labeled "tollbooth." Surprisingly, the gatekeeper, a shriveled up old man who looked as if the slightest breeze would blow him off the mountain, stepped out of the shed. The driver got out, paid him a small fee, he grinned a toothless smile and waved us on our way. We stayed three sweet days in Monteverde.

Several Costa Rican families from the gold mining fields of Guacimal first settled Monteverde in the 1940s, followed by a group of Quakers in the 1950s who developed a successful dairy farming and cheese production industry. The butterfly garden (El Jardín de las Mariposas) was a short hike from our hotel, and we spent one afternoon among the tropical butterflies. What fun to stand in the wire enclosures and have painted ladies, zebra longwings, blue morphos, swallowtails of many varieties, sulphurs, whites, glasswings, metalmarks, hairstreaks, and so many more flutter about our heads, alight on branches within reach, and occasionally even land on our shoulders.

Central America's forest types include tropical rainforests, dry forests, swamp forests, mangrove forests, pine forests, and cloud forests. The forests of Monteverde are cloud forests, and like all cloud forests, they are dense jungles high in the mountains. Constantly wet from both the cloud mist that forms around the mountains and actual rain, they are extremely lush. Unlike the lowland rainforests, which have a dry season and a wet season, the cloud forest is wet and green all year long. While Monteverde's cloud forest has around twenty-four hundred known species of plants, the flora and the fauna of cloud forests in general are the most diverse and complex in the world with as many as half a million species of plants. Although the tropical rainforest seems to have captured the popular attention of biologists and U.S. Americans, the cloud forest is probably more interesting biologically.

One of the biologists working at the Monteverde Cloud Forest Reserve took us on an afternoon hike through the preserve, pointing out various plants and animals. The tall *Cecropia* trees (*Cecropia* sp.) with their starburst leaf pattern, the oaks (*Quercus* sp.) with their large ridged trunks, and the zapote tree (*Pouteria vividis*) were the easiest to recognize. Another of the distinctive cloud forest trees was the enormous fern tree (*Cyathea* sp.) that looked its name, but the strangler fig (three species are common in this forest, *Ficus hartwegii, F. crassiuscula,* and *Ficus tuerckheimii*) was by far the most intriguing.

The strangler fig has one of the most remarkable interdependent life cycles of any plant in the world. Considered a keystone species in the tropics, it provides food for many animals throughout the year. The list of fig eaters is long. Birds, bats, monkeys, and even fish have been reported to indulge in the fruit. So much more than an epiphyte, more than a hanger-on, the strangler fig begins as a defecated seed (so it depends on the transportation of birds, monkeys, and other tree-top dwellers). It germinates in the crown of a tree, on a mossy branch, or in a humus-filled tree crotch. Here competition for light is less intense. To germinate, it depends on a bacterium that helps crack its seed coat. Then it sends its seedling vines sprawling about the canopy looking for a suitable trunk. Once it finds a solid trunk, it sends down roots. This may take four or five years, depending on the size of the host tree. Just as the root-vines reach the ground, they spit into many rootlets that grasp the soil like fingers grabbing earth. For years, the fig grows around the host tree, wrapping itself around it like an embrace. Finally the host tree dies, outcompeted, and using the dead trunk for support, the fig continues to grow (some are as old as three hundred years). Michael Roads (2002), in the chapter "The Spirit of the Forest" in *The Soul Unearthed: Celebrating Wilderness and Spiritual*

Renewal through Nature, writes that it is an illusion to think of these two plants as separate. He challenges the reader to imagine them as one, to disregard species boundaries. For a biologist this seems an enormous leap, but I can certainly admire the tree's astonishing interdependent life cycle.

The tree's connections to other creatures and to place continue. The hollow tree trunk provides a home for thousands of species of spiders, insects, snakes, frogs, rodents, and bats. Fungi and epiphytic plants also make their home in and on the tree. But the partnership between the tree and a small wasp (Agaoninae) is the most intimate. The wasp (each species of tree has a specific species of wasp) pollinates the tree in a complex and bizarre cycle. The wasp enters the fruit and lays eggs; the eggs hatch; the insects mature and mate. Females leave the fruit bearing pollen, find other trees to enter, and the cycle begins again. Without the tree, the wasp would not survive. Without the wasp, the tree could not pollinate. How many ways is this tree connected to other creatures and to place? Let me count the ways.

Many rainforest trees (and epiphytes) have complex relationships with insects, the biologist told us. Trees called myrmecophytes (ant plants) have complex mutual relationships with ants, and some are so dependent on one another that they cannot survive without each other. When the biologist loudly tapped the trunk of a *Cecropia* tree, swarms of ants (*Azteca* sp.) poured out, on the alert and ready to attack the suspect invader. These ants act as guards, patrolling and protecting the tree from harmful insects, climbing vines that might compete with the tree for sunlight and nutrients, and fungal infections. The tree, in turn, provides the ants with not only shelter but packages of food in special structures called Mullerian bodies. The biologists also related that these ants tend herds of mealybugs that they "milk" like cows. Truly, the cloud forest is a place of complex interdependences.

The dictionary of plants living on other plants in the cloud forest would take dozens of lifetimes to compile and define, our biologist guide said. He pointed out the bat-pollinated bull's eye lianas or sea bean vine (*Mucuna rostrata*) whose seedpods have whiskerlike hairs that cause itching when touched (and so is called "pica pica" or "itch itch"). We saw the infinite variety of other epiphytes, the rosettes of bromeliads (some seventy-two described species hang from trees in this cloud forest alone), the cryptic orchids, and the fanlike ferns. Our biologist guide recommended Alexander F. Skutch's *A Naturalist in Costa Rica* (1971) as a good reference and I wondered if it was as good as Adrian Forsyth's *Tropical Nature* (1984). Probably a little outdated now, *Tropical Nature* was, and remains, one of the most beautifully written books on the ecology of the tropics. In 2000 the most comprehensive resource, *Monteverde: Ecology and Conservation of a Tropical Cloud Forest* (Nadkarni and Wheelwright) was published. Written by a collection of scientists who have lived and studied in the Monteverde cloud forest, it is probably the most complete and comprehensive sourcebook on the region. The articles are accessible, interesting, and cover every imaginable topic from climate to plants that grow on leaves to golden toads to singing mice.

Inching our way through the almost impenetrable green, we came upon a three-toed sloth draped around a branch. Without our guide to point him out, we would certainly have missed him for he seemed a piece of the canopy, a clump of dark foliage. Most of Monteverde's mammal fauna are small, nocturnal, and difficult to see, and no better examples of this were the four species of mice that make calls humans can hear. Called the singing mice, one species make trills like cicada, another whistles, and the other two species make single-, two- or three-note calls. We did not see these secretive rodents, but we did see and hear our closer relatives, the primates. Jumping through the canopy like gangs of unruly kids, a troop of howler monkeys and some white-faced capuchins passed overhead. Near the end of the trail, in the dark shade of the dense lianas and vines, a male resplendent quetzal flew onto the side of a tree. The country's national bird, it is the archetypical tropical bird with its long green tail and red breast. Almost as soon as we spotted him, the bird flew back into the dense jungle and faded into the foliage. It seemed fitting to see this splendid bird in its deep lush-green home as our final image of this tropical country.

The Yucatan

The southern region of Mexico protrudes as a flat peninsula into the Caribbean Sea, supposedly the result of a meteorite that pounded the land over sixty-five million years ago. On the eastern side of the Yucatan, the well-known tourist spots of Cancun and Cozumel collect the jetsetters. On the northwestern tip, the old colonial city of Merida served as the hub of our explorations. In the city, we first visited the central plaza (the *zocalo*), which sits on the site of an ancient Mayan temple. We discovered that many places in this region were built over Mayan ruins. The yellow stone cathedral (stones from an ancient Mayan temple), the governor's palace, and the old Montejo family palace (now a bank) formed three sides of the square. The bas-relief on the facade depicted members of the Montejo family and Spanish soldiers standing on the heads of the defeated Mayans. I wondered what the citizens of Merida thought when they looked at this monument, those women in *huipiles* (white cotton dresses decorated with colorful embroidery) and the men in *guayaberas* (long pleated shirts that fit over pants) as they strolled beneath the laurels on the square. Would those of Mayan descent think of the terrible suffering and tragic losses of their ancestors? Would a wealthy man of Spanish heritage think nostalgically of a glorious colonial past? Would someone of mixed descent briefly contemplate the inevitable continuum of human life as one culture conquering another? Maybe there would be a slow-walking poet who would imagine that we might learn to be more gentle with each other and to not repeat the brutality of our past. She might think that a better way would be to imagine the mixing of two rivers of different colors that results in lovely new shades and hues. Or she might think of the strangler fig. The fig tree may eventually overcome its host, but the years of intimate connection between the two result in such a blending that they may become indistinguishable.

From artisans at the craft market, we bought baskets and straw hats and strolled along the square. A driving tour of the city took us to some of the city's monuments and buildings, the old churches, and the bullring. The architecture of stucco walls, the iron grill-work, carved wooden doors, and Moorish archways was typical of old Spanish colonial cities. At the Instituto Nacional Antropología e Historia, a mural by Fernando Castro Pacheco spread across the walls. The vivid scenes of Mayan slaves armed with little more than sticks and stones fighting the well-equipped, armored Spanish soldiers captured the tragedy of the War of the Castes. Moving from one wall to the next, the entire room was a bloody struggle.

The War of the Castes (Nelson 1964) occurred a few decades before the U.S. Civil War and had some of the same elements: an oppressed population of slaves, wealthy landowners, and an agricultural-based economy. Instead of cotton, the plantations were sisal, a cactuslike plant whose fibers were used to make mats, hammocks, and the hardy fabrics of sandals, baskets, purses, and such. In contrast to the U.S. Civil War, the native Mayan slaves, the imported black slaves, and the poor rose up directly against the wealthy Spanish landowners. Of course, this is an oversimplification. But the War of the Castes was a murderous one in which over half the population of Mayans were killed.

Because of the indomitable spirit of the Mayans, the region reflects a distinct independence from Mexico, and although it is not a separate country, strong separatist sentiments cast the region as different. I was surprised to learn as we strolled through the museum that the Mayan culture had enormous collections of scientific records, historical and sacred texts, and thousands and thousands of scrolls. In their pictorial script, all the knowledge of their architecture, astronomy, natural history, and medicine was recorded, and in less than a day, all their records were destroyed. The Spanish burned all their books. They destroyed not only the Mayan books and the Mayan culture, they took their land and made them slaves. That one group of people could so utterly destroy another so quickly is an act that repeats itself time and time again in our history. North America, South America, Central America, Australia, Indonesia—the litany of places where indigenous cultures were destroyed by Europeans is staggering. I felt like Wendell Berry (2002, 8) who said,

I am forever being crept up on and startled by the realization that my people established themselves here by killing or driving out the original possessors, by the awareness that people were once bought and sold here by my people, by the sense of the violence they have done to their own kind and to each other and to the earth, by the evidence of their persistent failure to serve either the place or their own community in it.

Each time I learn of another example in the long saga of cruelty that humans carry out when they take places that belong to others, I am shaken.

Of the many Mayan ruins in the Yucatan, the Puuc region south of Merida beyond the great limestone ridge and into the hill country has some of the most beautiful ruins. The Puuc culture dates back to around the fourth century. With over 150 ruins in the region, archeologists have discovered many sites connected by a raised roadway. The most intact ruins are Uxmal and Kabal. The fifty-mile drive through the flat countryside from Merida to Muna and then on to Uxmal was hot and dry, and even though the region was known as hill country, it seemed flat as a tortilla. The thatched-roof hovels and, in fact, everything lining the road had a white coat of chalk (limestone dust). The road passed the remains of an old sisal plantation, and I remembered the mural in the museum. Off in the distance in the overgrown fields, I imagined Mayan slaves cutting the sharp-edged, sword-like cactus in the deadly heat. That anyone could survive such brutal climate and working conditions was unbelievable. Although many old cotton plantations in the United States have been restored and glorified as part of some misguided need to reinvent a heroic, mythical past, I was glad to see this plantation folding back into the landscape, part of a memory so disgraceful it warranted fading.

The ruins of Uxmal consisted of elegantly carved and painted stones, temples, pyramids, platforms, square hutlike buildings, quadrangles, and many more structures. I thought how similar the basic designs of ancient and modern cities are. The great pyramid, the House of the Magician, could have been a Spanish cathedral in the center of town; the Chac Mools could have been the Christian saints carved in marble; the House of the Governor could have been the presidential palace; the intricate lattice could have been the carvings on the palaces and government buildings surrounding the church; and of course, the ball court most certainly could have been the soccer field. That people organize in such similar ways, whether indigenous Mayans or Spanish conquistadors, argues that we really are more alike than different.

That night from our hotel, the House of the Magician rose above the thorny scrub jungle like a sculpture. How lovely the stones looked illuminated at night, so lovely it was hard to imagine the city as a graveyard. Most scholars believe that extended drought caused the slow decline of the cities in this region. The water table may have dropped so low that cisterns even hundreds of feet deep into the limestone bedrock were unable to access water. Slowly the drought killed everyone off or forced them to move and the cities were abandoned. But how exquisite the patterns cast by the night lights. How lovely the city's bones.

At Kabal, the wall of repeating Chac masks, blocks of eyes with fanged mouths and curved predator noses, struck with fierce redundancy. Typical Puuc architecture, the wall seemed a desperate plea for rain. Perhaps the reason for its creation was that if they made the rain god's image over and over enough times, it would bring the rain—so many ways people hope for miracles.

By far the largest of the restored Mayan-Toltec ruins is Chichen Itza about 150 miles east of Merida. We arrived in the afternoon when the hordes of tourists and the heat were the worst. After fighting the crowds for half an hour, we decided to return to the hotel and get an early start in the morning. The walk back to the hotel was only a couple miles but it was like walking on a frying skillet. The village around the ruins was a long continual block of shops selling souvenirs and junk and more shops under construction. One of the shopkeepers said, "Pavarotti is giving a concert in a few months and we are going to make some money!"

Morning was the ideal time to explore Chichen Itza. Few people were up and about and it was cool. We purchased a copy of *Guide to the Ruins of Chichen Itza* (1971) by José Diaz-Bolio (at the bottom of the booklet, the phrase "Only one containing the theory of Mayan Art" appeared in red ink). Following the map, we tried to match the pictures to what we were seeing: the temple of rattlesnakes and jaguars, Culculcan's chapel, the wall of skulls, the platform of skulls, the temple of tigers and eagles, the red house, the temple of the sun, the sacred well called a *cenote*, the market, the house of deer, the temple of dates, the temple of the turtle, the thousand columns, the solar observatory, the ball court, on and on and on the chiseled stones went. Finally, we arrived back at the great pyramid called the Castillo in the center of the ruins. Resting in the shade, we watched kids climb the pyramid to the top and wave to their parents below. It was a far more enjoyable activity than reading the theory of Mayan art.

Our last day in the Yucatan, we traveled from Merida on a rickety old bus to Celestun, a small village on the Sea of Campeche. Near Celestun, the Ria Celestun Biosphere Reserve serves as an important conservation area, a breeding grounds for Caribbean flamingos, a wintering home for migratory waterfowl, and a nesting beach for sea turtles. Linda Hogan (1995, 84) writes about this "Estuary of Heaven" in a chapter entitled "Creations" in *Dwellings: A Spiritual History of the Living World*. She writes of the sea turtles who feel "the call of land in deep memory and so return to a place unseen." She writes of the flamingos on "boomerang wings" (89). And the essay ends with the line, "What does god look like? These fish, this water, this land" (98).

The bus picked us up at our hotel and after several pick-ups and drop-offs involving the driver's relatives and for what seemed hours, we bounced our way out of Merida towards Celestun. The flat countryside was treeless and dry as chalk, and the bus jerked along at a sloth's pace. At the pier, a small flat-bottom boat took us out into the reserve. The boat chugged slowly through the mangrove swamp on its lawn-mower-sized motor. All around us the brown, nutrient-rich waters of the lagoon flowed like a river of chocolate. As far as we could see, mangroves lined the shores, their roots hanging into the water like brown ropes. The mangroves that grew along the water's edge with aerial prop roots were the red mangroves (*Rhizophora mangle*) and its species name, mangle, is a good description of its roots. Several other species made up the mangrove swamp flora: the black mangrove (*Avicennia germinans*) whose roots look like straws sticking up from the mud, the white mangrove (*Laguncularia racemosa*), and a mangrove-like tree known as buttonwood (*Conocarpus erectus*). Dense squatty trees covered in tough leathery leaves, they were like the beams of a house, the supporting structures that held together the great mangrove swamp, and every creature in the detritus-based swamp depended on them.

Turning into a small stream, we entered a narrow passageway through the dense mangrove forest. The hanging roots and limbs formed a tunnel as we made our way toward a freshwater spring. At the spring, we left the boat and walked along a wooden walkway. Looking down into the pool, the water was crystal clear and the bottom was sandy white. As the waters flowed out and mixed with the dark estuarine waters, I understood why these places, *cenotes*, were sacred to the Mayans. There was fresh drinking water, seclusion and shade, an oasis in the swamp, a sanctuary to bathe and escape the tropic heat.

Leaving the spring and back out in the more open waters, flocks of flamingos fed in the shallows, their long pink legs lifting them above the waters, their long limber necks reaching down below the waters to fed on algae. Contortionists, they seemed all necks and legs. Some of the birds were young and although fully developed, they did not have the intense pink coloration of the adults. Several times we tried to get a little closer to them but each time they would take to the air, wings outstretched, long thin bodies elongated, like pink arrows shot against the blue sky. They would rise, circle around and settle back down further away from us, determined to keep a long, safe distance between themselves and humans.

The bus driver dropped us off in the village at a small restaurant on the beach. Lime soup and fresh baked *copia* turned us into garden slugs so we dozed in the shade until a troop of noisy boys riding a homemade bike-turned-cart came by. We persuaded them to give us a ride (a few pesos can be very persuasive to little boys) and we rode around in their cart for a while. Finally, the bus driver's niece returned from her visit with her aunt and we left for Merida. By then the temperature was well above a hundred degrees, so to cool off we converted our water bottles into misters. By placing our fingers tightly over the opening and squeezing, we could produce a fine cooling spray. Our water fight seemed to tickle the other passengers, and before long, everyone on the bus had been misted and was a little damp. We arrived back in Merida, a soggy bunch but considerably cooler. The next day we left the land of the Mayans and the mangrove swamps, but as with all beautiful places, this land would not leave us.

Panama

Thirty miles northeast of Panama City along the Panama Canal, Canopy Tower is an old military radar station converted into an eco-lodge by a Panamanian banker. I first read about Canopy Tower in the popular magazine *Birder's World*, and found its extensive web site (www.canopytower.com) informative. Built on the highest hill in the Soberanía National Park (about a thousand feet above sea level), it is an example of the expanding ecotourist business in Latin America (in fact, all over the world). The dining room and main gathering area on the top floor had all the trappings of a birder's paradise: comfortable couches, deck chairs, telescopes, a library full of books on birds and natural history, and framed pictures of birds photographed by Art Wolfe and other commercially successful natural photographers. Articles about the lodge and pictures of the owner hung on the walls. Clearly, the publicity reflected in the décor represented a lot of effort in giving it the image of a first-class wildlife observatory. The ground floor with its concrete base was an exhibition hall and the rooms on five levels were connected by metal stairways. Kind of an upscale barracks—Girl Scout summer camp rolled into one, with good, simple food, it was a pleasant lodge. But it was, first and foremost, a commercial enterprise. Its purpose was to make money. At prices comparable to those of a luxury hotel, it was affordable only by the affluent and that exclusivity bothered me.

I have often been troubled by this aspect of the ecotourist business, which I often perceive as rich patrons supporting rich owners. In my more utopian moments, I imagine eco-lodges owned by organizations whose sole purpose is conservation rather than by private entrepreneurs who are already rich. Despite the fact that ecotourism uses "Nature" to make money, it is an industry that is not as exploitive as the lumber business, the animal trappers, or the slash-and-burn farming common in the tropics. Since a number of people seem able to make a living employed by these ecotourist enterprises, it is clearly a far better economical means of reducing poverty than industries that destroy nonrenewable resources. Still, I wonder how much profit is being made and who really gets it.

I put aside my thoughts on nature for the rich for the moment and tried to enjoy the tower. It was not difficult. The first morning, I woke before first light.

Many of the guests had crawled out of bed and climbed to the deck to watch the birds bring in the morning. As I dragged myself up the metal ladder and peeked out the hatch, I thought of Margaret Lowman's words in *Life in the Treetops* (1999, 60). When she broke above the canopy in her crane-gondola for the first time, she cried, "What a view! Vines, orchids, goannas, more vines, tree crowns, birds, more vines and many layers of foliage were visible in every direction." The sheer overwhelming green of it all! As the sun floated up above the horizon, lighting the sea of trees below, I could certainly understand the appeal of treetop biology.

The group of experienced birders peering through their binoculars and scopes called out the names of dozens of birds so readily that we learned the names of the birds quickly. A tropical kingbird landed on the railing of the deck encircling the observation dome but most of the birds were in the canopy. One especially colorful bird, the blue cotinga, was a turquoise, iridescent spot far off in the green foliage, but there were hundreds more, more than all the birds of the United States and Canada combined, one birder said. For an hour we peered through our bins (as one of the birders called binoculars) at the vivid spots of parrots, parakeets, toucans, trogons, and flycatchers until the breakfast bell rang. Climbing down from our perch, a group of coatimundis, long-nosed raccoonlike animals, were also breakfasting, foraging for the bananas left them by the kitchen staff.

The first hike was along the lodge road, a three-mile blacktopped lane that wound down the hill from an elevation of about a thousand feet to sea level and intersected with the Panama Canal Highway. Cut once in the 1910s when the canal was built, the forest had grown back to a dense second growth. It was a typical lowland tropical rainforest. Like all tropical forests, the vegetation consisted of three distinct layers: the dense, most productive and diverse canopy; the second layer of epiphytes (ferns, orchids, and bromeliads) plus the smaller trees-shrubs; and finally, the dim forest floor. As we watched troops of monkeys move through the trees, the canopy was clearly the place these primates loved. Maybe that explains the appeal of canopy biology. It seems such a familiar home. First, mantled howler monkeys, then Geoffrey's tarmarins, and finally white-faced capuchins moved through the treetops, shaking the branches and rattling the leaves like a storm passing through. They were not happy to see us humans below, and several white-faced capuchins screeched and threw branches at us in an effort to scare us away.

Canopy Tower's web pages (canopytower.com/treelist.html) claims forty-five species of trees along the lodge road, and the guide pointed out some of them. Two of the largest, the amarillo (*Terminalia amazonica*) and the Panama tree (*Sterculia apetala*), rose over 120 feet high. With huge buttresses to support their massive broad tops, they seemed every bit the typical rainforest trees. But there was an infinite variety of trees shapes. The elephant's foot tree (*Jacaranda copaia*) had a corrugated trunk, hence its name, and the acabu tree (*Zanthoxylum* sp.) had spines covering its trunk. Palms of many species grew lean and tall throughout the forest, and the abundant balsa (*Ochroma pyramidale*) with its night flowers and chocolate-colored seeds had a broad canopy that produced a great deal of shade. Connecting it all like cables, the woody lianas and vines wove their ropey mesh into the green tangle. The winged seeds of the guayacan tree (*Tabebuia guayacan*) twirled down on us and the falling leaves had the look of autumn. Trees such as the cuipo (*Cavanillesia platanifolia*) and the kapok or ceiba (*Ceiba pentandra*) drop their leaves in the dry season much like deciduous trees that lose their leaves in fall.

A giant blue morhpo butterfly followed us, flashing its wings in a spectacular display of blue iridescent magic. Sharman Russell (2003) in *An Obsession with Butterflies: Our Long Love Affair with a Singular Insect* describes the morpho as "a bit of fluttering silk," and as if "a piece of sky had detached itself and flapped away." Red passionflowers hung from vines, their flower a maze of texture and attractiveness. If I were a pollinating insect, I would go for that flower in a heartbeat. As we walked along the road, the old tune "Old MacDonald Had a Farm" kept running through my mind with new words, "here an antbird, there a potoo; here a trogon, there a motmot." At the end of the lodge road, a converted golf cart hauled us back up to the lodge, saving us the hot steep climb up. What comfort, what luxury, a downhill walk and an uphill drive. Life does not get easier than this, I thought.

By noon the heat drove us inside so we rested beneath the huge ceiling fans and read for a couple hours. Later in the afternoon, we hiked the plantation trail and ended the day with a final bird watch on the observation deck. As the cool breeze blew the last few clouds away and the sky turned a soft mango color, we watched the top of a Russian grain freighter glide by on the canal. To see this enormous seagoing vessel moving through the jungle was eerie. To see it in the color of a rainforest dusk was surreal.

In contrast to our easygoing day, those ardent birders who had left early morning came straggling in at the end of the day looking like heat stroke. Obviously exhausted, instead of going immediately to bed after dinner, they spent hours, checking, reviewing, and discussing their bird list. This was my first encounter with the serious birder, and I was surprised at their devotion. It was not until I read Kenn Kaufman's *Kingbird Highway: The Story of a Natural Obsession That Got a Little Out of Hand* (2000) that I learned such obsession with birds is not unusual. Kaufman wrote of his journey as a teenager in 1973. Traveling 69,000 miles across the United States in a single year, he counted over 660 species of birds. His tale mentioned few people (although he had a small number of portraits of his birding friends and a few on-the-road stories). It was rather the telling of moving from place to place on very little money for the sole purpose of observing birds. He hitchhiked the freeways and traveled for days at a time to get to a certain spot to see a particular bird. He would leave that place, travel to another in search of another bird, leave that place, and travel to another, and on and on. Not at all like Odysseus, Jason, or the archetypical young man's travels, his wanderings were not for the acquisition of wealth, some valued prize, a beautiful woman, or even a story. He simply wanted to see birds. What an odd obsession. But then, obsessions are not things we make conscious choices about, and by definition, they are not driven by logic or reason. At any rate, those weary birders struck me as somewhat Kaufmanish, and while odd, at the same time, more than a little endearing.

The second morning, I woke early, stood alone on the deck, and watched a fire burning off in the distance. Through my binoculars I could see billows of white smoke and red flames flickering from the jungle. I knew the statistics. More than two-thirds of the Panamanian forests have been destroyed in the last forty years. Less than 1 percent of the old forests remain. Forests are cut and burned for banana and coffee plantations and pastures for cattle every day. Small farmers cut and burn, plant beans and corn for a few years, and when the soil gives out because tropical forest soil is very nutrient poor (most of the carbon, nitrogen, etc. is in the canopy), they move on to repeat the process. Unlike the affluent larger landowners who also destroy forests, these small farmers make a meager living, and even though they work hard, they remain poor. To witness the forest disappearing on such a glorious morning was a profoundly sad experience. To understand that its demise does not even sustain hard-working farmers was even sadder.

A Panamanian couple up from the city for a quiet weekend in the trees graciously offered to take us on a quick tour of the canal. I am always touched by the generosity of strangers in other countries. We found ourselves traveling the Canal Highway that parallels the fifty-mile canal. In the direction of the city of Colon on the Caribbean side, at Lake Gatun, the abandoned U.S. military base and a resort hotel were in sharp contrast to one another. The military base was completely deserted. The streets were empty, the buildings were boarded up, and the houses had that hollow, unlived-in look. No one was around. In contrast, the hotel was crowded with visitors. Kids wandered in and out of the swimming pool and guests milled around the tropical gardens and lobby. The image of the fading military presence replaced with folks enjoying life really appealed to me.

Reversing directions, we drove back towards the city of Panama on the Pacific side. Our Panamanian hosts pointed out the old site of the School of Americas, the infamous facility for a string of Latin American dictators trained to carry out the policies of U.S. corporate interests in Central and South America. The place gave me the creeps when I thought how so many of these men had sunk into brutality and cruelty. As we passed the buildings, I thought how strong a U.S. military presence dominated the last century of Panama's history. Once part of Colombia, Panama gained independence via Teddy Roosevelt and the Marines at the turn of the century (some historians interpret the action not as a fight for independence but as a U.S. military action to establish a secure base for U.S. interests in Central and South America). The canal, completed in 1914, was owned by the United States until President Carter enacted legislation giving it back to the country in 1999. Economically, the agricultural interests of companies like United Fruit were the ruling force, but more recently with the shift to oil and energy, the interests of Texaco and other oil companies have become dominant. As in other Central American countries, the United States has not done much to help the general citizenry, especially the poor and indigenous peoples, and everything to ensure the wealth of the old oligarchs (the landowning families) and always, the interests of U.S. businesses. Instead of educating leaders who might solve problems in ways that would help everyone gain, the United States often chose the political solution of military power that allowed a few to gain at the expense of others. "Fat brother," as Barbara Kingsolver calls an imaginary U.S. citizen in *Small Wonder* (2002), did not happen because he was lucky. He happened because he was greedy and did despicable things to accumulate his fat. He made choices that were shortsighted and selfish. Perhaps the United States might someday have leaders who are capable of helping us make more honorable choices. Perhaps if the United States outlasts or outcompetes all other countries, it would do so with the gentleness and grace of the strangler fig.

At the Miraflores locks, we watched several ships move through the locks and listened to the statistics on tolls and tonnage. A Chinese cargo ship passing through paid a toll of $30,000. As the mules (train locomotives) pulled the massive hull though the narrow channel with only inches to spare, I was not so much impressed with the engineering marvels of the canal as I was with the role the canal played in the understanding of disease. The fact that mosquitoes carried yellow fever and malaria was a significant milestone in the history of microbiology and medicine. By the 1920s, largely due to the studies of William Gorgas in the Canal Zone (Walter Reed and Ronald Ross in Cuba and Africa), scientists and physicians understood that infectious diseases were carried by vectors. They began to understand that by eliminating the vectors of disease, the transmission of such diseases could be interrupted and controlled. Truly a monumental discovery in terms of public health, that knowledge is still fundamental today. Even well into the molecular biological age when we know the sequence of the human genome and can treat diseases at the molecular level, controlling rats, mosquitoes, and other vectors is still one of the basic tenants of public health.

The last day in Panama, we hired a local driver to take us to El Valle, a small village in the central highlands. The driver, a young, good-natured fellow named Louis, turned his tape deck on loud and drove 160 km/hr (about 100 miles/hr) along the Pan American highway. We zoomed past small towns, whipped along the coastline, and sped through the brown dusty countryside. The road to El Valle turned off the Pan American Highway. Although paved, it was still a white-knuckle drive up an eighteen-mile narrow mountain road. My Spanish being poor, I had no way of telling him to slow down and lower the volume without sounding rude or stodgy. So we endured the music, which was actually OK, and the speed, which was, well, let's just say we adjusted.

Whizzing along the highway, a massive vulture migration caught our attention. Hundreds of turkey vultures glided on the thermals, making their way north in formations called kettles. Vultures travel thousands of miles catching an updraft and soaring, finding another updraft by visually detecting the presence of other vultures, and riding that current, then another and another. Perhaps our speed made me envious of the way those huge birds could travel in lofty drifting circles, spiraling their way from South America to Canada using so little energy. By angling their wings in just the right way and using the natural uplifting air currents, their flight seemed a marvel, a functional harmony of sky and wing. It seemed that humans might learn something from these wind-powered travelers. I was certainly more than willing at that moment to consider their mode of travel.

One of the village attractions, Indian petroglyphs, was back in the hills. Not especially old, the details of who did them and when got totally lost in translation, but the caretakers looked so poor we were glad to leave a small donation. Everyone we met—from the old man with his machete who guided us into the hills to his twelve-year-old daughter who gave the "lecture" on the petroglyphs to the little boy who tagged along to the villagers who passed us on their way down the mountain to town—were tiny. Not more than four feet tall, they looked like little brown elves. Walking down the trail, it felt as if we were traveling in the company of hobbits. What a wondrous escort!

A visit to the local botanical garden and zoo proved disturbing. The intense colors of the hibiscus garden were enjoyable but some of the crude cages were too small for the animals. The golden frogs in the constructed pond didn't seem crowded but some of the mammals were cramped. A fox was stuffed into a cage not much bigger than his body and the songbirds in a cage not much bigger than a small closet was just too much. Zoos have always depressed me, but when we saw a blue-gray tanager on the outside of the cage feeding what appeared to be his mate inside the cage, it was just too disheartening. We had to leave.

A quick browse through the craft market, lunch at a place called Santa Librada recommended by our *Lonely Planet: Panama* guidebook and it was time to head back to the city. On the drive back, we again crossed the Pan American Bridge. This direction offered a better view and we could see the Atlantic Ocean on one side and the Pacific on the other, probably the only place on Earth where the two oceans were visible simultaneously. A loop through the city, with its congested streets packed with traffic and people, could have been any city of the world. Along the beach, modern hotels and business offices of glass and steel twenty stories high looked out over the ocean. I wondered why people find skyscrapers so attractive and why we can't build forests like we build cities.

Louis dropped us off at our hotel near the airport, gave us affectionate hugs, and bid us a safe trip home. His head moving to the beat of the loud Latin music, he sped off into the evening. The welcome quiet engulfed us as we stood for a moment and watched the last rays of the sun dissolve from the Panamanian sky.

NATURE AS CONNECTION III

Indian Pipe (Monotropa uniflora). *Artwork by Eric Hinote.*

Kinship with the Natural World: Mitchellsville Gorge Trail, New York

6

❧

A SECTION OF THE FINGER LAKE TRAILS begins on the east side of the Mitchellsville Road next to Markham's Tree Farm and ends near Pleasant Valley Inn on Fish Hatchery Road. From Mitchellsville Road, it's all downhill (my favorite direction). The trail keepers have diligently marked and maintained the trail over the years and with permission from the landowners, cleared a pathway along Coldwater Creek, and built a sturdy bridge to cross the creek. Accessibility and a good path through lovely woods have made it one of the nicest three-mile hikes in the region.

One summer afternoon, we took a friend's grandkids on a hike to teach them the art of trail walking. Our small band of hikers, dressed in sturdy shoes, started at the edge of the tree farm and the bordering grass field. At the end of the field, the trail crossed a fence, and a narrow wooden stepladder allowed us to climb up and over into the woods. A sign off to the right as we entered the woods indicated that we bordered private land. The sign read, "Is there life after death? Trespass and find out." The land belonged to a local VIP, a wealthy publisher out of the city. Often seen driving around town in his Jaguar or his Rolls Royce, he reportedly flies into town in his helicopter. I wondered if he realized how harsh those words seemed to trail walkers who generally honor the rules and respect boundaries. While I would never begrudge anyone the privacy and security of their home, this vast acreage was more than home. Sometimes I think, not only do some little boys have to acquire all the cookies, they have to display them and then warn others to keep away from them.

We were soon beyond his property (I immediately felt better) and walking along the gorge. Several hundred feet deep, the ravine was a lush gully of treetops. At the bottom, a small creek trickled over gray shale. It was so shallow the rocks were barely wet in some spots. It had been a dry summer and the creeks were low. Only when the April snowmelt filled them would they come alive with a force that could tear off the gorge walls. Across the ravine an exposed bank looked like that was just what had happened some years before.

For about two miles, the trail was a soft auburn carpet of hemlock needles and green Sphagnum moss. Strewn with what looked like brown sweetheart roses, tiny hemlock cones littered the ground. Such tiny seeds for so massive a tree. I wondered how the phrase "From tiny acorns, mighty oaks grow" might sound if it were changed to "From tiny cones, mighty hemlocks grow." But it didn't have the right ring. Hemlocks are associated with darkness and death. And where hemlocks grew along the trail, it was especially dark. From its deep shade to its drooping branches, the eastern hemlock presents a somber image. The ground was also speckled with thumb-sized acorns. Smooth nuts with corrugated caps lay scattered among the palm-sized oak leaves, giving the trail yet another graceful ground pattern. Shagbark hickories, hickory nuts in their thick padded life jackets, added yet another color, a splash of emerald. I wondered why this was called leaf litter or forest debris, such terms implying waste rather than the beautiful art it is.

It was cool and the trail was almost clear of undergrowth when I spotted a cluster of Indian pipe sprouting up though the decaying oak leaves. Indian pipe (*Monotropa uniflora*), sometimes called ghost plant or corpse plant, has no chlorophyll so it cannot photosynthesize. Since it cannot fix carbon like most plants, it depends on a symbiotic fungus that lives with it to provide the essential nutrients. The fungus, a mycorrhizal fungus, lives entangled in the roots of oaks as well as with the Indian pipe. Using its enormous hardware store of enzymes, the fungi help the oak grow better and the pipe grow at all. Without the fungi or the oak, Indian pipe would not be able to exist. Scientists have not worked out the actual chemical dependencies between this threesome, but such relationships are common in damp deciduous forests. That plants and fungi could form such complex associations speaks to the magic of forest ecology and I marveled at the beauty of this basement-floor neighborhood of oak, pipe, and fungi.

Indian pipe is actually quite ubiquitous and found all over eastern forests, ranging from Maine to Florida. A member of the heath and wintergreen family, it has a long history of pharmacological uses by Native Americans, early settlers, and folk healers. Containing salicylic acid (aspirin), it was used as a fever and inflammation reducer. It also contains several powerful glycosides that in certain doses can act as a sedative or in higher doses can cause convulsions. In fact, it was once called convulsion weed or fit root because of these properties.

Once identified, the kids began to spot clusters of it everywhere, and they pointed it out in the same way kids like to use a new word, over and over again. Soon we were seeing the eerie white growth all over the place, and the old adage, when you look for something you generally find it, seemed to hold true. Shouts of "Indian pipe, here" were as full of delight as any cry of original discovery.

When I see Indian pipe, I am not only enthralled with its biology but am reminded of Barbara Hurd's description from a chapter called "Moon White Moment" in her book, *Stirring the Mud: On Swamps, Bogs, and Human Imagination* (2001, 106–7). She writes,

> One day . . . I found a small congregation of indian pipe sprouting out of the leaf mold. Two inches high, these albino plants resemble a sculpture of dripped wax turned upside down in the dirt. The color of breast milk, bluish, almost translucent, they are saprophytic plants, meaning they need decay in order to live. I don't know what it is about such ghostly whiteness that suggests silence, as if color were also sound and the absence of one means the absence of the other. Lovers of the damp, they don't look like pipes to me but like nuns, their heads bowed, lips open, mouthing a constant and silent syllable. If the moist ground below them could lip-read, it would see, leaning over it, a white wimpled chorus of "Oh . . . Oh . . .Oh . . ."

She goes on to further describe how she picks an Indian pipe and watches it die. Its death (107–8) "slow and linear, . . . like the way gangrene climbs a leg. . . . You'd think we could prepare, seeing death coming, climbing up our lives. The hints are all around us from the day we're born: we don't last. Our bodies are as impermanent as the indian pipe or a tin can or our own little visions of how the world works."

How amazing that this diminutive colorless plant in the hands of such a skillful writer serves as a means of transcendence and at the same time reminds us of our brief biological existence! That we can see such truths in the humble Indian pipe speaks to the powerful lessons Nature teaches and the great connections we have with all species, even a ghost plant.

As we walked along the trail, we spotted shelf fungi, cup and coral fungi, yellow, red, orange, and white mushrooms, and lichens galore. There were crustose lichens holding on so tightly to the surface of rocks and trunks they could have been part of the actual rock or the trunk or maybe just a stain (how aptly named crust); there were foliose lichens leafy and plantlike; there were fruticose lichens with tiny gray stems and red tops the color of ripe cherries. Called matchstick fungi, they looked like tiny matches. One white mushroom the size of a dinner plate made us stop and take a closer look. A white threadlike material (its mycelium or vegetative body) appeared close to the surface in and among the leaf mold. I remembered reading about a fungus (*Armillaria bulbosa*) discovered a few years ago. Billed as the largest organism on Earth, its mycelium was thirty-five miles in diameter. Like an enormous doily buried just below the surface of the

Earth, that fungus had spread its network of cells for miles. As we poked around in the leaf litter, I thought perhaps I might be standing on an even bigger one, a fungus fifty miles wide stretching all the way to Ithaca, or a hundred miles, two hundred miles, extending its lacy tentacles to New York City until only the ocean would stop it. Who knows, with fungi there are so many possibilities.

Mosses were also abundant, on rocks, near the base of trees, in hollows and crevices, in soft organic patches. There are many species of Sphagnum moss all belonging to the ubiquitous genus, *Sphagnum*, all green and cushy. This particular species covered mounds of decaying leaves and looked like green throw pillows adorned with stars. Walking on them gave me the same sensation as walking on an exercise mat: spongy, springy, and quiet. Maybe that is why some forests have such a profound silence. Maybe Sphagnum cushions help give the forest its softness and silence. I found myself thinking of the old Simon and Garfunkel song *Sound of Silence*, and changed the verse to "Hello Sphagnum, my old friend, I've come to talk to you again."

Actually, the forest is rarely noiseless but its sounds have always seemed connective in a sense. When things touch, they make noise and things are always touching in forests. Leaves rustle like paper. The wind touches them. Sometimes they rattle like loose stones, often they roar, and occasionally they squeak. A raucous squirrel, irritated that we had invaded his territory, shrieked his annoyance. His sound was the touching of cartilage in a voice box. A distant woodpecker tapped out a snare drum rap, the touching of beak to wood, bouncing off the tree trunks and filling the forest with hole-making percussion. The very nature of sound is touch.

The lyrical notes of songbirds—a cardinal, a robin, a vireo—echoed through the branches, but the cries of crows were the loudest and most raucous. Their language has always intrigued me, always remained a mystery, but sometimes I think I can hear words from my own language in their cries, like "crack, crack, crack the bat" or "here comes the cattle car cows." I know this is a fantasy, that I could listen to birds and understand their meanings, but sometimes, I imagine one wise, old, but aging well, crow sounding like Emily Dickinson; another rugged, weather-beaten ol' bird, like Mary Oliver; and yet still another daring, in-your-face bird, sounding the brash words of Sharon Olds.

When the air was still and there was a momentary pause in the forest noise, I wondered if the space between the sounds was perhaps as meaningful as the notes. This is one of the great differences between our towns and cities, the places we live crowded together, and the forests where there is abundant space (space between the notes). In the cities, there seems to be constant noise, the groans of machines always overlapping, never pausing, homogenizing our audio world. But in the woods, there is space and silence between the sounds. And it is in that space, the place between the notes, in the graceful curved line between the white and black, in that place of in-between that is so lovely.

As we entered a clearing, I noticed in the underbrush a dark blue Studebaker nearly covered by grasses and vines. Was the forest trying to cover an irritant in the same way an oyster covers a grain of sand, laying down layers of smooth calcium carbonate, laying down itself, until a pearl is formed? I found the sight comforting because in this green place, the automobile is foreign. The car is not the dominant feature. And in the forest, the forest prevails, transforming metal, gears, and petroleum into leaf, stem, and roots, changing all those inert mechanical things into the living. A biologist's dream!

The woodland trail narrowed into a grassy path, ran a hundred yards or so along a railroad track, and then entered denser underbrush along Coldwater Creek. Here were plants I recognized, mayapples each with their yellow-green crenellated platter-sized leaves and golf-ball hanging fruit, a patch of red bee balm with its flashy flower head standing tall among the brambles, wild raspberry bushes with purple blossoms, wild blueberries, and blackberries with their prickly vine and dappled white blossoms. In the dark damper soil, ferns of many shapes bowed their heads in praise of shade, their names a litany of descriptors: cinnamon, resurrection, leathery, sensitive, spider.

Along one especially spongy and shady section of the trail, a cluster of horsetail ferns grew like a stick choir. More like reeds, these primitive plants (*Equisetum* sp.) have been around since the dinosaurs and resemble bamboo stems. With their thin, segmented stalks and spiky green tops, they lend an air of surprise to the damp forest. Called scouring rush because the silica in their stems once made them useful for cleaning and polishing pewter, these prehistoric plants never seem out of place in the dank boggy soil. In the dim light, patches of horsetails stuck straight up out of the mud looking more like alien worms than benign ferns.

The trail crossed Coldwater Creek and then opened into grape vineyards. Lacy grape leaves draped over the trellis wires, and clusters of green Niagara grapes, thick and heavy in the August heat, filled the air with sweetness. The sweltering sun glared down on us as we walked the last bit of open trail. By the time we reached Fish Hatchery Road, we were more than ready for cold drinks at the Park Inn in nearby Hammondsport. As we all climbed into the car, the kids with their treasures—an oddly shaped rock, a cardinal feather, a large acorn, all collected along the trail—and us grown-ups with our treasures—the feel of the breeze on our arms, the green smell of the forest, the moments of calm, the flights of silliness—I thought that I would never make much of an ascetic. I could never give up my attachment to these woods, never stop enjoying the pleasure of the forest connection.

Social Connections: Osprey Nature Trail, Iowa

7

CALLS OF CROW, CARDINAL, AND WREN mixed with the low hum of motor-boat engines and water running over the spillway from the lake. Unlike the quiet ferns, we made noise. We talked. Sticks snapped beneath our feet and brushes rustled as we moved along the trail. We were a noisy lot. The occasional fish splashed. The mosquitoes were omnipresent. Their shrilly whine was like an unanswered telephone that kept ringing and buzzing until we felt we had to do something, if only to slap and wave them off momentarily.

The trail was damp as a cave, brown with leaf litter and slippery. Overhead the canopy of burr and pin oak, shagbark hickory, and elm umbrellaed the lesser trees of beech, basswood, mulberry, and dogwood. Little sunlight reached the forest floor but enough to support the ubiquitous poison ivy and mayapples that had bloomed and their leaves now yellowed the ground. And among these plants, the ginger leaves, the lovely shape of a water lily, hinted at a time when much of Iowa was under water.

Embedded in the limestone bedrock, fossil coral lay like a delicate lace collar. The coral was another reminder that Iowa was once an ancient sea. Coral, actually a marine animal, grows in colonies or reefs. The individual animal, the polyp, ab-sorbs calcium carbonate from seawater and deposits it on the outside as an exter-nal skeleton. As the animal grows by eating plankton and reproduces by budding, new coral forms on the outside of the reef. The skeletal colors are due to certain minerals, and pink coral, which was once used for making fashionable buttons (I wonder if they were called bone buttons?), is the result of traces of manganese in the calcite shell. In some coral species, the pink color is due to the presence of symbiotic red algae. The fossil coral found in the Coralville area, and for which the nearby town is named, was *Hexagonia profunda* and it had the shape of hexagonal cups, that pleasing shape like a honeybee's comb. Three hundred eighty million years ago during the Devonian Period or the age of fishes, this land was near the equator and covered by a shallow tropical sea. During that era the coral reef we were standing on was built.

Holding pieces of the coral in our hands, we examined them closely. The ridges were sharp and in the grooves, dirt colored the spaces brown. There was something intriguing about holding the remains of this fossil creature in our hands. Could we be touching the past, a time when we humans were only a misty gleam in Nature's eye? To contemplate a time when our species was not the masters of the Earth is a little like looking at an old family album and seeing the relatives before one's birth. To acknowledge a time and place without ourselves in the picture is both humbling and insightful. To imagine the forest as sea is to comprehend the illusive nature of place. To imagine that our land was once water is to understand the impermanence of all things and that we may also be impermanent, a species that may not last.

The Osprey Nature Trail on the McBride Field Campus of the University of Iowa wound up and down hills, crossed ravines, and circled around in a great loop. Sweat rolled down our faces and soaked our cloths as we trudged along, identifying the plants near the trail: wild geranium, wild strawberries, violets, false Solomon's seal, gooseberry, and trillium. We were a diverse collection of nature lovers—by profession, a nurse, a biologist, a social worker, an office manager, and a couple of retired folks—here to walk the trail and enjoy a few hours with Mary Swander, our knowledgeable guide, naturalist, poet, nature writer, and writing instructor.

Generally, people relate to one another in ways that differ from the usual on nature hikes. When I speak of nature hikes, I don't mean treks designed to climb some difficult peak, hikes to accomplish some great distance in a certain amount of time. I mean a communal walk where people move through a natural place with a sense of wonderment. It might be more a function of the people who go on such hikes and that the event selects for more congenial personalities, but perhaps place makes things happen. Real connections get made. In contrast to my usual experience with people whose egos are so dominant they smother any real interaction or diminish the desire to connect, on nature hikes, those kinds of interactions are less common. Power struggles, issues of dominance and competition, often dim. Ambitions and desires seem to give way to a broader sense of companionship. It may sound naive, but the old *Lord of the Flies* myth (the idea that humans revert to primitive, selfish killers in nature) is just not my experience.

The purpose of a nature walk is to enjoy the moment, to learn a little about the plants, animals, and geology, to become more aware of our natural world, and to reconnect with that world. In many ways, what happens is as spiritual, as renewing, connecting, and transcendent, as going to church, temple, or mosque. It is an event that requires the element of place and the connection to others. I find it a comforting phenomenon that nature trails are being built all over the country. I wished that, like churches and banks that seem to be on every corner, nature trails would become as numerous.

Too soon the Osprey Nature trail circled back to the picnic area, and we were in our cars speeding back to the city and our busy lives. And what did we accomplish by our hike? Certainly there are those who would take coral and make it into buttons, just as there are those who cut trees and make them into lumber and paper. We are an exploitive species. We transform things into useful objects. Some scientists claim we have survived as a species because we know how to exploit our environment, because we are the fittest, because we have selfish genes, because we can kill more effectively than any other species. Who am I to say? But I do know that some of us walk in nature not to find commodities, not to impose our will or our understanding of reality on the surroundings, not to fulfill some ambition to conquer the wild, but to connect with the natural world in respect. We walk for the pleasure of being in an aboriginal world and for the company of others who share a love of this world.

Belonging to Place: Life Birds, Vermont

8

❧

W E WERE GOING TO SPEND THE DAY LOOKING FOR BIRDS—lifers, if we were lucky. Lifers (or a life bird) refers to one seen for the first time. Since most birders (even the most causal) make lists of the birds they have seen, the term *life list* was coined to refer to those birds. Of course, no one, not even one's own mother, is really interested in someone else's life list, but life birds can be personal benchmarks. The remarkable thing about a life bird is that it can center an experience so firmly in place and time that it might be as significant an event as graduation, one's wedding, or the birth of a grandchild. I have heard birders say things like, "We first saw roseate spoonbills in Ding Darling when we were there with Hank and Sarah in '78," and their eyes might mist over with affection. The tone in which they described the event might range from warm affection to almost mystical. The bird serves as an anchor that holds time and place and the people who shared that moment together. When the bird is recalled, all the richness of the experience can be remembered.

So when I hear of a Canada warbler, I remember the gravel road from Goshen to Ripton and the noon sun beating down on the dusty willows and Sue in her floppy khaki hat jumping out of her Corolla saying, "Up there, scarlet tanagers, chestnut-sided warblers, Canada warbler!" I remember the lace collar on the bird's yellow breast and the way the sun hit the uplifted wing as it scratched beneath its wing like a little old lady looking for lost papers in her desk drawer. I remember the meadow of ripe grasses, purple asters, and goldenrods beyond a hedge row, and beyond that the hazy folds of the Green Mountains and the sky the color of cheesecloth. All these things from the mention of a tiny bird.

Sue was the model of the independent, hardy New Englander. She drove us around the Moosalamoo region, pointing out places of interest as we moved from one birding site to another. In the curve of the road, Warren Kimble's studio, a farm that once belonged to Thomas Davenport, the inventor of the first electrical engine (who died penniless, she added), the Brandon Free Public Library that was fully supported by the local community (Sue was, of course, a member of the board), the trailhead to the Long Trail (a trail I thought was part of the Appalachian Trail but which she pointed out was the other way around—the Appalachian Trail was part of the Long Trail). Sue had grown up in the area, moved away for a few years, but returned, so most of her life she had spent wandering the foothills of the Green Mountains.

The Leicester Hollow Trail crossed the Neshobe River and would eventually end at Silver Lake. A severe drought had lowered the creeks and rivers of the area, so the river was hardly more than a stream. We walked a short distance among the basswood, beech, birch, hickory, red and white oak, and all those wonderful deciduous northeastern trees that in summer are as lush as any green in the world, and in fall are the kaleidoscope that make New England autumns famous. A black dog the size of a pony came loping out from behind a nearby house and we froze. The owner quickly appeared and assured us that the dog was old and harmless. We walked on somewhat hesitantly, spotting a few common woodland species: an American redstart, gold finches, and eastern phoebes in the brush. The way the fellow had said "old and harmless" as if they were synonymous certainly did not reassure us (was it an unreliable narrator problem?).

On to the wetlands, Long Swamp Road and Short Swamp Road made a lazy gravel loop around a boggy lowlands west of Brandon. Chickadees and common yellow throats flittered in the underbrush, and the songs of red-eyed vireos and eastern peewees came singing from the woods. But by far the loveliest was the melodious tune of the hermit thrush. We were checking an old rotting tree for hairy woodpeckers when Sue said, "Listen, that's the hermit thrush." Not at all the gloomy question asked in *The Oven Bird*, "what to make of a diminished thing," (Frost 1969, 119–20), this bird's song was the essence of lightness. Sue told us it was often the first one she heard in spring. I imagine this might have been the bird that inspired Emily to write "Hope is a thing with feathers."

A short jaunt through a woodland, up a hill, and around a pond, revealed American wood frogs, a painted turtle whose underside was as red as a Turkish rug, and horse hoof fungi stepping up the side of a decaying tree. Few birds were around and the woodland spring flowers were gone, but the deeply loved leaves of bloodroot and heart-shaped wild ginger adorned the path. Bracken and interrupted ferns sprung from the moist ground around a shallow pond. Among the taller trees, a horse chestnut reminded me how once this land was covered with other chestnut trees, the American chestnut (*Castanea dentata*). Trees over two hundred feet high were common in these woods, in fact, common all over New

England. Logged out and the remaining trees decimated by a blight, the American chestnut became a ghost tree. A similar fate befell the elms (*Ulmus americana*) reduced by Dutch elm disease. With maple decline and beech blight, the tall trees of New England became a memory.

The fate of the tall trees in New England was related in Howard Mansfield's *In the Memory House* (1993). He traces the passing of the tall trees and the grief over their loss by searching the old writings for memories of the lost trees. He tells how the American forest went from a dark primitive place cleared for farmland and cut for firewood to resource lands logged for primary wood. I wondered, are we really a "plague species," a term Reg Morrison (1999) uses in *The Spirit in the Gene: Humanity's Proud Illusion and the Laws of Nature*. Are we destined to cut down our forests, to let them grow back a little, and then to cut them down again?

Moving on to a cemetery off Route 7, cedar waxwings, song sparrows, a catbird, and chickadees flittered in the thickets and white-breasted nuthatches crawled along the limbs of the hemlocks. A maintenance crew was out mowing and trimming the grounds. Walking among the neatly manicured stones and the well-organized plots, we came upon the back wall of the cemetery, and I caught myself thinking, "Something there is that doesn't love a wall" (Frost 1969, 33). This was certainly Robert Frost country.

Blueberry Hill was covered with wild blueberry bushes and picking paths crossed the hillside. The fields were maintained by the state wildlife department with periodic burns and shrub removal. Unlike the large supermarket hybrids, these berries were tiny, petits pois size, and it would take a lot of picking to make a pie, but they were certainly sweet and juicy. Picking a few and popping them into my mouth, I thought of Barbara Hurd's description in "An Appetite for Blueberries" (2002, 49). The star berry reminded her of hunger, and she asked the question, "Isn't it community in its largest sense that we hunger for? A community that includes the imagination?" She writes, "It is this longing to belong and the belonging that prevents spiritual starvation and propels us to protect special places."

We spread a tarp on the top of the hill and ate our sandwiches overlooking the slopes of the Green Mountains. As the orange wood lilies swayed in the breeze, Sue pointed out Mt. Moosalamoo, Brandon Gap, and Horrid and Rattlesnake cliffs where peregrine falcons had been released. She spoke of four great friends she had met many years ago at Audubon Camp. They lived all over the country, from Michigan to California, and every year they met in a new place. For a few days, these friends would explore the place and renew their friendships. I think this sense of community was based on the love of place and respect for the creatures that inhabit it, a community that allowed the imagination to make all kinds of connections.

Our final birding spot, west of Brandon near Lake Champlain, was where the flat and fertile farmlands (the only flat and fertile land in Vermont, Sue said) gave way to the marshes of the Dead Creek Wildlife Management Area. Shallow mud flats baked in the afternoon heat, and we could almost see the water evaporating from the cooking waters. The shore birds didn't seem to mind as they fed in the inch-deep waters. For a long time we sat beneath a small tree, watching the sun wink off the water and the sandpipers feed. On stick legs with their heads bent down, beaks probing and moving the muck, they seemed intent as potters obsessed with clay.

At the end of the day, we returned to the inn and sat on the porch, checking our bird list. We had several life birds. But more importantly, we had spent the day with a woman who had shared with us her sense of place and connection. And I felt, in turn, connected to that place. As the light faded and the stillness of the New England summer night turned evening's conversation into pleasant recollections, I thought, we find connections wherever we can. In the company of that small circle of bird lovers and to that community of women who loved the trees, the birds and the wild things, I imagined, I belonged.

SANCTUARIES IV

Sandhill Cranes. Artwork by Eric Hinote.

Private Lands: Vicksburg, Mississippi

9

WHEN SOMEONE MENTIONS VICKSBURG, what does it bring to mind? Does it remind us of a certain Civil War battle? Does it conjure up images of the old cotton plantations of the past or the riverside casinos of the present? Is it the river city with its old brick buildings or the malls on the outskirts near the interstate? Is it a place where someone might grow up (like Sidney Montgomory, a fellow we met on our trip), a place to work like the Corps of Engineers (I almost took a job with that agency), or a place to retire (one of my dearest cousins retired there), all personal references? Yet is that not what makes a place important to us, our personal references? Is that what makes a place endure? And how can we transform our personal experiences into something of value, something that endures and enlightens?

Eudora Welty, in a collection of personal and occasional essays called *The Eye of the Story* (1979, 299), captured it best in an essay on "Some Notes on River Country." She writes:

> Indians, Mike Fink, the flatboatman Burr, and Blennerhassett, John James Audubon, the bandits of the Trace, planters, and preachers—the horse fairs, the great fires—the battles of war, the arrivals of foreign ships, and the coming of floods: could not all these things still move with their true stature into the mind here, and their beauty still work upon the heart? Perhaps it is the sense of place that gives us the belief that passionate things, in some essence, endure.

A weekend along the Mississippi River in a place that captured my heart would endure in my memory forever.

In the heat of the August sun, we drove through the heart of rural southern Mississippi, from Mobile to Hattiesburg, Hattiesburg to Jackson, Jackson to

Vicksburg. The highways, once long empty stretches of road through miles of slash pine in the fifties, were busy and lined with businesses. How changed the landscape of the rural Deep South. Acres of longleaf pine became slash pine after the great cuttings of the thirties and forties, and now the highways were speckled with gas stations, convenience stores, and truck depots. In Vicksburg, we stopped downtown for sunscreen at an old drugstore full of Civil War medicines on display. The faded labels on amber bottles of tincture of iodine, arsenicals, herbal solutions, and root extracts were in sharp contrast to the brightly colored rows of Mineral Ice and plastic tubes of insect repellent, tooth paste, and Preparation H.

The river road where the glitzy casinos were beginning to gear up for the weekend and the Vicksburg National Military Park were our brief glimpses of the tourist attractions. The park road wound through blue and red markers, marble monuments, bronze statues, cannons, and grass-covered mounds and trenches as we listened to an audiotape that recounted the details of the famous battle. The siege of Vicksburg and the fall of this strategically located city allowed Grant and the Union to control access to the Mississippi River. According to the narrator, this led to the eventual defeat of the Confederacy. The tape droned on and on about how this regiment took position here and that unit moved there. Like a game of chess, the pieces of the war machinery were manipulated, but all I could think of was how green the grass had grown from the once blood-soaked ground where thousands of young men had died.

The back road to Eagle Lake crossed the Yazoo River and ran twenty miles through cotton fields and bottomlands with nothing but the occasional fish camp to indicate civilization. We had hardy pulled into the private preserve called Tara Wildlife, Inc. (I couldn't believe the name and dreaded its implications) when everyone jumped into their vehicles and took off up the levee for the first bird watch. The narrow levee road looked out over cotton fields, cow pastures, and backwater swamps. Perched high in the top of a dead tree across an open cotton field was a bald eagle. We all piled out of the cars and set up scopes to get a better look. Such a majestic creature sitting on the bare branch in his white-feathered cape looking out over the fields, he looked every bit the emperor of Mississippi.

Up over the levee and down into a slough, we came to a backwater pond, pulled out our binoculars, and watched as thousands of white ibises, snowy and great egrets, great blue herons, green and tricolored herons glided in to roost for the night. With the noise of cicadas and the multitude of birds, we could barely hear our own conversations as we began introductions.

"Hi, we're Mike and Laura. We're from Jackson."

"Bill and Sally. We're from Yazoo City."

"Look, green herons coming in off to the right, hey, I'm Sidney!"

As each flock sailed into the rookery like streaks across a canvas and landed as splashes of white against the dark green wax myrtles, the noise escalated to a deafening roar. And they kept coming. More and more birds glided in until the air was saturated with bird sound. Finally, the last rays of daylight diminished and the birds faded into the dusky night. The roar softened and the night became quiet and still. Only then did we reluctantly return to the lodge.

Dinner prepared by a jolly middle-aged woman with a deep southern accent was crayfish etouffee over spaghetti, fresh green beans, new potatoes, and pecan pie. It was like stepping back into my grandmother's kitchen. As we reviewed the bird list and continued with introductions, we met Jane and Terri from Jackson Audubon, Charles from the Jackson Zoo, and others. The evening passed quickly and we said good night with great plans for the next day.

I was up the next morning at dawn and watched a loggerhead shrike on the telephone wire. Barely visible in the early morning light, its mockingbird body blended with the gray morning sky. This Zorro bird with its black mask and razor-sharp beak is known as the butcher-bird because it impales its prey on spikes. Sometimes a barbed wire fence in its territory can look like a clothesline but instead of clothes, rows of lizards and grasshoppers hang from the barbs, a very efficient predator's larder. I remembered one afternoon in a south Alabama grass field seeing a shrike swoop down and catch something from the grass, then discovering the tiny bloody head of a swamp sparrow impaled on a sharp branch where it had perched to eat.

After breakfast, we meandered about a hardwood bottomland in search of woodland birds and spotted wax myrtle warblers (called yellow rumps), vireos, a yellow-billed cuckoo, Baltimore orioles, and a barred owl. Under the canopy of a mature hardwood forest, butterflies darted here and there. In a stand of hackberries, orange gulf fritillaries flitted from branch to branch, flashing their chrome undersides, and cloudless sulfur butterflies darted through the thickets like animated spots of yellow paint. On either side of the road, Spanish moss and vines hung from live oaks, water oaks, tupelo gums, green ash, river birch, pecan, and willows. In a clearing, a zebra swallowtail the size of a hand landed on a pawpaw bush. Its host plant, the shrubby tree was loaded with fruit. Sidney picked one of the pale green cucumber-sized fruits, peeled it, and took a bite. His slurp sounded so good, I had to try it, too. The beige-colored pulp globed around large black seeds was as smooth as sweet cream. Soon everyone in the group was slurping. Called false banana, the pawpaw (*Asimina triloba*) is actually a tropical fruit that was once abundant along the coastal plain but because of land clearing and development, it has almost disappeared.

Ms. Welty's descriptions (295–96) of the Mississippi River bottomlands have captured these botanical wonderlands with great clarity. She writes,

And the vines make an endless flourish in summer and fall. There are wild vines of the grape family, with their lilac and turquoise fruits and their green, pink and white leaves. Muscadine vines along stream banks grow a hundred feet high, mixing their dull, musky delicious grapes among the bronze grapes of the scuppernong. All creepers with trumpets and panicles of scarlet and yellow cling to the treetops. On shady stream banks hang lady's eardrops, fruits and flowers dangling pale jade. The passionflower puts its tendrils where it can, its strange flowers of lilac rays with their white towers shining out, or its fruit, the maypop, hanging. Wild wisteria hangs its flowers like flower-grapes above reach, and the sweetness of clematis, the virgin's-bower . . . and of honeysuckle, must fill even the highest air. There is a vine that grows to great heights, with heart-shaped leaves as big and soft as summer hats, overlapping and shading everything to deepest jungle blue-green.

How could one not believe in the magic of these bottomlands?

We were back on the levee in the afternoon looking for wood storks. One of the wildlife biologists first noticed the birds soaring off to the east. Flying in loopy circles, they became smaller and smaller, moving higher and higher until they were pinpoint specks in the hot white sky. Finally, they simply vanished into the heights. We raced off in that general direction and discovered a resting site farther down the levee in a shallow slough. Hundreds of birds filled the shallows, some perched in bald cypress trees, some stood motionless in the water, their stilt legs supporting large white bodies with black-tipped wings. In the 1930s there were sixty thousand nesting wood storks in the United States. Today's estimates put the numbers around five thousand, so those in that pond represented a significant portion of the U.S. population.

Some of the storks were feeding. One stork—with his wings outspread to block the glare of the sun—waded the pool like a cape-wielding matador. He disturbed something with his downward curved bill, snagged it, and swallowed it in one smooth movement. In the direct sun with no shade or breeze, the August heat soon had us back in our air-conditioned cars.

Turning off the levee, our caravan traveled down a dirt road that ran several miles through private pastures. The road passed through green fields where cattle grazed and where every cow had a companion bird. A single cattle egret fed along side its bovine partner. What odd couples these pairs made, hefty black heifers and small white bud-vase birds. Most of the cattle egrets fed on the ground, eating insects stirred up by the grazing cows, but occasionally one could be seen standing on the back of a cow picking ticks off its hide. The cattle egret is not a native bird but rather a recent African immigrant. They have only been around the South since the 1950s but have adapted well to the southern land with its cow pastures.

We parked the cars along the road and walked through the thickets to the banks of the river. The river looked like an enormous lake. At least a mile wide, it stretched out in either direction for miles before it bent around into green banks. In the distance, a tugboat pushed a couple of grain barges slowly up the syrup-colored waters. Someone in the group started humming "Ol' Man River. He just keeps rollin . . ." and we all giggled in pure delight.

Upriver, hundreds of white pelicans sunned on a long sandbar. Beneath their beaks, flexible food pouches stretched like empty yellow balloons as they raised their heads and preened. One of the largest North American birds, white pelicans migrate from Canada to Mexico, but unlike wood storks or vultures who travel in kettles, they fly in loose formations that change shape like wavy lines. The state bird of Louisiana, white pelicans came close to extinction in the 1970s because of DDT and other pesticides, but conservation efforts saved them and estimates put their numbers now back in the thousands. Not as numerous as the brown pelican, they feed in hunting groups, surrounding a school of fish and collectively corralling the fish. On the state seal, a white pelican is pictured feeding her chicks. The story I remember as a kid was that when a mother pelican's chicks are starving and there is no food, she plucks the feathers from her breast and lets the chicks suckle from her own flesh. What a powerful image of mothering this bird evokes.

With a heat index well over a hundred degrees and the humidity almost as high, we returned to the lodge and cooled down with sweet iced tea. For the final birding event of the day, we hopped into our cars again and caravanned to a place along the Mississippi called Buckhorn Sandbar. To get onto the sandbar, we had to climb down a steep thirty-foot bank. Although some of our less sure-footed members had difficulty, we finally all made it down, some by the seat of our pants and some with the help of our hardier members. The sandbar was at least a half-mile wide and completely covered with bird tracks. It looked as if someone had written a million Chinese novels on the sand, for there was not an inch of un-printed surface on that sandbar. As we sat on a gnarly old driftwood log near the river's edge watching flocks of egrets fly just above the surface of the river, the sun sank below the tree line. Sidney joined us and told us about how he grew up a few miles south of here, how he loved this place and would never leave it, how this place was like a soul mate, his soul-place. The sky turned maroon, then orange and purple. The water turned crimson, the sand turned pink, and even the air looked cherry-blossomed. Someone started a song, "Good to beat your feet on the Mississippi mud," and the evening air rang with laughter, music and color. When the sky finally darkened and lost its pastel, it came time to leave, and we trudged slowly back to the cars more than a little reluctant to see the weekend come to an end.

The next morning, just before daybreak as we packed our car for the trip home, herds of white-tailed deer moved along the fields at the bottom of the levee. In the dim morning light with a few stars still shining, the deer moved stealthily from the edge of the cut grass fields into the thicker vegetation. Like shadows, they faded into the trees and in an instant were gone. The morning mist was thick as we drove along the cotton fields past the tiny shotgun houses of the black farmers who lived along the dirt road. The dirt road turned into a paved road and then into Highway 61. With visions of wood storks, white pelicans, and white-tailed deer dancing in my head, I drove through the swirling morning mist. It was only when the fog burned off and we reached Interstate 20 that I felt as if I had awaken from a midsummer night's dream.

National Refuges: A Festival of Cranes, New Mexico

10

EVERY NOVEMBER FOR THE PAST SEVENTEEN YEARS, a group of volunteers called the Friends of the Bosque del Apache have put on an event called the Festival of the Cranes. We discovered the event was as much about the goodness and compassion of people as it was about birds. It was about Nancy, a landscape architect who sauntered across the desert in search of interesting plants; Ramona, a bus driver with four kids who loved birds and the refuge; Art, a retired professor who gave lectures on bird migration; Mary, a retired ornithologist who still wrote papers on bird evolution and led a field trip into Water Canyon; Jan, the director of a humane society who said the festival renewed her sense of sanity; Jane, a schoolteacher from El Paso whose grandparents taught her birding as a kid; and Toni and Meredith, two friends who lived in different states but met each year to renew their friendship among the birds. The festival was about so many generous people, both volunteers and participants, who gathered to honor the birds.

Throughout the year all across the United States, bird festivals (and there are hundreds) help raise funds for bird conservation. On the surface, the Festival of the Cranes was a fund-raising event that took place at the Bosque del Apache National Wildlife Refuge and nearby Socorro, New Mexico, and involved four days of field trips, lectures, refuge tours, art exhibits, and all the sort of events that connote festival. On a deeper level, it was a celebration of the coming of winter, a celebration of the return of the sandhill cranes and snow geese that overwinter in the refuge, and a thanksgiving for the place set aside to ensure the birds a winter home.

Probably the most spectacular events on the schedule were the fly-ins. Every evening at dusk when eight thousand sandhill cranes returned from the feeding fields to roost for the night in the shallow ponds of the Bosque, we stood bundled up in warm clothes along a dirt road bordered by orange salt cedars (tamarisk trees) to watch. They glided in, in twos, threes, fours, and in larger groups. They drifted in like a lace mantilla placed over the sky and allowed to float down. As the colors of sunset waned and the sky became a darker blue, the snow geese followed. The air was filled with their arrival honks and settling noise. Twenty thousand white flickering specks moved overhead and the sky trembled with wings.

Peter Matthiessen's *The Birds of Heaven: Travel with Cranes* (2001) presents the history of the sandhill cranes. One of fifteen species of cranes worldwide, in 1937 the population of these birds had dropped to twenty-five pairs in Wisconsin. With the efforts of such people as George Archibald and the International Crane Foundation, the populations recovered and estimates today put the numbers well over 650,000. The six subspecies of sandhill cranes have different distribution and migratory patterns. Some migrate, others don't, but their ancestors were migratory. Some winter in Florida, Texas, and Arizona; some summer in Nebraska along the Platte River. The birds at the Bosque del Apache were the greater sandhill crane and they breed in eastern Idaho, southwestern and western Montana. Making five-feet-wide ground nests out of marsh grasses, two eggs are laid; one fifth of the nests hatch both birds. The young cranes (called colts) feed and grow in the marshes and when the first cold snap kills the insects they eat, they migrate to New Mexico to winter. All sandhill cranes have complex social structures. Calls and dancing are the language the birds use to communicate and keep the social structure intact.

Ramona drove us through sections of the Bosque not generally open to the public. We saw a bobcat grab a sandhill crane and drag it into the brush in the blink of an eye; the remains of the kill, a pile of pale gray feathers blowing in the wind. We watched a pair of cranes dance, first like an awkward long-legged, square-dance couple facing each other, lifting their wings, hopping up and down and around, then finally walking off together in slow sync full of the elegance and grace of a long-married couple. In a leafless cottonwood full of yellow-headed black birds, the tree became a Christmas tree decorated with yellow and black ornaments.

Nancy took us on a plant walk along the Canyon trail. The miles of Chihuahuan desert covered in mesquite, creosote, juniper, and pinion pine were a warehouse of winter colors. A huge dry arrangement, there was every conceivable shade of brown. One of the showiest shrubs was the four-wing saltbush (*Atriplex canescens*) whose frilly branches looked like bundles of dried hydrangea petals. A closer look revealed that the petals were actually seeds and each had four parchmentlike bracts surrounding it. Tiny hooks allowed it to stick to passersby, a good means of dispersal. Other plants like Apache plume (*Fallugia paradoxa*), with its feathery pink antennae, fluff grass, rice grass, bush muhly, dagger and tree cholla, brickelbush, Mormon tea, pepperweed, snakeweed, and so many more trans-formed the hike into a litany of botanical delights. I will never forget the smell of the tangy sage, the subtle textures of all those dried grasses against a turquoise sky, and the way Nancy called out the names of hundreds of plants as if they were her dearest friends.

Not all events were part of the scheduled festival. The Leonid meteor show-ers, for example, peaked one night, and we drove five miles out of Socorro into the dark New Mexico desert, found a pull-off away from the road lights, and stood in the cold night air staring up into the sky. From about 3:00 to 4:00 a.m., shooting stars dusted the night sky. Every second, a meteorite would blaze across the black, leaving a faint dusky trail. Like fireworks without the boom, the shower finally faded with the morning. The shower didn't actually fade but the brightness of the sun made the shooting stars' light invisible by comparison. Sometimes I re-mind myself in the middle of a cloudless day that the stars are out. They are not visible because the sun outshines them, but they are there. So many things are like that.

Another day we saw rainbows, not just one or two but ten, all along the east-ern mountains beyond the Rio Grande. They began as rainbow dogs, small spheres of color, and grew into arches so vivid they looked like children's construction-paper cutouts. During the day, rain appeared as a gray mist high in the sky but by the time it reached the ground, it had dried. Imagine that, dry rain!

On the road from Socorro to Magdalena, Water Canyon was the place Mary took us to see canyon birds. The morning was cold and cloudless, and we spotted many birds typical of western canyons: acorn woodpeckers, northern flickers, dark-eyed juncos, stellar and scrub jays, spotted, green-tailed, and canyon towhees, bushtits, and even a Townsend's solitaire. We searched the pines for a Lewis's wood-pecker recently reported in the area but never spotted it. Driving back to town, a herd of pronghorn antelope grazed off in the distance. I wondered if they watched us speed across the horizon in our vehicles and thought of us as dust devils.

The day in Sevilleta National Wildlife Refuge was one in a true desert wilder-ness. Closed to the public except for a few scheduled educational tours and one day of open house each year, Sevilleta has the mission of keeping human impact to a minimum. The refuge sponsors long-term ecological research and the Mexi-can gray wolf research, but access is limited. Our ranger guide, an articulate young woman, explained to us that each of the over five hundred wildlife refuges in the United States has a slightly different mission. Some provide habitats for birds, wa-terfowl, woodland and grassland species; some refuges preserve habitats for other animals; some support research and are restricted; and some are more accessible to visitors. They form a web of land conservation across the country. In the centen-nial year, 2003, the National Wildlife Refuge system under the U.S. Fish and

Wildlife Service administered 538 refuges of one hundred million acres of land. A useful guide called *Guide to the National Wildlife Refuges* (Riley and Riley 1992) describes some of them and the history of the refuges is chronicled in *Smithsonian Book of National Wildlife Refuges* (Dolin 2003).

Our caravan of four-wheel-drive vehicles bounced over dirt and gravel roads, dry streambeds, gullies, and miles of arid hills. We had hitched a ride with Toni and Meredith because our rental car would not have made it up the first hill. With five distinct biomes (Chihuahuan desert, Great Plains short-grass prairie, pinion pine-juniper woodlands, Colorado Plateau shrub steppe land, and Rio Grande wetlands), the wildlife was diverse. Long eared, gray-coated mule deer grazed on a ridge; mountain bluebirds perched in the brush; red-tailed hawks and kestrels looked for lizards and mice. For lunch, we stopped on a high mesa overlooking the Rio Grande valley. From that sky-touching plateau, we could see the faint trail of the old cattle drives that had passed through on their way to Santa Fe.

Toni sat on a rock at the very edge of the mesa overlooking the vast rolling desert as we ate our lunch. She had a bag of homemade oatmeal-raisin-nut cookies, which she offered. I really wanted one, but didn't want to get that close to the edge of the cliff. She laughed when I said, "You're too close to the edge." She replied, "But the edge is always the most interesting place." I tentatively retrieved a cookie, but couldn't stay long near that precipitous perch. The cookie was delicious. I think such majestic landscapes awaken the senses in ways that nothing else does.

The canyon walls of dry Silver Creek were the color of milk chocolate and textured with engravings. In this dry land where a river could suddenly appear, carve its presence, and then disappear leaving only its writings on the wall, it was a reminder of the transient power of water. With the skill of a safari driver, Meredith drove us back to the visitor center over terrain that looked impassable. Bumping along the rough road, I thought how fortunate to share time and place with such wise and capable young women who so passionately loved the natural world.

With the festival ending and Thanksgiving a few days off, we could certainly be thankful for our National Wildlife Refuges. That there were people with the vision to set aside these lands for birds and other animals, for endangered and threatened plants, is a wonder. That there are landscapes, not manscapes, all over the United States that will be protected forever and will be homes for vulnerable species is truly cause for thanksgiving and celebration.

Preserves: Prairies of Iowa and Louisiana

11

W E WERE IN ONE OF THE OLDEST CEMETERIES in Iowa, the Rochester Cemetery in Johnson County, exploring the prairie flowers of June. The cemetery, one of the few remaining patches of tallgrass prairie in the area, bordered both sides of a dusty country road. Wild grapevines covered the wrought-iron fence and a species of milkweed (*Asclepias syriaca*) grew in the ditches. The purple clusters of the milkweed flower had a few monarch butterflies flying around them. Lighting for a moment then fluttering away, the monarchs danced around the milkweed. I thought of the harvest festivals where some Native American nations dance to honor corn, for what corn was to Native Americans, milkweed is to the monarch. And even more so. Milkweed is the monarch's host plant. They feed on the nectar, lay their eggs on the broad sandpaper surface of the leaf, and when the larvae hatch, the caterpillars feed on the plant. The plant even gives the monarch a means of defense. The toxic alkaloids, called cardenolides, that make monarchs distasteful to birds are acquired by the caterpillar as it eats the plant.

I thought how widespread these insects are. They can be seen all over the United States, from Maine to the Gulf Coast, from the Pacific Northwest to Mexico. It turns out that monarchs are either westerners or easterners. Eastern monarchs migrate to and from Mexico to all parts of the upper United States and Canada. In her book *Four Wings and a Prayer: Caught in the Mystery of the Monarch Butterfly*, Sue Halpern (2001) recounts how the monarch's winter roosting sites were discovered and how scientists and amateur lepidopterists worked out the biology of this population of monarchs. Western monarchs (those west of the Rockies) migrate up and down the Pacific coastal regions. In *Chasing Monarchs: Migrating with the Butterflies of Passage*, Robert Pyle (1999) tells of his adventures following them all over the West Coast, tagging them and working out their migratory pathway.

As the morning worked its way to noon, I became aware of the heat. The heat and humidity of an Iowan summer can be surprisingly uncomfortable. The day was beginning to feel like an August day many years ago when I was working in the salt marshes of Louisiana. A fellow graduate student, Sidney Crow, and I had been collecting samples near Golden Meadows, Louisiana. The town of Golden Meadows gets its name from the color of the marsh in late summer when, for hundreds of square miles, the marsh grass turns the color of a ripe wheat field. The salt marsh is actually a wet prairie and has been described in a book published nearly thirty-five years ago entitled *Life and Death of the Salt Marsh* by John and Mildred Teal (1969).

The day had begun flawlessly. We motored slowly across the lake with water and sky blending so completely it was difficult to distinguish horizon and sky, impossible to tell where water began and sky left off. The sun climbed higher and daybreak's colors dissolved into cloudlessness. The sky became the color of a turquoise stone. We were in the LSU Marine Science Department's small aluminum boat with our gear: trawls for collecting plankton and shrimp; a Peterson Grab for sediments; a Niskin sampler for water; probes for measuring pH, dissolved oxygen, salinity, nitrogen, and phosphate; plus BOD bottles and coolers to keep the samples stable.

Lake Chenier, our destination, took an hour of travel, and we had to cross a number of large estuarine lakes, bayous, and tidal creeks to get there. We began sample collection immediately upon arrival. Sid and I worked well together for he liked the jobs of working the heavy sampling gear, driving the boat, and trawling while I preferred the tasks of chemical analysis, data recording, and sample organization. Occasionally, we would pause to watch a great blue heron lift from the Spartina or a mullet jumping from the surface of the still waters.

Unlike the Iowa prairie, which may have hundreds of plant species in a single square meter, salt marsh flora usually consists of one or only a few species. In Golden Meadows, cord grass (*Spartina alterniflora*) is the predominant species. It stands about four feet high near the banks but inland and away from tidal flushing, it is shorter, perhaps only two feet high. No trees, no buildings, no telephone poles for miles around, we were the tallest things in the marsh. Like the Iowa prairie, the salt marsh is one of the most productive ecosystems in the world. Plants decay, producing a fertile soil abundant in nutrients. In most marshes, plant organics do not break down easily and they build up, forming peat. Like many prairie grasses such as the leadplant (*Amorpha canescens*), which has symbiotic nitrogen-fixing bacteria associated with its roots, providing it with the right form of nitrogen, marsh grasses often have symbiotic bacteria along their roots. Salt grass bacteria may be more than just nitrogen fixers. They may also be sulfur bacteria. These bacteria eliminate the toxic hydrogen sulfide that accumulates in wet or flooded anaerobic soils. Spartina like rice grows well in wet soils because of these bacteria.

Salt marsh and prairie grasses have to be tough to withstand the direct sun, and in the salt marsh, plants must survive the additional stress of salt. Salt marsh grasses have developed special mechanisms that keep the salt out altogether or that deposit it on the outside of their leaves and stems. Delicate species are not found in either the salt marsh or the Iowa prairie; plants with tough stems and extensive root systems are the ones that survive. In the prairie, roots of some plants may go down as deep as twenty feet, and in each square yard of prairie soil, there may be as much as twenty-five miles of roots. A grass called boneset (*Eupatorium perfoliatum*) forms roots that go down twenty feet, although most grasses average about six feet deep. In the salt marsh, roots rarely penetrate below several feet because of the toxic anaerobic nature of the soil.

That particular day, Sid and I were intent on our tasks of collecting samples and had established a rhythm common in fieldwork. The work became almost trancelike. We were so focused on collecting that we did not notice the dramatic drop in temperature and the darkening sky. Suddenly, a flash of light followed instantly by what felt like an explosion. Sid was knocked backward into the rear of the boat. The hairs on my arms stood straight up and it felt like they were being pulled out by the roots. Raindrops the size of eggs splattered us and the sky was nearly black. A second flash of light, another thunderclap, and I was knocked down. The tallest things around, in a metal boat, wet, we were in the middle of a lightening storm!

Sid shouted, "Get down!" (I was already down.) "I'm heading for shore."

"Sid, the probe is still down there," I hollered.

"Leave it," he said.

I knew if we lost another probe our field manager would have conniptions. He had given us a long lecture before we left on equipment expense, warning us that from now on those who damaged equipment were "guna-hav-ta-pay for it!"

Sid, seeing my hesitation in releasing the cable, said, "Forget it. We'll worry about it later."

We hunched down in the boat as best we could and he drove straight up onto the nearest bank. We crawled out away from the metal boat and sat shivering in the rain on the wet ground with the grass over our heads. Each bolt of lightening etched its way down the black sky and was followed by an explosion of thunder. The lightening may have hit ground farther north or maybe it was the vibration of the thunder, but after each burst, the ground shook like Jell-O.

Louisiana salt marsh soil is a dark gel, with the consistency of thick chocolate pudding, especially the soil inland away from the water's edge. Sid and I knew from experience the treachery of this sediment. Our first course in wetlands ecology, taught by professor Gill Smith had taken us into the salt marsh, and the first field trip was designed as a rite of passage. Gill, who was tall and thin with long broad feet like snowshoes, walked out into the marsh like a water bird and we followed like ducklings. Those of us who were stocky, compact, and with small feet (both Sid and I) were like wedges, and we sank in the mud up to our thighs. Panic would be a mild way of describing the feeling of sinking into that mud that seemed eager to suck us in. Would we become the bog women and men of the future? Sucked down into the mud and preserved for future civilizations to find? But we quickly learned to walk lightly, to watch for and to step on tufts of grasses, and to move rapidly, never letting our full weight stay in one spot too long.

Finally, after the storm passed, we collected our gear—minus the probe—and returned to Grande Isle and base camp. Our field manager never mentioned the lost equipment, I think, because he was glad it wasn't lost graduate students.

Lightening storms not only kill people (in Iowa there are on average seven deaths every year; in Louisiana it's even higher) but they also produce fires. Natural burns have always been part of grassland ecology. Deliberately set fires were common on the American prairie. Native Americans originally set the prairie on fire because the bison and antelope were attracted to the new grasses that emerged, and the animals were easier to hunt. Extensive controlled burning was also used by the settlers in the 1830s and 1840s. Today burn management is practiced in most U.S. national parks as a means of keeping plants viable. Although its use still has some opposition, it is well known that many species of grasses produce seeds that germinate only after exposure to fire.

Of the six major dry grasslands of North American, the best known are the tallgrass, the mixed grass, and the short grass prairies. Marianne Wallace's *America's Prairies and Grasslands: Guide to Plants and Animals* (2001) illustrates some of the plants in these habitats. (Billed for young adults, its illustrations are good for any age.) John Madson's *Where the Sky Began: Land of the Tallgrass Prairie* (1995) concentrates on the vegetation of the tallgrass prairie and presents some of the multitude of species found in to this grassland. In a square meter of tall prairie, there can be 150 or more different kind of grasses with about a dozen most common. Big bluestem (*Andropogon gerardii*) is the capstone species in tallgrass prairies, while blue grama (*Bouteloua gracilis*) and buffalograss (*Buchloe dactyloides*) are the dominant species in the short grass prairies, and little bluestem (*Schizachyrium scoparium*) and others makes up the medium or mixed prairies. Big bluestem, also called turkey foot because its seed head looks like one, can reach heights of nine feet. Other tall prarie grasses include slough grass, switch grass, buffalo grass, Indian grass, fescue, panicum, sideoats grama, needle and thread grass, sneezeweed, dropseed, and timothy (to name only a few of the hundreds). Prairies also have forbs, which are leafy plants, and forbs may include compass plant, rattlesnake master, gentian, and penstemon (again to name only a few).

The common names of the various prairie grasses (and aren't they wonderful) often reflect interesting facts or stories about them. Richard Manning in *Grassland:*

The History, Biology and Politics of the American Prairie (1995) relates the story of how timothy (*Phleum pratense*) was spread. Timothy, "a delicate wire stem topped by a dense, fuzzy seed head, cylindrical and fat like a caterpillar," was planted by Timothy Hanson, a herdsman (and a sort of Johnny Appleseed character) in the 1700s in a few eastern states. By the 1800s, it had spread to all parts of the United States. Another plant called the compass plant (*Silphium laciniatum*) gets its name from its ability to find the magnetic poles. In *Prairyearth* William Least Heat Moon (1991) describes how the compass plant turns its leaves on edge and points them toward the poles. He also relates how leadplant was believed to draw its color from ore deposits and when brewed could be used as a tea to cure pinworms.

While grasses give us the practical gifts of medicinal remedies, they also bring us other comforts. Grasses can sing to us, dance for us, and in their seasonal wardrobes offer us a visual calendar. They are truly some of our most beloved plants and efforts to restore prairies reflect this affection. Many preserves of tall prairie grasslands had been created throughout the Plains States. A tiny one called Walnut Creek Preserve in Iowa is described as "a place free of human meddling." Other larger ones, like the Tallgrass Prairie National Preserve in Kansas, are more in the tradition of national parks or scenic zoos with thousands of annual visitors. Even though there are thousands of preservation and restoration efforts (farmers, for example, are leaving the edges of their fields in native grasses, many landowners are planting native prairie grasses, and various projects have restored entire prairies [Stevens 1995]), these patches and strips are only remnants. The natural prairie lands under spacious skies are gone.

As our day in the cemetery came to an end and it was time for our group to leave this tiny tallgrass preserve, I reflected on the appeal of native prairies and untouched places in general. I thought of the writings of Aldo Leopold (2002) who in the 1940s wrote *A Sand County Almanac*, perhaps the most definitive plea for the preservation of our natural world. To leave places natural, to leave them as true wildernesses, seems a more enlightened way of behaving. We humans have exploited and misused lands throughout our brief and violent history on the Earth. It seems an act of contrition, a means of compensation for the damage we have done, to set aside places where humans are not allowed to interfere. It rather appeals to my sense of justice, and my sense of place expands when I think about the various preserves we have created, places where humans are not allowed to exploit, to meddle, or to even enter. It gives me great hope when I consider the many preserves (some no bigger than tiny backyards) around the country, around the world, where people are restoring the land to its native state (Jordan 2003).

ECO-MYTHS

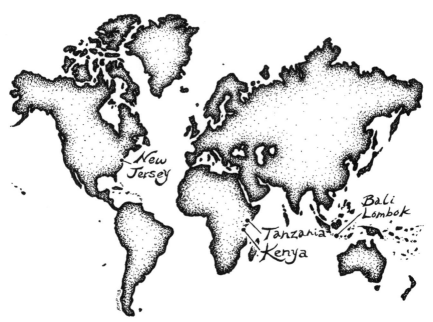

V

World Map: Bali and Lombok, Kenya and Tanzania, New Jersey. Artwork by Rachael Poston.

South Sea Island Paradise: Bali and Lombok, Indonesia

12

❧

I N THE 1980S, I HAD A RECURRING DREAM. Riding on a levee as far as I could
see, rice fields stretched out before me. The alternating rows of green stalks
and muddy water reflected in the brown water and created a double image of
rows and stalks. Tiny brown people with long thin arms stood up to their knees
in the water, their faces hidden by grass pyramid hats. Nothing happened in the
dream except I rode for a long time among the rice paddies. I thought perhaps the
dream came from news images of Vietnam. It was long after the Vietnam War, but
scenes from that time had made lasting impressions. Perhaps it came from the
1983 film *The Year of Living Dangerously*, with it portrayal of the 1965 revolution in
Jakarta and the takeover by Suharto. Or perhaps the image came from the movie
The Killing Fields, of Cambodia. Yet the dream was so peaceful, I was puzzled at its
origin and meaning. I saw that dreamscape in Bali in December 1998.

The Singapore airport was an island of consumer luxury. Slick, brightly lit
shops much like those in a U.S. mall offered clothes, phones, computers, electronic
gadgets, luggage, and gifts. The sushi bar, a red revolving counter in the shape of
a kidney bean maybe a hundred feet long if you broke it and stretched it out, had
every imaginable dish floating by as it made its slow orbit of display. What a contrast to the simple airport in Denpasar, Bali, where our flight ended. After forty-
eight hours of travel, we were grateful to get to our hotel and see that it was
comfortable (every bone-weary traveler's fondest wish). But like so many things in
that part of the world, there was more to the story. We would learn later that the
hotel, owned by members of the Suharto family, had been built on Hindu temple
land, ancient land that represented one of the holiest sites in Bali. The building of
the hotel had caused much resentment and anger among the Balinese, and our stay
there would result in some uncomfortable situations.

The hotel grounds overlooked the Hindu temple, Tanah Lot. Perched on a rock outcropping, the temple was accessible only during low tide, when visitors could walk across the tidal flats to the pavilions. Legend had it that the surrounding rocks were inhabited with sea snakes, but that did not seem to bother the visitors who climbed over them or the fishermen who threw their nets from the rocks. From the edge of the high cliff the dark outline of the classical temple with its multitiered thatched pagoda roofs (called *merus*) lightened with the dawn. In the morning mist the five-roofed (always odd numbers) central pagoda rose like a stack of umbrellas, each higher one smaller than the one below it. With the sunrise, the rocks and ocean, the cliffs and fields became more than just dark outlines as the details of the landscape became visible.

We moved on to explore the lush gardens. As we walked a paved pathway, two big guys in cowboy hats drove by in a golf cart and hollered, "Howdy. We're trying to get in a round of golf 'fore it gets too hot. Where ya'll from?" Well, of course, they were from Texas. Much of the land surrounding the hotel, we discovered, was a golf course and by early morning, the heat and humidity made walking intolerable. Drenched in sweat by the time we had made a single loop around the grounds, I thought that this was definitively not my kind of place—hot, humid, and crawling with golf-playing Texans.

To conceptualize this tiny South Pacific island imagine several volcanic peaks sticking up from the sea squeezed in the middle of a three-thousand-mile archipelago of over thirteen thousand islands stretching from the tip of Vietnam to Australia. The land around the volcanoes is about 70 miles wide, 140 miles long, and home to over three million people. Most of them can be seen riding mopeds at some time or other on the narrow streets of the island's cities. Never have I seen such traffic congestion. But I thought I had seen it all, when a mom and dad and three little ones clinging to their parents all rode on one tiny moped. Now *that* is modest transportation, I thought. Unfortunately, so many of my memories of traveling about Bali were of crowds, traffic, and the exhaust-filled highways.

Our first outing to an open-air theater was the Barong dance. A dance-drama, the Barong recounts the battle between good and evil. Good, represented by the mythical lion Barong, defeats the evil witch Rangda with great dancing and much flutter. The written program described a strange and incomprehensible plot probably lost in translation so I just ignored the text and enjoyed the performance. The music by a group of musicians known as a *gamelan* (maybe "jug band" would be a good descriptor) consisted of various strings and percussion instruments. My Western ear, not well adapted to Eastern harmonics, found the music jarring. But the masks and costumes were dazzling. Believed to be magical, the masks were works of great craftsmanship. The eyes bulged, the mouths bared teeth or delightful grins, the cheeks glowed. They seem to embody the character; some were funny, some beautiful, some frightening. And the costumes were transforming. The monkey-men became real monkeys; the paper tiger, a real tiger; the tusked creature, a real boar; and the feathered thing, a real bird. As I watched the characters move in their masks and colorful costumes, I thought how like the animals in the musical *The Lion King*. I later learned that Julie Taymor, the creator of the animals for the *Lion King* had studied in Bali. Perhaps she learned the magic of transformation right here in this Barong theatre.

Balinese are known as fine artisans and skilled wood and stone carvers. Shop after shop sold woodcarvings on the streets of Ubud. But with so many items, all looking alike, they appeared mass-produced, and the temptation to consider them cheap junk was hard to resist. In truth, they were not mass-produced. Each one— thousands upon thousands, all looking alike—was hand-carved by individual artisans, not only masks but decorative items, trays, boxes, furniture, doors, all sorts of things. Each really was a little different from the others. Unfortunately, too many replicas of anything, no matter how finely crafted, no matter how beautiful, can render them common and uninteresting. With over six billion humans on Earth at this time, I wondered if this principle held true for us.

Like the woodcarvings, the temples (called *pura*) seemed like endless clones. In two days we must have walked through a dozen of the twenty thousand Hindu temples on the island. Finally, we told our guide, as respectfully as we could, that we were not particularly interested in any more temples—so he took us to cremation ceremonies. The first ceremony for a middle-class woman felt like a family funeral except for its colorful and celebratory nature. All the relatives, dressed in their finest attire, sat on simple wooden chairs lined up against the wall and visited. Young women in brightly colored sarongs served the family members small cakes and some drink that I think translated as fruit punch. We were offered refreshments but respectfully declined. As we left, I noticed a dead plucked chicken hanging by its neck from a string in the middle of the compound. Our guide explained it was an offering.

The second cremation was the funeral preparation of a wealthy man. We watched men perched high on a wooden scaffold constructing a two-story bull, much like a Mardi Gras Krewe might build a parade float. The body to be placed inside the bull would be carried litter-style by all the male members of his family from his house to the site of cremation. With musicians, food, and building costs, this type of cremation was very expensive, our guide said, and only the very rich could afford it.

The last cremation ceremony was a communal one. Kind of an arts festival, many people gathered to collectively honor their family members. Our guide said that some bodies were initially buried and then dug up to be cremated. Burial was an intermediate step to the time when enough money could be raised for a proper cremation. Musicians played, offerings were prepared, and the costs were shared. The grounds were wet and muddy that day from the rain and so many people tromping over the same bare spots. As we walked about the site, my sandals got very muddy. Mud oozed up through my socks. Somehow the memory of cremation ceremonies became entangled with the feel of mud between my toes, hearing the tinny discordant music, seeing the damp offerings, and imagining images of digging up the dead. It has remained a strange and unnerving memory.

After so much preoccupation with death, our guide turned to showing us how the people of Bali lived. A typical family compound with its surrounding stucco walls enclosed several buildings, the family temple, sleeping huts, and kitchen. Poorer families lived in single-room thatch huts. Floors were generally bare ground and the beds were bamboo racks. Women in these huts pulled up the grass-matted walls like shades, leaving one side open to the breeze. A visit to a local market was like attending a flea market. Open-air stalls offered everything imaginable: sandals, cotton shirts, trousers, fabrics, mats, bowls, and spoons, and foods such as rice, vegetables, and fruits. To my Western eye, everything looked grimy. When we passed the food preparation area, I was shocked at the flies buzzing on pieces of open meat in the heat, and the odor was appalling. Fruit juice in a dirty bucket was served by dipping a hand-held cup into the bucket. Mangy dogs loitered around everywhere and fed on strange piles of brown material. As a microbiologist, I wondered why everyone wasn't ill.

On the way to Mount Batur, offerings to the gods littered the roadside and small leaf boats containing rice balls and flowers lay decaying and wilting in the sun. Offerings were everywhere. On the dashboard of the van, our driver had a small woven leaf basket containing a cigarette, a coin, and an orange hibiscus. And always crowds of people moved along the roadside, sometimes walking, sometimes standing and talking, sometimes sitting in open huts, the people of the island were always outside. The heat and humidity insisted on such placement. Along the roads, irrigation ditches were full of rushing water on its way from the highlands to the rice fields. The sight of an old woman, thin as a reed, bathing in an irrigation ditch was as humbling a sight as anything I have ever seen. When we arrived at the top of the mountain, the clouds were so dense the view was little more than smoky white fog. But we tried to imagine the green valley below sculptured in banana plantations and lush jungle. The clouds grew denser and denser until the mist blurred even the open road.

A day trip to the northwestern coast and a loop around the western end of the island revealed a claustrophobic landscape. It seemed every space was occupied with either huts or rice fields. I had imagined immense rainforests on the island but was surprised to learn that little of the lowland rainforest of Bali remained. Bali Barat National Park was the only uncultivated or uninhabited place we encountered in our journey, and we were able to travel only a few miles along the edge of the park. Stands of *Corypha* and *Borassus* palms, acacia, and large deciduous trees (I believe the species was *Planchonia valida*) grew along the road, but we saw no birds or wildlife at all. Since there was no way into the park—no road, no trail—the small remaining pristine land described by Whitten et al. (1997) was not accessible to us.

In the lowlands, every inch of land was planted in rice, and in the highlands, rice fields also occupied every available ground. The difference was that the highland fields were terraced. Even on the steepest hillside where growing anything seemed almost impossible, terraces were dug into the slopes and rice grew from the step pools. We observed every stage of rice agriculture. We watched oxen pulling a plow through the muddy waters as farmers readied the soil for planting; we saw farmers calf-deep in brown water planting the individual seedlings of rice; we watched them sling their sickles to harvest the rice stalks and then dry the grains on large canvases in the sun. Everything was done by hand. Every sprig of rice was planted by hand. Every single grain of rice was harvested and processed by hand. It was the most labor-intensive agriculture imaginable. And the system of irrigating the rice fields was astonishing. No matter where you looked there were channels and tunnels and aqueducts and weirs. The Balinese farmers had been engineering and controlling their waters for thousands of years. It was enough to make the U.S. Corps of Engineers look like rank amateurs.

All of Indonesia except Bali is Islamic, and at the bat cave, we encountered our first hint of anti-Americanism. A group of teenage boys hanging around the cave recognized us as tourists and asked where we were from. As soon as we said the United States, they began shouting something I could not quite understand but the gist was that Clinton shouldn't be bombing Islamic targets in Iraq. Our guide hurried us away as quickly as possible, clearly concerned. Earlier that day and the day before, we had passed several gatherings that appeared to be political rallies. When we asked, he confirmed that yes, they were political rallies and quickly changed the subject. There was obviously political tension on the island but he was not about to discuss it with his American tourists and risk scaring us.

On the trip to the island of Lombok, we encountered another nasty bit of shuffling. The airline ticketer took one look at our tour packets and said we couldn't get on the scheduled flight. He told us to go back to the main desk. At the main desk, they told us to go back to the check-in counter. We were hustled around for a bit, until finally after some persistent complaining, we were issued new tickets and allowed to get on the later afternoon flight to Lombok. I suspect they saw that we were staying at the politically incorrect hotel and just bumped us off the flight. When we finally got to Lombok, our luggage, of course, had been lost. Discussions with our hotel staff left the impression that Americans were not especially liked and complaining did no good. To retrieve our bags, we had to catch a ride to the airport and retrieve them ourselves.

Our travel packet included a tour of the island, so we tried to forget our ill treatment, and enjoy the day. Traveling in a minivan, we rode with a wealthy family of four Asians who lived in Jakarta. The father was a businessman, the mother, a bridge player, and the two tall, attractive twenty-year-old girls went to Yale and the University of Chicago. They were majoring in architecture and art history. After a brief discussion of the dangers of living in Jakarta, we seemed to have very little to say to one another. I hate to admit such feelings, but I developed a sense of resentment toward these folks. What I would have given to have had the money to go to such fine schools when I was young! Even with an academic scholarship at a small state college, I felt more than a little envious of their affluence. Their air of aloofness, obvious wealth, privilege, and superiority was annoying. In a moment of ungraciousness, I imagined they were probably linked with the Suharto family and that the old "who-you-know" rather than "what-you-know" had gotten them their wealth. If I was a little envious, what might the average citizen of Bali or Lombok who had almost nothing feel, I wondered. And would they resent me as well?

A visit to a native Sasak village revealed round houses made of straw. Sasak village women grew cotton, harvested it, spun it into fibers, dyed it with natural plant products, and wove primitive wall hangings. For a few bucks, they sold them to the tourists. As we walked through the dirt paths among the hovels, I kept thinking that my camera and accessories probably cost more than what these women made in a year.

My encounter with six-year-old Kari proved to be enlightening. Kari peddled wraps on the beach and made a few dollars a day. She spoke a little trade English and kept saying, "vety cheap, only five dollas." I asked her if she went to school. "No," she said, she wanted to "get married and have children." I suspect she could not have afforded school of any kind. As we sat on the beach looking out at the blue waters of the South China Sea, she reached over and stroked my arm. In broken English she said how beautiful my white skin was and how she wished she had such skin. This gorgeous dark-eyed child whose complexion was the color of creamed coffee, wished for my sagging, freckled, blotted skin. It almost broke my heart. What strange things we wish for, she for white skin, I for an education at a prestigious university. What illusions these things we desire.

The last day in Bali we stayed at the "palace of a local royal family" in Denpasar. The air-conditioner pumped out cool, humid air that gave the tiny room a moldy smell. The toilet moved when sat upon and in the tin shower stall the rusty faucet sprayed lukewarm water in all directions. Hordes of mosquitoes attacked us whenever we walked outside and the only place to eat was a hut that sold cold drinks and crackers. But more distressing was the group of women who parked themselves at our door and waited all evening to sell us sarongs. Our guide must have alerted the neighborhood women that "rich Americans" were staying there, because by late afternoon seven or eight women with piles of stuff had camped out on the doorstep. We could not leave without literally stepping over them. Hawkers had bothered us much of the time in Lombok, but this was by far the most intrusive.

Often a dilemma for Americans traveling in Third World countries, the disparity of wealth can create uncomfortable situations. What am I saying? The disparity of wealth always creates problems. It creates envy, hatred, leads to war, murder, and all sorts of cruelties and atrocities. Yet we place our greatest value and power on wealth. Throughout history, enlightened people have tried to shift the emphasis away from wealth or to make it at least more equally distributed, but we still don't seem able to manage it on a personal level, a national level, or a global level. I tried to be more understanding of the women outside the door, but it made me sad that the last impression of this place was being stuck in a moldy room to avoid being hassled to buy something.

The most confusing thing about traveling in this part of the world was the incongruity of what I had read regarding Indonesia and my actual experience. Some of the most important anthropological and biological studies in the world had been done here. Work by Margaret Mead on the social and cultural behavior of Samoans (while under some dispute as to its accuracy, still represents a turning point in modern anthropology); studies of tribes in Papua New Guinea fill the anthropology texts; and the work by Wallace and Darwin on evolution and natural selection represent the very foundation of biology. The idea of South Pacific Islands as paradise also runs through much of our literature and popular culture. My senior prom had as its theme *South Pacific*, and everyone wore flowers around their necks and in their ears. But my experience did not reflect an Eden. The islands of Bali and Lombok had so many people, so much poverty, and a landscape so transformed by humans there was little pristine world left. Few spaces left uncultivated, they did not feel like island paradises. The heat and humidity slowed life down to a belly crawl and the elements of decay, claustrophobia, and confinement seemed pervasive.

Why I dreamed of such a landscape so many years ago, I do not know. I still have no idea of its meaning, if dreams, indeed, have any meaning at all.

The islands of Bali and Lombok in the vast archipelago of Indonesia were not places that moved me in any way except to make me grateful to be going home. But, perhaps, the lesson of some places is to make us appreciate our home. Some places teach the lesson of limits. Like the thermostat that keeps temperature regulated by detecting too high and too low, some experiences act as gauges and make us aware of our limits. The knowledge that those limits have been so wide for me as an educated, American woman—that I have been able to live in considerable space, comfort, freedom, and safety—makes me a person of exceptional privilege. This was a truth Bali and Lombok revealed.

Survival of the Fittest: Survival Camp in New Jersey

13

H OW HOT CAN A NEW JERSEY BEAN FIELD get in August? We learned that pretty awful is about as good a description as any, and that all journeys are not enlightening experiences. Some are just plain miserable disappointments with no redeeming qualities other than to reveal one's idiocy, and humbling as that may be, it is not a truth I especially enjoy acknowledging. We arrived at the designated interstate exit, called a number to get directions, and made our way to the campsite. What a surprise to find it was a weedy spot bordering a bean field with a falling-down barn not much bigger than a thirty-foot cube. The barn (could it be a fire hazard? I wondered) was to be our classroom for five days. We were given a tent and told to pitch it on a small grassy slope along with a hundred other participants. The word *overcrowded* came to mind as we tried to find a soft patch of ground among the other tents and discovered that stones lay hidden under the deceptively tender-looking grass. As we struggled to erect our two-person tent in the drizzling rain, I wondered if anyone here understood the connection that plagued medieval societies (plague being the operative word here), the connection that crowded living conditions lead to disease.

The bathroom facilities, six porta-toilets—smelly, and about twenty feet from where the meals were prepared—were the next surprise. Then we discovered the drinking water. As I looked at the beat-up old plastic containers full of water, I hoped the safety of the water was not reflected in the condition of the containers. Meals were mush in the morning (sorry, an oat mix) and vegetables and rice at noon and six. When I looked down at a cardboard box full of oranges and saw dark fuzzy cultures, I thought, "Oh my god, I'm going to die here in this bean field of aflatoxin poisoning." The heat was getting to me. It was probably a culture of *Penicillium* and not *Apergillus flavus*. Other than the moldy fruit, there was actually little a self-respecting microbe could live on. There was no sugar, little fat, and little protein, but certainly, the temperature was high enough to grow thermophiles. And the reason for the simple cuisine, we were told, was that it helped cleanse the body. Who are you kidding, I thought, it was cheap, no, *very* cheap food.

With no place to sit except the ground in the rain, we ate our first saltless, flavorless meal, and learned that each of us would have meal duty for one day. To be decided among the assigned groups, some would peel vegetables, some would cook and keep the fire going, some would be responsible for clean-up. No luxury eco-lodge here.

After the evening meal, we sat in the hot barn on hard backless seats for five hours listening to the rules, procedures, and the schedule. Even with the sun gone, the heat was intense. Finally, the leader of the organization appeared. Dressed in loose fitting, all-weather pants, a light short-sleeve pullover, and barefooted, he had mastered the L. L. Bean wilderness look. His hair was smartly trimmed. He was very clean, dry, and his toenails looked manicured. He proceeded to give a performance that would have gleaned the admiration of the best evangelical preacher or motivational speaker on the circuit. I thought it odd that he looked so fresh since most everyone else was damp from the rain and wilted from the heat until I realized where he had come from and went back to during breaks. He came from the air-conditioned farmhouse behind the barn. Off limits to all participants, supposedly because the instructors stayed there, I imagined it plush and comfortable inside. As the evening wore on and he began to sweat, he took a long white cloth and wiped his brow like Pavarotti. For an instant, I thought he might even throw it into the audience.

The leader was a successful writer of books on survival and an instructor of wilderness skills. He went on and on with his list of accomplishments. While he told his stories, I idly watched bats fly in and out of the barn, and I caught myself drifting off into thoughts of these creatures. I remembered Linda Hogan's wonderful chapter "The Bats" in *Dwellings: A Spiritual History of the Living World* (1995, 22). She writes, "an ink black world hanging from a rafter. The graceful angles of their dark wings opened and jutted out like an elbow or knee poking through a thin, dark sheet. A moment later it was a black, silky shawl pulled around them." In a single genus, *Chiroptera*, bats always evoked in me a deep sense of mystery. Everything about them is enigmatic: they way they use sound to see (it's called echolocation); the way they fly as if the air were only imagination (no other mammal flies); they way they sleep (upside down). It was as if nature did not want us to forget that half the day is night and lest we forget, made the most beguiling creatures to remind us.

Like ghost stories made up to scare us, there are lots of myths about bats but bats are really just pollinators or insectivores, so who could think ill of creatures that love flowers and eat mosquitoes. As the little carnivores zoomed and looped inches above our heads, I tried to think of as many names of the nine-hundred-fifty-plus species of bats. I could remember fruit eating, vampire, fishing, evening, pallid, seminole, myotis, spotted, silver haired, red, hoary, northern yellow, funnel-eared, free-tailed, big brown, little brown, big eared, bulldog, ghost faced, spear-nosed, sword-nosed, fringed-lip, long-tongued, hog-nosed, leaf-nosed, leaf-chinned, slit-faced, tube-nosed, horseshoe. Not bad, I thought.

When the bats disappeared, I began observing the other participants. Most of them were twenty-something white guys, maybe fifteen young women, and a few middle-aged fellows. Some of the bat names might have easily fit them. One fellow could have surely been a funnel-eared bat, another, a hog-nosed bat. An older woman (perhaps a silver-haired bat) looked more like a leftover flower child than a bat. In her dress of the bygone 1960s, she seemed like an old tie-dyed shirt snagged on a branch in the river of time. Most of the young men in various costumes ranging from the wilderness adventurer to the paramilitary look were very serious, intent, and enthralled with the speaker's presence. Then there was us. Under the misconception that this was to be an experience about spirituality and nature, I was especially eager to learn the folklore, medicinal, and nutritional value of local plants.

Around 11:00 p.m., the man finished his spiel and we staggered exhaustedly to our tents for the night. The roar of cars on the nearby freeway droned all night long and the stony sloped ground made for a restless night. The next morning, I thought I might have an inkling of how cults exert power over their followers. Using sleep and comfort depravation, I could see where it would weaken one's thinking process. As I drank a cup of unsweetened, unmilked tea to dispel the aches of my damp joints, I thought I might try to strike up a conversation with some of the others students. But before I had time to complete my thoughts, we were back in the barn. And the leader was back on stage telling a story of how he prowled the predawn to see fox, deer, and other animals. The man could certainly spin a tale.

The morning grew hotter, and there was little shade around the barn so even when we took fifteen-minute breaks from the lectures, there was little relief from the heat. Like good Boy and Girl Scouts, we learned how to make a fire from milkweed fuzz. We stood in a circle in the hot sun watching a young man make fire by rubbing two sticks together, but with a hundred people only a few could actually see the demonstration. Lunch was again tasteless and it was back to the hot barn for more lectures on how to make rope from weeds, how to build a shelter, how to filter water, Lyme's disease, and a host of other topics considered survival skills. Another demonstration in the sun and back to the barn. With the heat, the lack of sleep, and the lectures on stuff that I thought common knowledge or at best summer-camp level, I began to get annoyed. But as I looked around I was amazed to see the young men soaking it up. They seemed eager to learn the most basic things. They asked questions that I expected everyone would know.

By late afternoon, the heat was overwhelming and I knew this wilderness survival experience was not for me. This was not about nature, there was no wilderness here. It was not about native plants. This was not about spirituality. It might have been about a sort of survival, a Navy-Seals-down-in-enemy-territory survival, a male-stereotype "lone-wolf" survival. But this was clearly not my idea of survival. I kept having this crazy thought that I would really learn more at bag lady school.

So what was this place about? Could it be about making money? At $600 per person (what I paid) with one hundred people, the organization may have grossed $60,000 that week. Probably with $500 for food (an overestimate in all likelihood) and $100 rent for the bean field, they may have netted about $59,400 profit. From their brochures, they operated at least twenty other sessions (and I understand are expanding) so the figure could climb to well over a million dollars a year. It does not take an Enron accountant to know they had a very lucrative business.

I have never been so glad to leave a place in my life. With a short acknowledgment that we were in the wrong place, we left (knowing there was no chance for a refund). Later, over a cold glass of sweet tea, I thought how foolish I was to be taken in by such an event. Angry with myself for being so gullible, I should have known better, but I wondered about the young people. It was disturbing that so many young men and women seemed to buy into this idea of survival. To accept that wilderness survival equates to living in grubbiness, eating tasteless food, having little connection to those around you, and like the rash of TV survival shows would have us believe, survival goes to the toughest competitor, I found disturbing. Perhaps these kids would never read the Athabaskan Indian story *Two Old Women: An Alaska Legend of Betrayal, Courage and Survival* by Velma Wallis (1993), and learn that while there are many ways of surviving, making community is what humans do best to survive. I felt saddened that these young men and women were learning such selfish and narrow ideas—but then, there seems to be a lot of that going around.

Africa as Wilderness: Kenya and Tanzania

14

THE WRITINGS OF SO MANY WESTERNERS—from coffee plantation owner Karen Blixen (*Out of Africa*, Dinesen 1952), bush pilot Beryl Markham (*West of the Night*, 1983), journalist Elspeth Huxley (*The Flame Trees of Thika*, 1959) to fiction writers like Ernest Hemingway (*Snows of Kilimanjaro*, 1936)— have created an image of colonial East Africa and perpetuated a myth of colonial nostalgia that grips the region like a phantom memory. With the images of great white hunters, safaris to kill big game, country clubs of white Europeans served by black servants, and plantations where white men (and women) paternally over-see native tribes, the popular literature about Africa often has the quality of *Gone with the Wind*. The most well-known exception is Barbara Kingsolver's fictional *Poisonwood Bible* (1998), whose setting is actually West Africa but whose story told by the wife and daughters of an American missionary presents a far more realistic Africa.

Even Western scientists, like the well-known primatologist Jane Goodall (*In the Shadow of Man* [1971] as the first, plus her many other works), anthropologists Louis and Mary Leaky and family (Mary Leaky's autobiography *Disclosing the Past* [1984] is probably the most widely read), and other writers have not really dis-pelled the myth. Their writings have helped build careers for themselves, added to the scientific understanding of human origins and certain wildlife biology, and saved some endangered animals, but against a background of population explo-sions, AIDS, poverty, and devastating environmental degradation, their contribu-tions (if I may be so blunt) seem small.

Yet in the great paradox that is East Africa, these nature writers and scientists (some who have only visited Africa for short periods of time) manage to capture at times a sense of place as strong and multifaceted as any place on Earth. That their writings evoke both a profound sense of home on the template of the exotic and adventurous perhaps speaks to the miracle of the land itself. To write about such a place with its historical and cultural complexities; the impact of the early Persians, the Arabs, the Portuguese, and the British as foreign powers; the hundred or more tribes that make East Africa their home; and the natural wonders of jungle and grasslands and their wildlife is a daunting task. It would be tempting to accept the idea expressed in the phrase so often used to describe East Africa as the cradle of humankind. Certainly, the fossil records support this but in that ever-changing river of Science, all the facts are not yet in. What may be at work when writers relate a sense of home is not really the place of origin of our species but home as a sense of intimacy with nature and closeness to a captivating natural world.

"Jambo," said the man in khakis holding up the sign bearing our names. Glad to see our guide waiting for us at the Jomo Kenyetta International Airport, we would begin our travels from Nairobi. A few giraffes and zebras sauntered out in the distant brush but mostly the road from the airport into Nairobi was lined with half-constructed buildings and more going up. And the high-rises as we entered Nairobi gave the city the appearance of an "any-city-in-the-world."

After a short rest, our guides called the group together and described the routes and rules of our travels for the next twelve days. Part of the five million tourists who visit East Africa annually, we would be going to the national parks and reserves. We would spend the afternoon around Nairobi and the next morning begin an eight-hundred-mile loop through Kenya and a second loop through Tanzania.

Karen Blixen's farm in the foothills of the Ngong Hills and the Giraffe Center were on the outskirts of Nairobi. It was 1995, a time before the bombings of the American Embassy in Nairobi and Dar es Salaam in Tanzania, before the September 11th terrorist attacks on the United States, and before the bombing in Mombasa. The city and surrounding area was peaceful, a colorful, easygoing place, yet bustling at that decisively slower pace typical of tropical cities. Every road we traveled was tangled with people—people walking, waiting for buses, gathering to talk or hang out, men in white shirts, women in colorful skirts and wraps carrying straw baskets, and kids in shorts and bright shirts. What seems prosperous and peaceful can sometimes be a short distance from poverty and violence.

The road to the high plains of the Aberdares passed through fertile Kikuyu tribal land. Small shacks with metal corrugated roofs and small cornfields lined the highway. At Thika, we walked to the banks of the rusty Thika River and watched it thunder down the Chinia Falls, turn to white churn, and disappear into the jungle greenery. The cabana that sold drinks had orchids but nothing remotely looked like flame trees (*Spathodea nilotica*). Back on the road, the farmland and jungle soon gave way to the moors of the Aberdares.

At the Aberdares Country Club, a troop of baboons foraging bananas on the fairways of the golf course had everyone chuckling as our band of ecotourists pulled into the clubhouse. Built on a plateau overlooking the Aberdares plains, the colonial-style clubhouse was constructed of light stone with a long, sloping, red-tile roof. Yellow-flowered groundsel bloomed along the walkways and peacocks strutted about displaying their many-eyed tails. Giant lobelia grew on the trimmed lawn like succulent candelabras. Lunch among the lush hanging orchids on the porch surrounding the clubhouse provided a view of the vast moorlands. Like an undulating sea, the moors rolled on to a distant horizon of soft blue mountains. No wonder Westerners want to remember (or imagine) the old colonial days with fondness.

With an overnight bag, we made our way to the Ark. The three-level lodge looked very much like its namesake. Built over a waterhole and salt lick, the wooden-plank walkway leading into the entrance of the ark was speckled with mousebirds. Inside everything was rich red wood. Cedar and brown olive wood gave it the feel of a sturdy ship. The idea was, animals would come for the salt and a good wallow while the guests, enclosed and protected by the reinforced glass, could watch the floodlit grounds below from the observation decks. As the sun set, we noticed ibises feeding in the shallow pools. They cast thin abstract shadows on the pink waters. When night fell, the doors were locked and a soft buzzer sounded whenever an animal approached. A rare black rhinoceros appeared around midnight and everyone got up to watch him nibble on the salty clay. His coat of dried mud gave him the appearance of a ghost. I thought, as I wandered sleepily back to bed, what a fitting metaphor for so many endangered species.

The next morning we were off to northern Kenya. The Mt. Kenya Safari Club with its photographs of William Holden and the great white hunters on the walls could have been the setting for the character Rachel in Barbara Kingsolver's *Poisonwood Bible*. The book (Kingsolver 1999) was published after my trip, but when I read her description, I imagined Rachel with her platinum blonde hair sitting at that bar with a martini in hand. Rachel's "birds for the amusement of the guests" were on an island in the middle of a muddy pond. Saluis storks, saddle-billed storks, and sacred ibises covered the trees and a few gray-crowned cranes perched in the branches. These cranes were once everywhere in East Africa in numbers reaching into the millions according to Peter Mathiessen in *The Birds of Heaven* (2001, 234). At the end of the millennium, he reports, populations had steadily declined to between eighty-five and ninety thousand, the result of hunting and loss of wetlands. His description of a family of four birds crossing the Ngorongoro crater, "the morning sun flashing in the vivid semaphore of broad and white wings against the high dark forest rim, the nape on fire," is a verse of praise for these magnificent birds.

Mt. Kenya's snow-covered peaks were the background as we rode through the high grasslands of the Aberdares. At a market-rest stop on the equator, a fellow showed how water ran clockwise through a funnel in the northern hemisphere. He took a few steps back and showed how it ran out of the funnel counterclockwise in the southern hemisphere. For a few shillings, it was a clever demonstration of how, as someone in the crowd remarked, "water always knows where it is."

The landscape turned arid and the villages became abode. The guide warned us not to take pictures of the villagers, and I noticed a few unfriendly stares as we sped through some of the towns. A man driving three heavily laden camels reminded us that we were entering desert lands. We were heading north into the scrub deserts of Kenya, a region where tribes have lived in traditional and isolated existence for centuries. The attire of the women changed from the colorful *kangas* of the central highlands to long somber robes and their heads were covered, though not their entire faces. The Islamic influence was obvious and we were reminded that the Ethiopian border was less than two hundred miles away, and the border of Somalia, less than that.

The game reserve, Samburu, was the first chance to see African wildlife in a natural habitat. The reserve is actually three national reserves—Samburu, Buffalo Springs, and Shaba—that together make up over three hundred square miles of typical African savanna. We stayed two nights and ventured out on morning, afternoon, and evening game drives. This was what most people think of when they imagine Africa: herds of elephants, reticulated giraffes, lions, zebras, oryx, impalas, waterbuck, kudos, and gazelles grazing on the savannahs. The fact that Africa's wild animals exist only in the parks and reserves (Kenya has fifty, Tanzania has twenty-one) did not diminish the experience of seeing these animals, but it was a surprise to learn that there are no more wild animals free to roam the lands of East Africa. Animals are relegated to the game parks, and while game parks are not really zoos, they are certainly limited spaces. The idea of "born free" is no longer a reality.

Our lodge on the Ewaso Ngiro River was a pavilion with a string of cabins along the river. From the path leading to our cabins, we could see the surging red waters of the mighty river at flood stage. The currents whirled and ripped at the banks. Enormous red waves rose from the surface and massive logs emerged to be swept downstream as if they were sticks. Along the walkway, a troop of vervet monkeys greeted us, parading and showing off their new infants. After dumping our suitcases, we quickly headed back to the vans for an evening wildlife drive.

Our first sight was a troop of baboons sitting in the shallow stream cooling off. Others lounged on the banks munching palm nuts. I do not know exactly why my primate cousins intrigue me so, but I certainly understand why so many scientists choose a life of watching them. Away from the river, the landscape changed from riverine to dry savanna with vast stretches of grassland sparsely dotted with acacia trees (*Acacia* spp.) and doum palms (*Hyphaene thebaica*). Beneath some of the trees, termite nests as tall as chimneys rose like red monoliths. A long-neck gerenuk rose up on his hind legs and chewed on the green shoots at the top of an acacia tree. We disturbed a family of wart hogs and they scampered off to the safety of thorn bushes, tails straight up in the air like little flags on stiff poles. Then we saw the elephants. A small herd with many newborns grazed in the tall green grass that had sprung up from the recent rains. It was the typical social group, a gathering of females led by the biggest matriarch. To see these creatures carefully keeping their massive bodies between us and their infants was to see maternal protectiveness on a colossal scale.

Around the table that night, one of the travelers related the story of the Adamson family who helped set up these reserves. He told us about Joy Adamson, who had been murdered in nearby Shaba, trying to restore leopards to the wild, and George Adamson who had been killed by bandits just a short six years ago. I knew the story of Diane Fossey (*Gorillas in the Mist*, 1983), but did not know about the Adamsons (House 1993). It was a poignant reminder of the dangers in some regions of the world and the risks some people take to save wild animals.

Early morning, the savanna was a vast aviary. Weaverbirds (the red-rumped buffalo weaver) had built long teardrop nests in the thorny acacia trees. Another species of weavers, the masked weavers, had nests that looked more like round fuzzy tennis balls. Guinea fowl like bright blue chickens wandered in and out of the brush and off and onto the road. Large birds like the Somalia ostriches, cori bustards, and the hammerkop wandered the grasslands looking for insects and grubs. We watched a three-foot-tall secretary bird stomp through the grass, pound its feet to flush out a large insect, and snap it up in its predatory beak. A falcon and several tawny eagles on distant branches were dark spots against the sky, but when a red-billed hornbill flew directly in front of the van and landed in an acacia tree no more than ten feet from us, I almost expected it to squawk "hello." Perched in the thorn branches, great blue-eared and superb starlings turned the trees into Mardi Gras trees. The savanna starlings gave new meaning to the name *starling*.

In the late afternoon, I walked from my cabin to a nearby clearing to watch the Samburu dancers. To a single drum beat, sixteen young men and women draped in long red skirts shuffled slowly out of the forest into the ring. The young men carried wooden spears and the women had walking sticks. Heads held high, chins up, they moved in a wavy circle and began to chant-sing. Their voices, clear and innocent as a children's choir, made a provocative music. The women's vividly colored beaded headbands wound tight against their round dark-chocolate faces flashed in the sunlight when they moved their heads in a kind of owl-like motion. The rings of beads around their necks jiggled up and down like hula-hoops. With the jangling of the neck rings, the young men began to leap into the air. Stomping their feet, the dancers became enveloped in a cinnabar haze as the dust rose like red smoke. It was spellbinding.

On the long drive to Lake Nakura, we began a conversation with our driver. A tall, thin ebony man with sunken cheekbones, he spoke Swahili, so the guide translated. He had twenty-five brothers and sisters; his father had children by five different wives, and his grandfather was a Mau Mau warrior. My early misconception of the Mau Maus was that they brutally slaughtered thousands of innocent British settlers. Even the name Mau Mau conjured up visions of black hordes ready to murder whites. But like so many stories, the Mau Mau insurrection was mostly propaganda (Clough 1998), a greatly exaggerated myth perpetrated by a colonial agenda. In truth, twenty-seven white settlers were initially killed in 1950—but the reaction to the event resulted in the deaths of over 11,000 Kikuyu tribesmen and 2,000 African loyalists, and over 20,000 Kikuyu were put in prison between 1952 and 1956. The Mau Mau revolution was a reaction to British rule and led to the establishment of an independent Kenya in 1964.

The Aberdares grasslands and wheat fields changed to a lush green when we descended the eastern escarpment of the Rift Valley. One of the largest and longest valleys on Earth, the Rift stretches four thousand miles from Lebanon to Mozambique. An area of tectonic-plate movement, the rim bulges up six thousand feet and sinks two thousand feet in the middle as a great high crack. Dotted with volcanoes, boiling springs, alkaline lakes, unusual rock formations, salt deposits, and all those geological features that indicate plate movement, its geology reflects a land of instability. This region of the valley with its fertile volcanic ash soil had been transformed into green patches of farmland.

Lake Nakuru is one of many alkaline lakes of the Rift and is most noted for its flamingos. About two million flamingos, mostly the lesser but some greater flamingos, feed on blue-green algae (*Spirulina* sp.), cyanobacteria (*Arthrospira* sp.), and small crustaceans (*Artemia* sp.). To witness the sheer number of birds was almost indescribable. As we walked along the shore, the birds were a vast sea of pink and the sound was deafening. A predatory stork called a marabou swooped down on the birds looking for young flamingos, and the sky became a pink cloud. Waves of pink rose as the stork kept scaring the birds. Up they would go in fright, then settle, then up again as the hunter's swoops caused the continual scattering of birds.

Sarova Lion Hill Lodge was a cluster of cabins built on a hillside overlooking the lake. We settled in and closed our eyes for a short afternoon nap. Just as we dozed off, the sound of someone in our room woke us and we opened our eyes to see a baboon rummaging through our suitcases. He scampered off when we shouted, but some of the others travelers were not so lucky. We later learned he had gone to other huts, rummaged other suitcases, and made off with their clothes. Underwear littered the hillside, and we noticed two boys in our group wandering the hillside picking up their shorts and shirts, collecting their scattered clothes.

From Lake Nakuru we traveled to another Rift Valley lake. The highest lake of the Rift, Lake Naivasha, was in sharp contrast to Lake Nakuru (Willock 1974). Fresh waters and surrounding lush greenery made it far more biologically interesting. We boarded a small boat and set off to explore the lake. Bulrush, or papyrus (*Cyperus papyrus*), grew in thick feathery stands along the edge of the lake, and the lake's surface was covered with purple lotus (*Salvinia molesta*), water hyacinth (*Eichhornia crassipes*), water lettuce (*Pistia stratiotes*), and a floating fern (*Azolla nilotica*). Birds loved these aquatic plants. A tiny heron called a squacco heron squatted down among the stems and a gray goliath heron over five feet tall fished among the papyrus. A lily trotter walked the lily pads with the smoothness of an ice dancer. Pied wagtails, sandpipers, coots, black crakes, wood hoopoes, lilac-breasted rollers, egrets, fish eagles, pelicans, cormorants, and malachite kingfishers, the bird list went on and on. But the feature creatures of the lake were the hippos. Partially submerged, they looked like floating rocks. They formed gray flotillas and oozed through the water, raising their watery heads occasionally to look around, snort, and flick their pink ears. Careful to maintain a safe distance from the animals, we circled and circled the aquatic behemoths like a curious water bug.

At the entrance to the Maasai Mara National Reserve the driver stopped and went into the station to check us in. From out of nowhere, half a dozen Maasai women descended on the van. An ochre dust moved into the van as they thrust their necklace-laden arms through the windows. In shrilled voices, they repeated, "cheep, cheep, cheep, make deal." We could not help but laugh. Every time they started screeching, we burst into laughter. It was a loud and crazy scene. One older woman, rather shy and modest, looked sort of embarrassed at the spectacle and when our gaze connected, she rolled her eyes in exasperation. We left the women traders behind and made our way to the Mara Sopa lodge.

On our first game drive onto the Serengeti plains, we encountered a leopard. Unfortunately, we weren't the only ones. A dozens other white vans appeared and soon they were swarming around the cat like cabbage moths. The leopard paid the gawkers no mind, crossed in front of our van, and sauntered off into the brush. I wondered if the cat was as exasperated as I was with too many tourists.

Probably the most famous grassland in the world, the Serengeti is a fire climax ecosystem (fire maintains it). It supports a number of grasses—a bunch grass called red oat grass (*Themeda triandra*) and several short-grass species, pan dropseed

(*Sporobolus ioclados*) being the most common. Arid tolerant trees with thin-leafed canopies form arbor islands on the grassland. Trees like the sausage tree (*Kigelia africana*), the umbrella thorn tree (*Acacia tortilis*), and the ant gall or whistling thorn tree (*A. drepanolobium*) with its protective symbiotic ants stood alone or in small clusters. But what every visitor comes to see are the plains animals and they were bountiful. A pride of lions lounged around a scraggly yellow bark acacia (*Commiphora africana*). Wildebeests in long lines stretched across the flat lands like dotted lines, calm now after their frenzied thousand-mile migratory trek. Topi on hilltops looking so picture perfect they could have been a pen-and-ink drawing stood alongside gazelles that grazed on golden grass. Impalas, buffalo, giraffes— the panorama of hoof stock stretched across the plains. And big birds were everywhere. Bustards, crowned cranes, and secretary birds strutted in and out of patches of burn. The evening ended as we watched a giant ground hornbill meander along a ridge overlooking a tent camp. It was almost like watching a small child wandering around a playground.

Maasai villages called *manyattas* speckled the Serengeti. We entered the circle of five-foot-high oblong mud and dung huts through a gap in the thorn bush fence that surrounded the village. Inside one of the huts, it was surprisingly cool, much like an abode house. A small hallway opened into a main room where a bowl of grits sat on a flat stone in a smoldering dung fire. A young woman cradled an infant in the dim light, light that came from a single hole in the roof. The smell of cattle and dung was strong. Our guide explained that the leader of the village was a wealthy man with 250 head of cattle. I had read about the extensive problems of overgrazing and wondered what would happen to a culture whose wealth and value lay in something that ultimately could not be sustained. But, I thought, is that so different from our own oil-based economy?

When the village's young men danced for us, they danced very differently from the Samburus. Tall, thin, and elegant, they leaped straight up into the air, legs and arms held rigidly down by their sides; they seemed to defy gravity. Their circle dance was athletic and vigorous, and in short thigh-length red wraps with shoulder cloaks and wooden sticks, they looked like invincible stick warriors. When they leaped into the air, I noticed the soles of their sandals were old tire treads.

The little kids and some of the women gathered and let us take their pictures. Their black heads glistened like coal. Some of the women had strings of colorful beads that hung from their long-holed earlobes down to their shoulders. An old woman sat in the shade of one of the huts and when I started to take her picture, she put her hand over her eyes. I felt embarrassed that I had intruded and wanted to apologize. But how could I do that? I didn't speak a word of her language. I could only drop my eyes, back away, and hope she would excuse me. As we left the village, several young men asked if we had medicines. I didn't even have an aspirin.

Back in Nairobi, the second leg of our journey took us into Tanzania. The day was cloudy so the peaks of Kilimanjaro were hidden. Only a fleeting glimpse of the mountain was visible as we sped towards Arusha. Lunch at a coffee plantation-turned-dining-room had black waiters in white gloves and white jackets catering to noisy demanding white tourists. Glad to leave this scene reminiscent of the film *White Mischief*, we drove through Arusha and on to Tarangire National Park.

At the lodge I rested while my traveling companion wandered off to look around. When she returned she told how she had saved a snake. The pencil-size green snake had climbed the wall and frightened the couple assigned to the room. The staff was ready to kill it but she lifted it gently off the wall and put it in the bush. Being a docent at the zoo, she had had a lot of experience handling the zoos snakes, but I wondered if it was a harmless African green snake or a green mamba, a species in the same family as cobras. Her spontaneous reaction to save an animal was admirable but perhaps risky. Yet I am grateful for those fearless individuals who rescue the vulnerable creatures of the world.

On the afternoon game drive, a tree full of bee-eaters startled us out of our heat-induced drowsiness. In the branches of a baobab tree (*Adansonia digitata*), the birds decorated it in splendid colors. Trees that look more dead than alive, baobabs can live over a thousand years. Like some cactus, the thick trunks retain water, which allows them to survive long periods of drought. The huge wrinkled trunk, the dense, knobby stick branches, and the nearly leafless canopy made "root tree" a good name. The contrast between the scrawny acacia with its thorns and small fernlike leaves and the massive baobab with its dead-looking branches reminded me that trees adapt to harsh conditions in myriad ways. On these dry grasslands, the tree is the exception to the rule, and each tree is a monument to a long struggle for survival.

From the Tarangire National Park to the Ngorongoro crater, our route took us along Lake Manyara and through many habitats. Open grasslands gave way to acacia, thorn bush, and baobab woodlands, and then marshlands appeared. From the village of Mosquito River with its lush jungle forest of date palms, tamarind, giant fig, and mahogany trees, we climbed up the side of the extinct volcano. Dark by then, the headlights of our van caught a swarm of termites, illuminating them like snowflakes. It was like driving through a snowstorm. At the end of the road and at the top of the crater rim, the lodge was a welcome rest stop after a long day of travel.

Morning began with a slippery descent down the slopes into the Ngorongoro crater. On the eastern side of the Serengeti Plain, this twelve-mile-wide caldera is a world-renowned conservation site. It reminded me of a terrarium. The crater floor consists of flat grasslands, acacia woodlands, and a central soda (or alkaline) lake called Magadi. A lion kill had taken place earlier and we watched the succession of diners. After the lions had fed, vultures spotted the carcass, and one by one they glided in on huge black wings. Like a battle of broken umbrellas, the birds struggled for good feeding positions. Then the hyenas appeared and the corpse became a frenzy of struggle. Fur and feathers flew all around the bones.

Moving on to the hippo pools, the van skidded and slid in the mud. It swerved in the slick tracks and suddenly, we were stuck. The inexperienced driver, a kid about fifteen, tried to back up and gun the engine, but the bald tires spun wildly in the muck. The van became even more deeply stuck. To lighten the load, we all got out and some of the other drivers and guides came over to help push the van out of the mud. This was the only time we were ever allowed to leave the safety of the van on the savanna. It was exciting to stand on the banks of the hippo pools and look down at the massive creatures that stared back up at us. Nothing separated us. For an instant I felt the excitement, the danger, the intimate connection a big game hunter might feel to a wild animal. Its intensity was surprising. But just as quickly, I realized that game hunting was a vestigal connection at best.

We ate sandwiches in an open area, watching shrikes dive-bomb other tourists who had made the mistake of picnicking under their tree. The afternoon passed quickly as we bounced about the caldera observing the terrain and the wildlife. Returning to the lodge late in the afternoon, we watched the sunset turn the crater into a bowl of honey. From that high rim, the crater below seemed such a peaceful place. But what seemed tranquil to us in that high safe place was just the beginning of the other half of the savanna's life cycle: night and the awakening of the nocturnal creatures. As I watched the plain darken, I thought what sense it made to place our gods in the sky, places of serenity and peace far above the messy conflicts of biophilia.

Our last dinner in Nairobi was at a restaurant called the Carnivore. Our guide reminded us for the umpteenth time that we were required to leave him and the driver a hefty tip. The noise, the crowds, the platters of bush meat, and the guide's persistent remarks about gratuities brought to mind the image of the scavengers over the lion kill. The afternoon exploring the shops of downtown Nairobi also seemed tinged with an element of carnivorous tension. The hotel staff instructed us to remove all our jewelry and watches and to be very cautious. Nothing happened but I felt a constant edginess on the streets of that city. For all its natural beauty, East Africa was a place of too many tourists, complex tensions, and a heavily impacted environment. Perhaps the discomfort of sloughing off the familiar, of negotiating different personal boundaries, and of not understanding cultural differences threatened my sense of security. Whatever the reasons, making connections to this place, whose wilderness had diminished to game parks and preserves, was not always an easy thing to do.

THE LEGACY
OF CORPORATIZATION

VI

Temperate Rain Forest With Douglas Fir (Pseudotsuga menziesii). *Artwork by Eric Hinote.*

Sprawl: Ft. McDowell in Arizona 15

W E WERE VISITORS ON THE RIDGES OF SAGUAROS AND CHOLLA, where white mallow seeds drifted on the wind like snowflakes and wrens perched in the ironwoods, still as ornaments. The sky was a blue screen against the green leafless branches of the paloverde. The branches etched a dendritic drawing into the sky. Like veins in a leaf, a river's distributaries, or blood vessels in the body, a thing that begins in full and works its way into smaller things—or like the reverse, a thing that begins small and becomes larger like branches of a tree, an artery, or a river's tributaries—there is something so appealing about this graceful pattern of change.

Ft. McDowell Mountain Park is northeast of Phoenix in the northernmost edge of the Sonora Desert. Probably the best-known and best-studied U.S. desert, the Sonora Desert stretches south into northern Mexico and west into Baja California. It is one of the most beautiful deserts in the world. Biologists such as John Alcock (1985, 1990) and Gary Paul Nabhan (2002), to name only two, have spent years walking and studying its unique vegetation and wildlife. Their writings contain the careful, accurate descriptions of good scientists but also reflect a deep respect and concern for the land. It is clear they love this desert. Their work argues the case that science, generally thought to be objective and remote, might best be practiced using the traditions of the humanities, with passion and love.

A coyote howled across the miles of scraggly brush, a cry that felt infinitely lonely. A call to ask if another of its kind was present in the vast dry emptiness; it was answered with silence. In that silence was the reason we had come: to find emptiness, to become intimately reacquainted with emptiness, to become empty ourselves. Deserts have always been places of meditation, places of solitude, places to find one's self or God or whatever it is that needs to be found. The desert has always been a place where the visitor could shed the ordinary world, empty herself, and let another reality take its place. Deserts are places of transcendence.

The spatial arrangement of vegetation in deserts is sparse. Plants in the desert give each other room. Usually, there is a foot or two of space separating plants. Botanists explain this as a function of water or, rather, the lack of it. Because annual rainfall is less than six inches (that is the way a desert is defined), the stress of too little water prevents plants from growing too close to one another. Some plants produce toxic compounds that keep seeds from germinating, thus preventing them from growing too close. This gives the landscape a generous feel. With little crowding, space is open, and each plant seems important and maybe even a little special because it is surrounded by empty space. Certainly, the immediate lesson of the desert is spatial and that all creatures need space.

Another lesson the desert teaches is silence. No traffic, no machines grinding and groaning, no human voices, no sound of water like the surf at the beach or waves and currents on a river, the desert is a quiet place. A few birdcalls, the occasional coyote howl, and sometimes the wind were the only sounds. It is the silence, the vast space, and the beauty of the landscape that create the reverence and sacredness much like that in our hallowed buildings. What makes cathedrals, churches, temples, mosques, and other such buildings transcendent are the same elements experienced in the desert. Conceived and fashioned by humans, the vaulted and painted ceilings, the stained glass, the golden icons, the carvings, and all the artistic embellishments seem poor imitations of the beauty of the natural land. The sky at dawn or dusk, the red and brown earth, the multicolored stones, the plants of all shades of green, brown, and yellow—all these are untouched by human hands, unshaped by human minds. The natural land is as pure and aboriginal a sacredness as our early concept of the divine. Perhaps, when our species first moved from the outdoors to the indoors, into homes and cities, we desperately missed our original home. Perhaps we keep building in an effort to recreate this home, to reclaim our paradise lost.

Five miles south of the park, a real estate development called Fountain Hills oozes out into the desert like an oil spill. The road that leads to the park passes through this development. The first sight as the road enters the suburb is a huge fountain that spews thousands of gallons of water a day high into the dry air. A golf course, many huge red-tile roofed, pastel-colored adobe houses costing hundreds of thousands of dollars, malls, and shops, this is where thousands of affluent people call home. Now here comes the hard part. What do I say to the people who live in this place, who call it home? What do I say to the lady who directed one of the university's programs and had an office down the hall from me? She is a really nice person. They have another home, a summer place, in Maine. What do I say to the retired couple from Minnesota who bought a house here in order to spend their last days in sunny Arizona? What do I say to the pleasant fellow who worked in the firm that owned the apartment building I lived in? He bought a home for his family here, wanting his kids to have a safe place to grow up.

Because they are wealthy, educated, and capable, because they are good people, because they need safe homes, all the becauses, and I still feel disappointed with them. All the admirable qualities and yet they want to turn the desert into a sub- urb. Couldn't they have made homes in places already suitable for houses? Restor- ing old neighborhoods in downtown Phoenix would be so much wiser than sprawling out into the desert.

But they are not alone. The statistics are staggering. Urban sprawl is engulfing our country. The picture of the night sky from the Hubble Telescope reveals the light of our electric nation. The rest of the earth, all the other places on the planet like stars in the daytime sky, dim by comparison. Duany et al. (2000) in *Suburban Nation: The Rise of Sprawl and the Decline of the American Dream* as well as a report by Smart Growth America (Ewing et al. 2002) give the horrifying statistics. Even the popular press has begun to run articles on sprawl. A picture-graph of the sprawl around our cities (Mitchell 2001) shows this with the clarity and urgency of a siren. We are devouring our natural land. Over one million acres are currently lost every year. In eight years this is equivalent to all our National Wildlife Refuges. In the Deep South, where "sprawl is king" and where the sprawling freeway city is the norm (Tibbetts 2002), the problem is even worse than in the Southwest. Do we have such a need (or greed) for space that we are willing to sacrifice our natu- ral places? I have to believe that we are more capable of making wiser choices about what we do when we make home.

As we walked among the plants and stones under the cloudless Arizona sky, I thought of my visitor status here in this desert. Humans are always visitors in such places. We have no right to turn the desert into a suburb or to take its plants, rocks, and soil for decoration. We have no right to transform them into places that answer our selfish needs. Deserts are more than places for our personal transcen- dence, more than our need for entertainment or recreation, more than our need even for homes. If only we could learn to take ourselves out of the center, to just imagine ourselves as visitors, respectful, considerate visitors.

Impoverishment: Hudson Bay, Canada

16

၁၇ဇ၇

THE PLAN WAS TO GET AS CLOSE TO THE HUDSON BAY AS POSSIBLE. We would drive to Cochrane, then take the train to Moosonee on the shores of James Bay. The drive through the flat, drab, industrialized region surrounding the Great Lakes was tedious, and until we reached Algonquin Provincial Park, there was little natural scenery.

Algonquin Provincial Park with its lakes and dark green forests resembled the landscape of the northern Adirondacks. Its flat topography and dense hemlocks that lined the roadside made it difficult to see anything but the first few rows of tree trunks. Ontario's first park, Algonquin Provincial Park is a mixed forest of conifers such as hemlock, balsam fir, and white pine, and hardwoods such as sugar maple, yellow birch, and beech. A few remaining old-growth stands of white and red pine (once the great forest ecosystem of Canada) occur, but logging continues to reduce the forest. Several places along the highway had canoes for rent. Stopping for cold drinks, a cheerful shopkeeper told us, "You could travel thousands of miles without portaging more than a few feet in these lakes." He said, "The only way to see moose is to get into the back country and the only way to do that is by canoe and I, good salesman that I am, can rent you the best canoe around, yeah, you betcha." But it was late in the afternoon and we had miles to go before we rested, so we passed up the chance to canoe those dark, moose-inhabited lakes.

The small hotel on a lake we dubbed Loon Lake was a pleasant overnight. Just at sunset, a pair of loons glided in and called to each other all night long. It was one the few relaxing moments on a road so riddled with construction and development that any hint of wilderness was gone. We arrived in Cochrane the next day, located the train station to validate our tickets, and spent the rest of the afternoon exploring the town. Main Street was a long stretch of stores and several blocks of warehouses broken by railroad tracks. The sky was gray, it was cold and rainy, and any hopes of seeing the northern lights were dashed by the lousy weather. The next morning we caught the Polar Bear Express to Moosonee, the only way into this town other than by plane.

The train ride was a three-hour journey through a spectacular boreal forest. For hundreds of miles no towns, no buildings, nothing but forest, rivers, lakes, and bogs rolled by the windows. The motion of the train lulled me into a kind of trance, and as the landscape rolled by, I found myself thinking in the rhythm of the train. I thought, "The train rocks through miles of muskeg where Sphagnum, black spruce, and tamarack grow. This is a wet land, a cold land, a land where the hand of frost lifts ground like a plow. In the fens, the lichens cover branches in black lace and giant dragonflies hover over spongy bog. Birch trees like winter candles tremble in the Arctic wind and jack pine from old beach heads rise above the boreal sog. This is a dark land, a tea-brown water land, a land molded hard by permafrost, where moss turned peat becomes lignite, the charcoal gray of old burns."

A sudden jerk of the train and I was back to seeing the boreal forest through the eyes of a biologist. The boreal forest or taiga is one of the world's largest biomes. Its great band of green encircles the arctic tundra, extending deep into Canada and Siberia. One might imagine the Earth's North Pole as a balding person's head. The Arctic is the bald spot and the ring of hair below the bald spot is the taiga. One-third of Canadian land is taiga, and its millions of acres are forested by evergreens. As few as eight species of trees make up the vast taiga (white, black, and red spruce, balsam fir, jack pine, birch, and tamarack) but over five thousand species of fungi (and lichens) make their saprophytic home in the boreal forest. The trees grow literally covered in the green drapery of lichens. It might be thought of as a lichen woods, and the phrase, "Lichens Rule!" seems fitting. The ground called muskeg is a liquid soil covered with Sphagnum moss. Cotton grass and shrubs in the heath family, the most dominant vegetation, grow from the spongy moss mats.

The end of the line, Moosonee was clearly a poor town, a trading post, a gateway-to-the-tundra sort of town. The one grocery store sold wilted vegetables and bruised fruit and the dairy case had only a few cartons of fresh milk. But it seemed to be the place where most people hung out. Round, plum-faced Cree women with little black-haired kids rolled up and down the aisles filling their shopping carts with cans. Across the street a car wash by the high school senior class attracted the town's pickup trucks and jeeps. A couple yard sales also gathered a small crowd of women but from the looks of things (modular matchbox houses surrounded by chain-linked fences), there was probably little to buy. In a small museum, a few frayed artifacts and plaques told the history of the town's frontier and fur trading past. Everything in the place was dingy and dusty. As we strolled around town, I thought, when people are barely making ends meet, historical societies and museums are probably the last thing they have the energy to spend on.

When I considered the riches taken from this land, the huge fortunes made by those in the Hudson Bay Company, I wondered why some of that wealth was not reflected in the town. The Hudson Bay Company is the oldest active European company in the world (*A Brief History of the Hudson Bay Company*, n.d.). Begun in 1670 as a French fur-trading enterprise, it traded beaver pelts with the Cree Indians right here on the James Bay. The company's monopoly and control of massive amounts of Canadian territory have made it a political and economic force for over four hundred years. It currently owns retail businesses like K-mart and Outfitters in Toronto, has interests in Canadian oil resources, and its assets are conservatively worth billions. But the company and their investors had no attachment or commitment to the land and no interest in the native people who lived on it. That this is the place of origin of one of the Western world's oldest and richest companies, that the company exploited the land and left the indigenous people so poor, illustrates the social injustices and disparities that results from a way of acting and thinking that seems to have evolved smoothly from colonial imperialism to modern corporate businesses. If our modern business organizations continue to have no other commitment than short-term profit for the few and making only the few rich, what a sad world this will be.

We did not linger long in Moosonee. After a day of exploring the little town, we caught the train back in late afternoon and returned to Cochrane. Back to Toronto and then to the States, we wondered why we had gone. Yet, like with all trips, there is usually something to be learned. One lesson might be that exploitation of a land without some commitment to its conservation and to the people that call it their home can give rise to a landscape of poverty. If people continue to take from a land without giving back, that land is bound to become a place of "nothing left."

Extinction: In Praise of Trees, Washington

17

ALONG SECTIONS OF HIGHWAY 101, the trees are as tall as canyon walls. The straight black trunks and deep green foliage of the ten-stories-high evergreens are so dense little light can penetrate. With only the tiniest bit of sky overhead, the car's headlights kept snapping on automatically. Then suddenly the sunlight would nearly blind us as we entered long stretches of road where every tree had been cut. The open fields full of stumps and dead branches were covered with magenta flowers. But as bright and colorful as they were, my thoughts turned to battlefields and cemeteries, and the familiar line "In Flanders Fields the poppies grow" became "In Olympic Park the foxgloves grow."

Long stretches of sunlight broken by the short tunnels of trees illustrated the reality that the ancient evergreen forests of the Pacific Northwest were becoming a memory. In the early 1990s, 16 percent of the old-growth forests remained; ten years later, less than 9 percent remained. The sections of cut and managed forests with every plant the same age had the quality of an assembly line. Lined up in straight rows with a precise distance between each tree, they looked like a drill team. Forest managers have not yet learned that a community of all infants, all teenagers, or all young adults is not a community. And a community without its elders is certainly no community. What works for the mass production of automobiles does not work for the forest. But then, this was not about what works for the forest.

Because so many of the old trees have been lost, species that depend on them have declined. Populations of northern spotted owl, for example, which require old trees to nest, have plummeted. Laws such as the Endangered Species Act, which were enacted to help protect species from extinction, did not really protect the old trees. As a result, the owl became a surrogate species, a means of saving the old-growth ecosystems. Corporate interests and certain wealthy landowners claimed that the laws and the environmentalists were the cause of economic loss. They turned the northern spotted owl into a symbol of job loss, economic declines in the timber industry, and environmental extremism. Reaction to this nasty bit of propaganda in turn resulted in the spotted owl becoming even more of a rallying symbol for environmentalists. The story of this conflict was told by William Dietrich (1992) in *The Final Forest: The Battle for the Last Great Trees of the Pacific Northwest*.

That a small bird could become a pivotal symbol in the fight to preserve old-growth forests against the mighty timber industry might on the surface seem like a David and Goliath story but, of course, modern conflicts are far more complex than that. Being cast as the evil giant was not in the best interest of the timber industry so the issues were made more complicated and the cast of characters began to take on more shades of gray. Money can always muddle the clearest waters.

One group of people who were often portrayed as villains in the conflict over the old-growth forest was the working folks of the small towns. People like the cutters, the truckers, and the small sawmill workers who depended on the timber business for their survival were cast as the bad guys. In Dietrich's *The Final Forest* (1992), they seemed more like the spotted owl, victims. His portraits of these likable, hard-working, honest folks who believed themselves to be the tough independent spirit that made America great provoked such sympathy, it was difficult to blame them for anything.

An easier target for villainy might be the corporate managers of the big lumber companies. Dietrich wrote of one corporate raider named James Goldsmith which purchased Crown Zellerbach, sold off the company's pulp mills and some timberland to pay for the acquisition, logged excessively on the remaining land, which caused massive erosion and land damage, and then sold it off—making millions in the deal. Another easy target for villainy might be the U.S Forest Service which, between 1950 and 1990, sold 76 percent of the country's old forests to the timber businesses. One of Dietrich's many characters sympathetic to the timber industry asked what role did (and still does) the U.S consumer and the foreign demands for wood play in the forest's destruction? No one wants to wear the bad guy label, but everyone wants a home, toilet paper, books, and the infinite variety of wood products on the market, he argued.

Regardless of who the real villains were (and still are) in the fight to preserve the old trees, the spotted owl and the loggers became the symbols of the two polarized factions. How ironic that the two most sympathetic groups ended up bitter enemies. How often in history do the rich and powerful manipulate events so that the little guys end up fighting one another? Perhaps growing up in the South, I can appreciate the tragedy of decent folks being cast as the bad guys and exploitive economic policies perpetrated by a few inflicting a heavy toll on the ordinary citizenry. So as we drove through the clear-cut forest, my thoughts kept turning to battlefields and cemeteries. The clear-cut, treeless fields spoke of battles lost.

The local coffee shop in Forks, the center of the old-growth forest controversy in the 1980s, also spoke of battles lost. The atmosphere in the cafe was not friendly and the sullen expressions of the locals who sat in the dark booths in the smoking section suggested that they might still view ecotourists as the enemy. I was reminded of the poignant and bitter words of Ann Goos, a candidate who lost a close election for the Washington state legislature and was spokeswoman for the working folks of the small lumber towns (Dietrich 1992, 242). She said, "That's their solution for our future! . . . Make the entire peninsula a playground. Cater to the urban tourist on the intermittent weekends when the sun shines. Make their beds, cook their food, carry their high-tech yuppie outdoor gear into the forest for them, dawdle along behind their motor homes. Yes, Bwana. It turns . . . [my] stomach."

One of the reoccurring themes in *The Final Forest* was the strong sense of place among some of the pro-timber people like the loggers and the small landowners as well as the environmentalists. Of the environmentalists Dietrich presented (and some were not especially likeable), probably the most admirable was a former political scientist and philosopher, Lou Gold. Gold was captivated by the forest. He lived in the forest not for a summer week but for years and grew to love it. He spoke and wrote about the importance of place. His concept called bioregionalism involved focusing on a particular piece of ground, cherishing it, caring for it, and anchoring in it. A shift away from the migratory short-term exploitations that characterized American economics in the past, his ideas were not really new but they provided another way of thinking about how to live in a nonexploitive, sustainable manner.

Ten years after the telling of *The Final Forest*, we had come to the Olympic Peninsula to see the ancient evergreens, the western red cedars (*Thuja plicata*), the Douglas fir (*Pseudotsuga menziesii*), the Sitka spruce (*Picea sitchensis*), and the western hemlocks (*Tsuga heterophylla*) before they were gone. We would try to see some of the champion trees of the park identified by the American Foresty Association (Record Trees in Olympic National Park, n.d.). The first tree we visited lived at the end of Big Cedar Road several miles north of Kalaloch Lodge. It stood over fifteen stories high towering above the other tall evergreens. In the rain, its branches dripped like fresh paint and the huge red roots glistened as if polished. If we had made a human chain around the base, it would have taken ten of us. We walked around the tree several times staring up at its massive cathedral top and marveling at the weathered ridges and grooves in its enormous trunk.

The second tree, another western red cedar, was miles off Highway 101 far back into the managed lands of the national forest. Turn after turn onto progressively narrower and narrower gravel roads, we finally found it. Hardly alive, it had little foliage remaining. Like a very old woman who had lost her teeth, her body fat, her eyesight, her hearing, until little was left but bone, the tree stood almost a ghost among acres of replanted trees. Some years ago, loggers had recognized the tree as old and did not cut it. Scientists dated the tree at around a thousand years old, a long time to be in one spot. It seemed so much alone surrounded by the young clones. Brenda Peterson (2001, 242) in "Killing Our Elders," from a collection of women writing on the green world entitled *The Sweet Breathing of Plants*, quotes a Nez Perce Indian woman. She says, "If you cut those ancient trees, you lose all your ancestors, everyone who came before you. Such loneliness is unbearable." That old tree certainly evoked the essence of loneliness.

Kalaloch Lodge was built on a cliff overlooking the Pacific Ocean. Below it, a sand beach appeared and disappeared with the tides and was littered with boulders and enormous white weathered logs. A warning sign referred to them as beach logs and cautioned beach walkers of their danger in the surf. Near the dry bone-colored logs, seagulls rose like leaf litter and settled back down on a sand spit near the mouth of a tidal creek. The reflection of hemlocks along the creek banks turned the waters black.

Kalaloch Lodge was near the Hoh Rainforest, the Queets Rainforest, and the Quinault Valley Rainforest. Although they have different names, they are part of the larger Olympic rainforest that lies along the westernmost edge of the Olympic peninsula. The only rainforests in the continental United States, they border rivers that originate near Mount Olympus. The rivers flow westward, empty into the Pacific Ocean, and make valley funnels whose topography attracts rain. What makes a rainforest is, of course, rain, and at an annual rainfall of 160 inches in the river valleys, this means that it might rain nearly half an inch a day. Actually, summers are drier with rainfall about a tenth of that in winter, but every day we were there, it rained. The constant dripping of water through the trees was the voice of this temperate rainforest.

In the Hoh Rainforest was a third ancient tree, a gigantic Sitka spruce. Called the Rainforest Monarch, it stood 270 feet high, 13.5 feet in diameter, and was 550 years old. We patted its butter-churn trunk, walked around it, and marveled at the silvery underside of the sharp needles. Three trails—the Hall of Mosses Trail, the Spruce Trail, and the Hoh River Trail—made the rainforest accessible. The downside of that accessibility was that it was too crowded. With nearly a quarter-million tourists every year, we planned to avoid the crowds by getting an early start. By midmorning the trail was packed with kids and families. The visitors weren't litterbugs or especially noisy or any of the other things tourists can be to make a place feel congested, it was just the constant close encounters that spoiled it. Continually moving off the trail to let folks by or moving out of someone's way is not the way to walk the rainforest.

With our trusty plant guides in hand (Hanify and Blencowe 1977; O'Connor 1962; Hutten et al. n.d.), we found the Hall of Mosses Trail aptly named. The trail crossed a stream full of coho salmon fry wiggling in the cold clear water. Up a steep slope, it opened into a hardware store of mosses. Mosses covered the ground, mosses engulfed fallen branches and rocks, and mosses hung from the trees. Practically every space was filled with mosses so beautifully described by Kimmerer (2003). Stair-step moss, Oregon beaked moss, and common green Sphagnum greened the forest floor. As I flipped through my guide book, the list of ground mosses was extensive: clear moss, flapper moss, pipe-cleaner moss, bent leaf moss, badge moss, electrified cat's tail moss, lanky moss, common haircap moss, juniper haircap moss, branched moss, contorted hairy cap moss, Menzie's tree moss, broom moss, and crane's bill moss. Could there be so many mosses that hugged the ground?

Among the ground mosses, liverworts elbowed their way onto the dance floor. Species like ring pellia, conehead, and lungwort grew together in green profusion. And among the mosses and liverworts, ferns squirted up like emerald fountains. Sword, deer, lady, maidenhair, and bracken ferns were common. In the few places where there was no moss, a shamrock called Oregon oxalis and bunchberry dogwood made their stand. The only nongreen was the occasional lichen such as reindeer, frog pelt, freckle pelt, and matchstick lichen. (The list of scientific names of plants would bore even the most dedicated reader to tears, so I have spared the reader this list. Besides, the common names are so much more fun.)

In the dim understory, shrubs were abundant. Huckleberry, salal, salmonberry with its thimble-size yellow berries, clusters of Devil's clubs with its wicked thorny trunks crouched in the darker corners. Vine maple with its frilly leaves gave the forest a lacy look. On stumps and fallen logs another battalion of mosses battled for territory. The guidebook listed curley heron's bill moss, wavy leafed cotton moss, lover's moss, broken leaf moss, small flat moss, fan moss, blue pouchwort, jagged notchwort, Pacific fuzzwort, and my favorite, fairy barf.

Not by any means an expert on bryophytes, I was not really sure which ones were really there but it certainly seemed as if everywhere I looked there was a different moss or lichen. On a blowdown log the size of a shed and almost as long as a street block, these mosses were a campground of squatters. Called nurse logs, these logs also provided nutrients for young trees and many seedlings sprouted from them. My guidebook was definitely beginning to take on a well-worn look as I turned the pages looking for pictures to match the thousand-plus mosses of this rainforest.

Almost every tree along the Hall of Mosses Trail was enormous, and another group of mosses (the tree mosses) tangled in their canopy. Some hung like green draperies; others wrapped the trees like sweaters. Big leaf maple trees with leaves the size of dinner plates were covered in a spike moss called Oregon selaginella. One of the most unique mosses of the region, it draped around the branches and hung down like dingy curtains. Licorice ferns protruded from the trees trunks like green fuzzy feathers. The giant hardwoods were covered with a different repertoire of mosses, and the evergreens, Douglas firs, and hemlocks supported yet another collection of mosses.

As we walked along the trail, I looked up into the evergreen canopy and thought how astonishing that we ground walkers had missed this world for so long. This perpetual green umbrella of an ecosystem high above the forest floor has only been explored in the last twenty years. Although canopy walks have been built in forests all over the world, canopy biology is still an infant discipline. In the Northwest, a group of scientists (Canopy Database Project, n.d.) has been actively studying the ecology of the evergreen canopy. One of the best-known tree climbers, Nalini Nadkarni, and her colleagues (Finkel 1998) have described a distinct ecosystem with arboreal earthworms (could they be skyworms?), species of beetles, ants, wasps, spiders, and mites specific to the canopy. They have also discovered roots of three of the seven major trees in the Olympic rainforest growing in the canopy beneath epiphytes (sky roots)! Maybe such discoveries will change our whole concepts of earth and sky. Certainly, my notion of ground as the best place plants can grow has changed.

These scientists (Lyons, Nadkarni, and North 2000) have reported the abundance, the spatial distribution, and the distribution of the nonvascular epiphytes in these old-growth forests. On hemlocks alone, mosses were most abundant in the lower canopy; certain lichens called alectoroids were dominant in the upper canopy; and another type of lichen called cyanolichens was most abundant in the lower to midcanopy. That epiphytes could have such distinct patterns of associations on particular trees evokes a profound sense of spatial preference in life. Not only do these plants prefer a particular species of tree, they prefer a particular place on that tree. The sheer order in the botanical world never ceases to astound me.

The Spruce Trail, also true to its name, was a little more open than the Hall of Mosses Trail, and had stands of spruce, red alder, and cottonwood. Large alders look a lot like birch trees with their white bark, but the white color is really a lichen covering a naturally brown bark. Nitrogen-fixing bacteria live in the roots of the tree and allow the alder to grow in poor soil. Because of this, they are often the first colonizers or pioneer trees where forests have been cut.

The Hoh River Trail was a longer trail and accessed another that eventually led to Mount Olympus. Trekking through the ever-widening puddles, we heard the high-pitched whine of a Roosevelt elk and smelled an unmistakable sour odor, but the understory was too dense to see her. As we searched the green, I thought of Elizabeth Bishop's poem "The Moose" (1983). How the sudden appearance of a wild creature can alter one's awareness, can shift it from the ordinary to the sublime. Not that the rainforest was ordinary, but the appearance of a large wild creature anywhere can move one to another state of awareness. Even though we could not see her, we knew that somewhere among those dripping leaves, a creature of the primeval forest stood, and she was probably aware of us. The only other creatures we encountered on the trail were several groups of hikers and a few dark-eyed juncos. A pack of ten rambunctious young men passed us, moving along like an army. The juncos chattered and pecked at things along the path, and I thought, how remarkable the variety of creatures that found this trail the place they wanted to be.

The Strait of Juan de Fuca with Vancouver Island a misty hump across the channel, was another watery world. Tankers and cargo ships floated along the straits like wisps of clouds. Bald eagles flew along a beach littered with seaweed (brown, red, and green algae) and sea grasses. (I like to think of them as the trees of the sea.) Fronds of the giant kelp (*Macrocystis integrifolia*) draped like green-brown streamers over rocks and piles of flotsam. Could this be the same kelp I had seen in Patagonia? Other kelp such as feather boas, ribbed, winged, and bull kelp added to the litter. At the end of a long yellow-green stem, the reproductive structure of one species ballooned like a light bulb. Sea braids, mermaid's cups, and sea fern (red algae) lay entangled in heaps among the rocks together with tangle weed, sponge weed, and tube weed (green algae). One species with air bladders the size of jalapeno peppers begged to be popped. So we tap-danced along, squashing the air pockets, sliding back to a time when we were little kids, a time when all the magic of the world lay in sand, and the only reality was the joy and innocence of a beach.

On the rocks, limpets clung to the sides like little suction cups. Tiny blue Chinamen hats, they grazed the algae fields. Periwinkle snails covered the rocks like warts and the razor-sharp edges of barnacles filled in the vacant spaces. So many things seemed to be hanging on for dear life around the water's edge. The beach was deserted; we were the only ones for miles. What pleasure to walk along a shore without hordes of people, without hotels or restaurants or the awful amusements (strange word to describe these things) that sprout up when too many people gather at the water's edge.

Leaving the Olympic peninsula, we drove three hundred miles east, moving through seven distinct environments in a single day. From the ocean through the rainforests to downtown Seattle was as startling a transition as any. To experience the swelling of a two-lane country highway into sixteen lanes of speeding traffic was more nerve-racking than interesting. The freeways that connected the mega-city's suburbs, like freeways all over the country, were little more than murals of a homogenized corporate landscape entwined with off and on ramps. Away from the urban corridor, the drive through the rugged peaks of the Cascades with their snowy peaks and glaciers was a more enjoyable transition.

The road made wide curves around pine-covered mountains, but almost be-fore we realized it, we were beyond the mountains and the land was desert. Then almost before we recognized desert, the arid land became an orderly landscape of fruit orchards. Around Wenatchee, the broad Columbia River wound its way among acres of apple orchards. Arches of white spray drenched the trees as Columbia River water was pumped onto the orchards. I thought of the tiny stick-ers on apples, "Washington Delicious," and remembered how sweet those apples were, especially in fall and winter. From Florida to Maine, from Wisconsin to Ari-zona, Washington apples fill the bins of every grocery store in the country. Those apple trees seemed to link the country at times. Water into the sweet pulp of ap-ples, it was as if the Columbia River and its tributaries reached all over the nation by way of the trees and by way of the apples.

Apples seem to have a special place in our lives. One of the best writings on the apple is Michael Pollan's *The Botany of Desire: A Plant's-Eye View of the World* (2001). He almost overwhelms the reader with information on nearly everything pertaining to apples, from its Kazakhstan origins to the portrait of John Chapman (Johnny Appleseed) as businessman-eccentric to the use of apples primarily for liquor to the narrow genetic code of the sweet cultivars Americans now eat. Surely, phrases like "American as apple pie," "the Big Apple," and "An apple a day keeps the doctor away" must come from our close involvement with and passion for apples.

The final transition in landscape occurred when we climbed from the Colum-bia River gorge onto the high prairie lands. The car grunted and groaned up the steep slope and a black-billed magpie flew by, its long black tail streaming like a banner against the brown canyon walls. At the top of the plateau, vast fields of wheat spread out for hundreds of miles. Not a tree in sight, the road rolled on like a silver ribbon to Spokane through pale green wheat and barley fields. The hori-zon was an unbroken velvet line between grain field and sky.

We turned back to the "Bavarian village" of Leavenworth and spent a few days walking some of the trails. The town, a touristy little place, had a busy main street of German shops and eateries, but a block off the main street a quiet waterfront trail ran along the Wenatchee River. The mosquitoes were so bad we were unable to walk much of the dense trail, but we did find a relatively bug-free spot on the bridge to Blackbird Island and watched violet green swallows feeding on the in-sects. They zoomed over the waters, up the banks, and under the bridge, their emerald green and violet backs spangling in the evening sun.

As I watched the river moving on its liquid journey below the swallows, I thought of all those lovely rivers of the west that Kathleen Moore (1995) writes about in *Riverwalking: Reflections on Moving Water*. Her writing is more than descriptions of rivers. She contemplates our relationship to place. In a chapter "The Brazos River," she writes of how she and her husband learned to square dance in order to fit into their community and how difficult it was to do those country-western dances. She writes that their dance should have been "a medicine dance, a healing dance, a dance of longing for a life that is connected to a way to make a living, and a living that is rooted in the land, and a community so connected that life depends on it. (108)" She also writes of finding reluctant answers from the river, but always her sense of place seems so alive in the life-affirming waters of rivers.

The best trail, the Icicle Gorge trail, was a three-and-a-half-mile loop that paralleled the Icicle River, crossed at the Rock Island campground, and looped back along the other side. Through stands of Douglas fur and orange-bark Ponderosa pine, we walked, then on to the edge of an open meadow where Indian paintbrush colored the hillside red, down into a low-lying cedar swamp, and through dense hemlocks where red cross-bills and white-breasted nuthatches flittered in the branches. A brief stop to look at broomrape with its epiphytic stems sticking up like pink straw, we continued on. The trail dipped and rose and opened up onto vistas where the view of the Icicle River tumbling over mountain boulders was a white rush. The river shoved its way from the glacier to the Wenatchee River, then to the Columbia River, then to the apple orchards, then to every corner of the United States as Washington apples. Even in the remotest wilderness, on an isolated mountain trail, the most unlikely connections are possible, I thought. I wondered if it was the ability to recognize these connections and to understand that trees (and rivers) are often the connectors that give us a broader sense of place. If we lose them, if we cause them to go extinct, we will lose our most vital connections.

More Extinction: A Pygmy Owl in Texas

18

ONE OF THE FEW THINGS I LIKED ABOUT TEXAS was Molly Ivins until I attended the ninth annual Rio Grande Valley Birding Festival in Harlingen, Texas. A field trip to the King Ranch and seeing the Ferruginous Pygmy Owl added a few more items to my small lists of likes. Held annually for the last eight years, this festival is supposedly one of the finest in the country, with some of the best birders as speakers and guides plus dozens of field trips to many of the area's wildlife refuges, management areas, sanctuaries, and preserves of the lower Rio Grande Valley. With over a thousand participants attending, I thought it was too big. But after all, it was in Texas.

At 5:00 a.m., we climbed aboard one of the buses and drove off into the dark. By the time we arrived at the King Ranch property, the sun was up and the morning light had painted the mesquites and shrubs a soft peach. A watering hole with ponds and metal water tanks sparkled with morning dew. The tall grasses looked like glass. The fence wires gleamed with bangles of water beads and a spider web the size of a soccer goal glimmered in the breeze. Perched on the edge of a water tank, a vermillion flycatcher watched us for a few moments and flittered off in search of breakfast insects.

The bus moved along the dirt road through several bump-gates, and the mesquite-shrub habitat give way to grasslands. Near these transition zones, wildlife was bountiful. White-tail hawks flew overhead and white-tailed deer peeked out at us from the tall grasses. Nilgai antelope (an exotic species imported from India by the ranch for hunting purposes) loped off as we approached, and a flock of wild turkeys sauntered across the road. The toms displayed their gorgeous tails, opening them like fans and moving around to strike provocative poses. On a fence further down the road, a rare Cassin's kingbird sat among half a dozen western kingbirds and scissortail flycatchers.

The oak lands were our main destination. These live oaks, like oaks on barrier islands, were stunted and gnarly. What salt spray does to barrier island oaks, aridity does to these oaks. Covered in weathered green mosses, the grove looked like an alien world with spikes and drapes on every branch. Ball moss (*Tillandsia recurvata*) grew like cockleburs from the surface of the bark; air plants (*T. pruinosa*) looking like Medusa heads grew from the crotches; and Spanish moss (*T. usneoides*) hung down like mop heads.

We spent nearly an hour in the grove looking for the pygmy owl but to no avail. While we stood about scanning the trees, I recalled what I had read about the King Ranch (Aston and Sneed 2004). Currently owning nearly a million acres worldwide, the ranch began in the mid 1800s as a land grant to Richard King and Gideon Lewis. King and Lewis never paid money for the land but acquired it through some legal maneuvering and paying off taxes. (The details were a bit fuzzy, as you might imagine.) While most people recognize the names of Carnegie, Morgan, and Rockefeller, few recognize this cattle baron's name or his descendants (Kleberg) perhaps because they left no university, no foundations, no libraries or visible legacies for the public good. A Confederate supporter, making money by supplying the military with cattle for the troops, King was pardoned after the Civil War by the president. His grandson, a congressman for many terms, made sure the family's business interests were looked after. In other words, big business and political connections seemed to be the template on which the ranch prospered. A chapter by Alex Shoumatoff (1978), "The King Ranch," in *The Rivers Amazon* describes how the ranch via the FUNAI (the National Indian Foundation) in the 1970s dispossessed the indigenous peoples, the Urubu Indians, of an enormous land area in the Brazilian Amazon. They cut, burned, and cleared the rainforest, an area the size of a small state, to create pastureland for cattle. The ranch, now a big corporate business, generates huge profits from oil (in the past fifty years, oil and gas royalties from Exxon alone amounted to over a billion dollars), cattle, timber, and crops (grain sorghum, cotton, and sugar). The ranch has just now begun a venture into ecotourism.

With no luck spotting the owl, we left and tried another site. From the oaks along the road, a keen-eared birder thought he heard the owl call. We stopped, scanned the trees, and in a few minutes, someone spotted the owl. Up went the scopes and everyone struggled to find it in their binoculars. It sat, "a softball sized bundle of brown and white feathers," a description that comes from David Wilcove (2002). Wilcove writes that the populations of pygmy owls went from "common in the mid-1900s" to "no reliable spot to find the species in the United States" in the 1970s and 1980s. So the Arizona owl was added to the endangered list. Like with the spotted owl of the Pacific Northwest, developers protested that the owl would have a devastating effect on the economy, and conflicts among developers and the environmentalists flared. An attempt called the Sonora Desert Conservation Plan was created to "bring order to the chaotic pattern of growth in southeastern Arizona," Wilcove writes. But frankly, I wondered if any plan would really stop developers and habitat destruction. I wondered if the King Ranch would sell tickets to the last pygmy owl edging towards extinction.

As we left the owl and rode back to town, I also wondered if this bird would experience the same fate as the Ivory-billed woodpecker or the northern spotted owl. Few of us seem morally able or willing to make the connection that those who create the corporations which exploit the world's materials are the ones who are decimating Earth's habitats and destroying the wild creatures. We who create the freeways lined with corporate chain stores and drive huge SUVs and refuse to invest in renewable and less damaging technologies; we who vote for politicians who rescind the Clean Air Act, weaken the environmental laws, and refuse to make policies based on sustainability; we are the ones who are destroying the Earth's wild creatures.

The sight of this small beautiful bird hanging onto a tree on the King Ranch in the big state of Texas, and that some of those watching the bird were affluent from corporate profits, did not escape my sense of paradox. But with all the paradoxes we live in, I hoped that collectively we might someday soon gather the courage to say, "We must change our lives." As Linda Hogan (1995, 42) writes in *Dwellings: A Spiritual History of the Living World*, "we must see life and other lives not as containers for our own use but . . . in a greater, holier sense."

BIOREGIONALISM: THE ETHICS OF "IT ALL BEGINS AND ENDS AT HOME"

Live Oak (Quercus virginiana) *with Epiphytes. Artwork by Eric Hinote.*

Home as Region: A Southern Fringe, The Gulf Coast

19

OR NEARLY TWO THOUSAND MILES, the southern coast of the United States makes a great arch stretching up from Brownsville, Texas, through Louisiana, through small bits of the Mississippi and Alabama coast, reaching south down to the tip of Florida. Dozens of rivers flow through the coastal region into the Gulf of Mexico. The biggest, the Mississippi River, empties its load about in the middle of the arch, and creates the largest delta in the country. All along the Gulf Coast, long thin barrier islands lie just off the mainland. They are unique habitats and protect against storms and hurricanes that come up from the Caribbean. They go by names like Padre, Matagorda, High, Cheniers, Grande, Chandeliers, Cat, Ship, Horn, Petit Bois, Dauphin, Santa Rosa, Crooked, St. Vincent, St. George, Dog, and Sanibel. If we were to draw the Gulf Coast as a three-colored rainbow, the innermost blue band might be the barrier islands. The mainland cut with tidal creeks, river mouths, and bays would be the green-yellow band. The outer red band would be the uplands.

Florida: A Barrier Island

Part of the Gulf Islands National Seashore that runs along the Mississippi and Florida coasts in eleven separate units (Bowden 1994), Ft. Pickens is on the westernmost end of Santa Rosa Island. I have walked the park for thirty years and consider it one of my most cherished places. In the 1970s, it was quiet and isolated. It might even have been considered a wild place in those days. It is no longer. Thirty years have passed and the park is bustling with visitors. One recent Sunday, so many cars jammed the single road leading into the park, the bumper-to-bumper effect was like an urban rush hour. I had read about the national parks of the country becoming congested with crowds, traffic, car fumes, and snowmobiles in winter, but thought that was in Yellowstone or the Grand Canyon, places that tourists frequented. Not until it happened in my own backyard did I think of overcrowding in parks as a reality.

Summertime is worse with the beach babes, the orange, purple, and chartreuse rent-a-beach-buggies puttering up and down the island, and the newest attraction, the helicopter rides, but winter is getting to be congested as well. To get to the Ft. Pickens park means passing through strip malls and shops, go-cart tracks and water slides, and rows and rows of hotels, condos, and seaside homes. Finally, the buildings end and the sea oat–covered dunes stretch out undisturbed for seven miles to Ft. Pickens. Developers have built right up to the parkland, making the contrast between development and natural shore very distinct. Whenever I cross into parkland I always breath a sigh of relief.

Even on early weekday mornings, the joggers and bikers can disturb a quiet walk. As annoying as it is, I have to remind myself when I see groups of campers wandering from their RVs along the trails of Battery Worth that they have as much right there as I do. This is public land. Just because I may have walked it for years, may know it better, and love it more passionately, it belongs to them as well. Our public lands belong to all of us. What we do with them may define us as a nation of shortsighted exploiters or a nation of compassionate citizens concerned with healthy environments.

I remember a beaching of sea crabs one summer twenty years ago. The size of a man's hand, soft fawn-colored with darker mottled markings, they washed ashore by the thousands. Never before had I seen so many crabs. We scooped them up in a dip net, easy as picking up Easter eggs, boiled them in lemon and crab boil, and ate them with great delight. They tasted wonderful. I would never think of doing such a thing now, but in those days when life seemed so abundant, like manna from the sea, those crabs were a jubilee feast.

I remember fifteen years ago when I first began to notice the monarch butterflies. Thousands of orange-and-black gliders drift in and move along the shoreline during the month of October on their way to Mexico, where they winter in the Sierra Madres near the small town of Angangueo. They feed on milkweed (*Asclepias humistrata*), golden aster (*Chrysopsis godfreyi*), goldenrods (*Solidago* spp.), October flowers (*Polygonella polygema*), and the multicolored lantana (*Lantana camara*). They roost at night in the pine trees, and one fall I discovered the location of several roosting trees. Since the 1990s, I have noticed fewer and fewer monarchs every year. Their decline is due to habitat destruction, such as the burning and cutting of the winter forest habitats in Mexico, the elimination of the milkweed host plant from cornfields in the Plains states and the ever-expanding urban sprawl all over the United States. The newest threat, a genetically engineered Bt corn cultivar that produces a pesticide, actually a toxin, that destroys their intestinal tract, adds another hurdle on their migration route. Having to move through such an obstacle course, it is a wonder any monarchs survive. Every fall I watch for them with the anticipation of a holiday.

One spring, I spied dozens of great blue herons perched in the top of a single tall pine. I almost expected the pine to bend over, but it didn't, of course, because great blue herons, though they look enormous, are mostly fluff, weighing less than seven pounds. They build stick nests the size of trampolines in the tops of the pines. Every spring, least terns, plovers, and black skimmers nest on the sugar white beaches and up in the dunes among the sea oats (*Uniola paniculata*). I am always dazzled by the flutter of these birds when they nest near the road. Like paper airplanes we launched as kids, they dart over the road and in and out of the dunes. Wisely, the biologists have begun roping off the nesting areas to protect them. I once saw a sea turtle lumbering back to the waves after making its nest and laying eggs in the sand. In the early morning light one spring, millions of migrating dragonflies winged their way from who knows where to who knows where. I have watched brown pelicans flying along the shoreline in formations of astounding synchronization. Looking like ancient pterodactyls, when they feed they fold back their wings and plunge headlong into the water like darts. Their story is one of the great comeback stories, for in the 1970s their populations had declined to only a hundred birds because of pesticides that caused egg thinning and breakage during incubation. Thanks to a ban on DDT and PCBs plus the Brown Pelican Recovery Plan, they now inhabit the Florida Gulf Coast in healthy numbers.

In the last few years, I have begun to watch the passerines. Neotropical birds on their way north in spring and south in fall use the woods and thickets of Ft. Pickens as a stopover. A new field in biology called stopover ecology reminds us that to move is the nature of animals. From nomadic humans to ruby-throated hummingbirds, from humpback whales to green darner dragonflies, animals migrate. Some may travel only a few miles, but move they do. The fleeting sight of the many warblers, orioles, indigo buntings, an occasional painted bunting, red starts, scarlet tanagers, and a rare scissor-tail flycatcher reminds me (as so well described in Scott Weidensaul's [1999] *Living on the Wind: Across the Hemisphere with Migratory Birds*) that much of a bird's life is spent on the wing. That some of these tiny birds travel from South America to North America (and some even from the Arctic to the Antarctic) twice a year is a source of wonder that astounds me every time I see them.

One spring I remember walking the trail from Battery Langdon, where the tall pines and the live oaks begin, to the fort at the westernmost end of the island. The trail (now part of the Florida National Scenic Trail system) crosses several miles of pine-oak scrub, a freshwater marsh, and some brackish water creeks. With the conradina (*Conradina canescens*) in bloom, its pale lavender ruffles among the elegant

Florida rosemary bushes (*Ceratiola ericoides*), the island had an almost English garden quality. Along the ground, false reindeer lichen coated the white sand in gray-green puffballs. Thickets of yaupon and wax myrtle entwined with fox grape and saw greenbrier grew along the trail, and at the edges of the tea-colored ponds and creeks, an uncountable variety of grasses and aquatic plants created a liquid landscape. Duckweed (*Lemna minor*) and mosquito fern (*Azolla caroliniana*) adorned the surface of the ponds in a pale green lace. The dark stalks of needle rushes (*Juncus* sp.) and the tall, tasseled grass (*Phragmites australis*) supported the swaying bodies of redwing blackbirds. Slash pines, a few sand pines, and shrub-size live oaks (short because of the stress of airborne salt spray) grew along the trail. Their branches and the thickets were full of warblers—prothonotary, yellow, magnolia, and hooded warblers. A yellow-billed cuckoo landed in the oak branches, so close I could almost touch him, his six-inch black-and-white tail hanging down like an image from an Escher drawing. All the wonders of the island are part of the landscape I carry with me as memory.

Alabama: The Great Bay

Mobile Bay, Alabama, is another place to see fall and spring migrants. A place where freshwater from rivers and seawater from tides mingle in a slow merger and flow out to sea, the Mobile Bay basin contains many habitats: rich coastal plains, freshwater cypress swamps, bottomland hardwoods, tidal marshes, and a barrier island with sandy beaches. At the mouth of Mobile Bay, the barrier island, Dauphin Island, and the Ft. Morgan peninsula protrude into the bay, almost landlocking the vast shallow waterway. One of the largest estuaries along the Gulf Coast (it's called a drowned river valley estuary), Mobile Bay stretches over thirty miles from the gulf waters to its northernmost shore. Its watershed, the sixth largest in the country, has a delta of over 185,000 acres, and some of the great southern rivers (the Mobile, Alabama, Tensaw, and Tombigbee) empty into it.

Many weekends I have spent on the shell mound at Dauphin Island searching the oaks for painted buntings, orchard and Baltimore orioles, and the twenty-five-plus species of warblers that pass through. Like other wooded areas right on the coastline, these are the first bits of vegetation transgulf birds encounter when they arrive from South America or the Yucatan. Although I have never seen a fallout (and, in truth, I'm glad, because it can mean birds fall from the sky and die of exhaustion by the thousands), sometimes I have seen some very worn-out-looking birds. I try to imagine what it might be like swimming a thousand miles against a current, which is what these birds do (many no bigger than a chicken egg) twice a year. If there is a storm or a strong oppositional wind, many of them do not make it.

Migrants can be seen almost anywhere on Dauphin Island. One April afternoon, scarlet tanagers spotted the lawn of a house right along the main boulevard. I nearly ran my car off the road into a ditch rubber-necking those birds. Across the bay, Ft. Morgan, another nineteenth-century fort-turned-park, is also great for watching migrants. Bird-banding stations have been set up for some years, and every spring and fall the data generated give ornithologists and conservation groups an idea of population trends.

On the eastern shore of Mobile Bay, small bays, creeks, and inlets make the bayshore a desirable place to live. Towns like Magnolia Springs, Fairhope, Montrose, Daphne, and Spanish Fort have suffered from intense development, but there are still some places that remain natural. Where the Tensaw River flows into the bay, an old settlement and early battlefield site has been transformed into historic Blakeley State Park. Yellow fever epidemics and rampant land speculation doomed the city of four thousand in 1821 to a ghost town. Today, the park is a preserve of bottomland and upland forests with miles of hiking trails and a long boardwalk bordering the river that makes swamp walking a joy. Bald cypress and tupelo edge the river. Patches of spider lilies, pickerel weed, and arrow arum grow among the cypress knees.

One spring day, with a group of birders led by Lucy Duncan (she and her husband, Bob, are two of the best birders in the region), I paused beneath a stand of ancient live oak trees. Looking up into the thick canopy, trying to spot a great crested flycatcher, I was struck by the multitude of creatures in the arms of those hundred-year-old trees. On the upper branches, epiphytes lived like crowded city tenants. Resurrection ferns (*Polypodium polypodioides*), brown and withered, after a good rain would uncurl and become a green fur coat. Mixed in with the ferns, the green-fly orchid (*Epidendrum conopseum*), whose delicate creamy flowers bloom in summer, looked like aerial clumps of lily leaves. In Florida they bloom around July 4th and are called the Fourth of July fern. Wiry Spanish moss (*Tillandsia usneoides*) hung down like gray tinsel. Orange, pink, and beige lichens splattered the trunk and spilled over the larger branches like big paint spots. The lives of bark and root fungi—their secretive tubular lives as invisible as stars in the daytime sky—could only be imagined. Describing the life cycles of these creatures would fill volumes, perhaps even entire libraries. And these were just the plants and the fungi. The birds, the mammals, the insects, and the multitude of other organisms that make up the community on these trees were even more numerous. I once read an insect survey that reported over 150 different types of insects living in Spanish moss alone. Having looked at oak trees most of my life and adored them, I had never before really thought about how many creatures depended on them.

Another live oak called Inspiration Oak in nearby Magnolia Springs told a sadder tale. In 1990 the property owner wanted to cut down the five-hundred-year-old tree to build a filling station. With a trunk over 27 feet in circumference and a canopy 165 feet wide, the tree was massive. Local environmentalists tried to prevent its cutting. But in defiance and with the attitude that it was her land and she could damn well do with it what she wanted, the landowner hired someone to girdle the tree. He took a chain saw, cut a deep circle around the trunk, and the tree died. Arborists tried for three years to save it, but it eventually died. It stands today surrounded by a chain linked fence, a charcoal skeleton. The branches are leafless and the color of ashes, the entire canopy is a void, and nothing fills the space but grayness. Even the opportunistic fungi don't seem to want to reside there. I read (Sternberg and Wilson 1995, 101) that one of the arborists planned to inject the tree with preservatives so that may account for its lifelessness. The structure remains "as a reminder that centuries of life can be suddenly ended in a thoughtless act of anger."

Yet another live oak in Daphne, called the Jackson Oak, is alive and well and protected as a champion tree. Part of a nationwide project, champion trees (Champion Trees, n.d.) are selected in every state on the basis of age or size and preserved as historical monuments. This beautiful old oak, honored with a surrounding walkway and lots of space, stands with its arms open wide, holding all the creatures that make their homes in live oaks. Every time I see it, it fills me with such joy at its presence. At the same time, it disturbs me to realize that we have come to the stage that we must depend on government programs to save the old trees of the South. We can no longer depend on the kindness of strangers or on landowners.

The U.S. Fish and Wildlife Service has published a brochure describing the Alabama Coastal Birding Trail (*Alabama Coastal Birding Trail*, n.d.) with its loops around Mobile Bay. Listed are many places to walk, observe birds and other wildlife, and enjoy the natural beauty of this great estuary. Birding trails and IBAs (Important Bird Areas) are also being created by state Fish and Wildlife organizations throughout the country. On the Gulf Coast, Texas, Georgia, and Florida have birding trails much like Alabama's. Such efforts may help save some of the special places from developers. If the public knows about these places and grows to love them, maybe it will be harder to destroy them—or at least that is the idea. Awareness equals stronger support for preservation efforts, Julie Brashears thinks. Julie, coordinator of the Florida Birding Trail for the Florida Fish and Wildlife Conservation Commission, says, "My vision is for the birds to save the world." And who knows, they might.

A Mississippi Pine Savanna

The Sandhill Crane Refuge in Gautier, Mississippi, is located several miles inland near the Pascagoula River. Once the most common biome along the Gulf Coast, the pineland savanna stretched unbroken from the Pearl River to Mobile. Cut by

Interstate 10, it has now been nearly decimated by development. Pinelands can be both thick pine forests and the more open pine savannas or grasslands; they can be dry or boggy with standing water. One January weekend, a group of us gathered at the pine savanna refuge to search for the Henslow's sparrow. Slushing around a field full of winter dried pitcher plants, we got to see this elusive bird.

Bogs like this are extremely productive. As many as sixty-two different plant species have been reported to occur in one square meter. Below the brown grasses, sundews, dewthreads, butterworts, and foxtail clubmoss crouched close to the ground. Orchids, such as the spreading pogonia or rosebud orchid (*Cleistes divaricata*), the rose pogonia orchid (*Pogonia ophioglossoides*), the yellow-fringed (also called orange-fringed) orchid, the pale grasspink orchid, and the tuberous grasspink orchid, all call this wetland home. Redroot, bog buttons, hatpins, and swamp coreopsis transform the fields into a painted meadow. One of the biologists in our group said, "Sometimes, I dream I run naked through this bog." Clearly, this place evokes passion.

In our knee-high rubber boots we made entrapment circles in the wet field and succeeded in flushing a few birds. The bird's attempts to hide in the thick clusters of grasses, gallberry, and wax myrtle were no match for the determination of our obsessive group of birders. Much of the morning we tramped through the fields and managed to get a few dark views of the bird, but it was not until a graduate student captured one in a mist net and held the bird between his fingers for us to see that I realized how beautiful the tiny bird was. In her rusty-brown olive coat, dark streaks, and subtle yellow splotches on the side of her throat, held up against the golden grassy background, the bird was a small miracle. To watch the feisty, warbler-sized bird trying to escape by pecking the hand of the scientist was to witness the indomitable spirit of survival.

The field where the student had set up his capture net was drier than the first field and there was no standing water. Covered mostly in winter-dormant wiregrass (*Aristida stricta*) and toothache grass (*Ctenium aromaticum*, named because it produces a substance that numbs a toothache when the base of the plant is chewed), the field was like a meadow of spun gold. Among the golden grasses, the dried-up catch tubes of the white-top pitcher plants (*Sarracenia leucophylla*) looked like brown pipes protruding from the ground. They reminded me of bagpipes, and I imagined eerie bog music coming from them at night. The Henslow's sparrow is right at home in these bagpipe bogs. Reported to winter in wet prairies, they especially like pine savannas with wiregrass groundcover, pitcher plant bogs, marsh borders, and broomsedge meadows. A few months after our trip, I ran across an article in the American Birding Association journal, *Birding* (Reinking 2002), that gave details about the distribution, breeding habitat, and general biology of these little-known grassland birds. But no article could compare to the experience of slopping through a pine savanna, catching a glimpse of the sparrow in the bog grasses, seeing it at eye level in the hands of a skillful bander, and then watching it fly away when released.

Alabama, Florida, Georgia, and Mississippi's Pine Forests

The southern uplands that stretch east of the Mississippi River through the Florida Panhandle, north into Alabama and Georgia (and even farther north) go by various names—red hill country, sandhill country, wiregrass country, pine barrens, to list a few—but they are all basically pinelands. The topsoil is sandy, highly acidic, with nutrient-poor underlying clay, so it will support little else. The forests of the South have been cut so many times there are few old-growth pines left and the forest landscape has a scraggly look. One of the largest continuous public pine forests is Blackwater River State Forest in the Florida Panhandle with the adjacent Conecuh National Forest in Alabama to the north, Eglin Air Force Base to the south and a twelve-thousand-acre land connection (recently purchased by the state from International Paper Company). From the gulf shore through Florida into Alabama, it is nearly a hundred miles long.

While extensive, these public lands may not be enough to provide adequate habitat for certain species of endangered plants and animals of the pinelands. Private landowners often resent environmentalists and the laws that regulate their land. The landowner who cut Inspiration Oak in Baldwin County, Alabama, is an example. Or they are like St. Joe Company (the largest landowner in the Panhandle) who is selling off its lands to developers (Ziewitz and Wiaz 2004). The Endangered Species Act prohibits landowners from engaging in any activity on their property that might harm endangered animals, and as a result some landowners, fearing such regulations, have cut down old trees to prevent the presence of endangered species. A new approach called "Safe Harbor" (Safe Harbor Resources, n.d.) was created. Supposedly, by guaranteeing the landowner's right to change his or her mind without the burden of incurring regulatory restrictions, many landowners could temporarily commit their lands to protective management practices. The idea was that it would buy time for endangered species. But there are serious concerns that this policy weakens the Endangered Species Act and allows corporate interests and developers to avoid the law (Southern Pines Ecosystem Project, n.d.).

The natural pine forests actually include several variations: the drier sand pine scrublands, the slash pine flatwoods, and the longleaf pine ecosystem. The longleaf pine ecosystem is probably the most endangered of the pine forests with as little as 3 percent of the original forests remaining. One of the finest writings on the longleaf pine forest is Janisse Ray's *Ecology of a Cracker Childhood* (1999). She writes with passion, deep concern, and sound biology about this ecosystem.

Many folks are working to restore the longleaf pine ecosystem. Don Schueler (1996) in *A Handmade Wilderness: How an Unlikely Pair Saved the Least Worst Land in Mississippi* tells how he and his partner, Willie Brown, transformed cutover land into a healthy longleaf pine forest. The story begins in the late 1960s when they purchased eighty acres of land for what was to be their own private Shangri-la. They built a house, made connections with neighbors, and had all the domesticated animals like chickens, guinea hens, cattle, and horses typical of a farm. But it was to be more than a farm, more than a weekend retreat. In an evolving ecological awareness, they removed slash pine, control burned, and tried to put things back to a more natural state. For twenty years, they worked to make "The Place" a healthy environment and to restore the longleaf pine forest. In the late 1980s after Willie Brown died of AIDS, Schueler began to envision the land as a preserve. He purchased additional land, expanding it to 240 acres, and the Nature Conservancy agreed to make "The Place" "The Willie Farrel Brown Nature Reserve." The tiny longleaf pine seedlings have grown into tall trees with healthy canopies. The midstory now has typical of longleaf pineland shrubs, and the understory has the herbaceous plants of a healthy longleaf pine forest. Gopher tortoises live in the uplands and the pitcher plant bogs are thriving. Their handmade wilderness (now over three hundred acres) is a marvel. That two fellows (and "city folks" at that) could recreate a wilderness by their own labor restores my faith in the compassion of people and makes the idea of ecosystem restoration more than just a wishful dream. If two guys could transform a virtual wasteland into a healthy longleaf pine habitat, the message is that habitat restoration can be done by anyone, not just government agencies with big budgets and large staffs. What a hopeful message.

One spring morning we treked off into the pine forest of Blackwater River State Forest in search of red-cockaded woodpeckers. The charred trunks of the huge loblolly pines and longleaf pines were in sharp contrast to the open understory of bracken ferns and sand post oak. The winter burn was still evident on the trees as black bark, but it was almost erased by the spring green understory. As we hiked along the red clay road, we listened for the distinctive tapping of the bird. The bird nests only in pines infected with red heart disease. This fungal infection causes the tree to rot and soften, allowing the bird to more easily drill into the wood. After the lumber industry culled most of the decaying trees, the population of the woodpeckers dropped dramatically, and by the 1970s, the bird was listed as endangered. By allowing rotting diseased trees to remain, population declines have slowed, but woodpecker populations have never recovered and the birds are still considered endangered.

Once as many as forty million birds lived in the pine forests of the Southeast. Estimates by the FWS put the numbers now around twelve thousand, or about 3 percent of the original populations. Action by the timber interests in Florida have recently tried to remove the red-cockaded woodpecker from the endangered list. The red-cockaded recovery programs in Eglin Air Force Base, Blackwater River State Forest, and Cunecuh National Forest have reported limited success with their programs. Increases of 250 active clusters of birds in the mid-1990s to currently around 360 represent improvements, but these small gains are a far cry from a real recovery. Books such as Scott Weidensaul's *The Ghost with Trembling Wings: Science, Wishful Thinking, and the Search for Lost Species* (2002) and Christopher Cokinos's *Hope Is the Thing with Feathers* (2000)—to mention only two of the most recent ones—have presented the plight of vanishing species and the extinction of so many species, but such concerns do not seem to affect the attitudes of some in the timber industry.

We spotted two black-and-white checkered birds hanging on the side of a lighter-colored pine (an indication that the tree had red heart disease) looking like downy woodpeckers but with white cheek patches. Nearby, several Bachman's sparrows, another rare grassland bird species, flitted up and down in the understory, never staying long enough for a really good look. A few brown-headed nuthatches and pine warblers moved around in the pine branches. Seeing these pineland birds, we considered the day a great success.

Several hundred nature trails in the western Florida Panhandle and surrounding region have been compiled and described by Jack Jordan and James Burkhalter for the Longleaf Pine Chapter of the Florida Native Plant Society (Florida Native Plant Society, n.d.). One of the most beautiful trails is the Clear Creek Nature Trail. I learned of the trail one spring when James Burkhalter (the Panhandle's leading plant expert and director of the University of West Florida's herbarium) led a group of Florida Native Plant Society members on a plant walk. On the Naval Air Station of Whiting Field, it includes several habitats: a mixed pine-oak uplands, a transitional upland-lowland forest, and a tupelo swamp. The first part of the trail is slash pine, longleaf pine, and species of oaks (live, water, laurel, sand post, black jack, and turkey). Horsesugar, chinkapin, persimmon, yaupon, pawpaw, sassafras, sparkleberry, gallberry, and dahoon holly (to name a few) make up the lower shrub understory. A short section of cane brake (the native bamboo, *Arundinaria gigantea*), magnolias, a cluster of sourwood trees, and then a patch of red cedar and Atlantic white cedar lead to the boardwalk. Constructed above the wetlands, the wide boardwalk allows the hiker the luxury of strolling over the spongy swamp with ease.

I returned many mornings to marvel at this wetlands. One particular morning I remember vividly. Looking every bit the image of the dark southern swamp, the thick black tupelo trunks rose from the oily water. The oils on the surface of these waters are natural plant-microbial lipids. Refracting light, they made fluorescent streaks across the ebony surface. In the more open area, the bog vegetation steamed in the morning sun. Water lily pads were green saucers holding drops of sparkling water. A bullfrog hopped and created black ripples. Ripples from the touchdowns of waterbugs, mayflies, and dragonflies intersected and made more circles. The water's surface became a canvas of overlapping rings.

The ovate blades of golden club (*Orontium aquaticum*), with its small yellow flowers on giant asparagus-like stalks, emerged from the water alongside the dark spikes of *Juncus*. Small crepe-paper blooms of floating yellow bladderwort (*Utricularia biflora*) popped up from the water to form a duet with a tiny pink butterwort. Greasy carnivorous plants, butterworts are covered with glandular secretions that capture gnats and are called pings (from their genus name *Pinguicula*). I wanted to shout, "Praise be, could it be pink pings!" But what I had hoped was the rare Godfrey's butterwort (*P. ionantha*) turned out to be something else, probably the tuberous grasspink orchid (*Calopogon tuberosus*).

The leaves of white-top pitcher plants rose like veined funnels, and alongside their catch-tubes, bulbous maroon flowers that looked like wax candles drooped in the heat. Hatpins sprung up like pincushions. Branches of sweet bay covered with gardenia-sized flowers and the white bristly racemes of the blooming red titi draped across the walkway. A prothonotary warbler flashed yellow in the willows, and a green heron settled in the branches of a dead tree. Hunching its blue and dark maroon shoulders down into itself, it seemed to withdraw like a turtle into its shell.

I have come to understand as I walk these wetlands how time here is an essential element of place. In the wetlands, it is either day or night, morning or evening, spring or fall, winter or the dreadful oven of summer. I know the place, I know the time, and I know the harmony of their entanglement. All of this gives me a profound sense of comfort. When I think of the places we occupy where there is no sense of time—places like casinos, the computer, television, or corporate chains, environments where everything looks the same—I lose my sense of time and, thus, place. Time is suspended in these artificial places and the effect is disorienting and alienating. In *Swampwalker's Journal: A Wetlands Year*, David Carroll (2001) celebrates the element of time. He gives dates and times, and as I read his passages, I can be in the swamp or the marsh or the bog, totally immersed in it, experiencing it again, and know where I am. To me this is amazing grace.

Not long ago, I returned to the Clear Creek Nature Trail and was turned away. It was a spring morning and I wanted to see the blooming of the swamp flowers. The road to the trail was blocked with orange painted cement barriers and guards patrolled the area. All nonmilitary personnel were forbidden to enter. "National security," one big guard said with his hands on his hips in a posture of self-importance. We had lost access to one of the most beautiful nature trails in the area. I wondered how many more things would be lost in the name of security?

About nine miles south of the Clear Creek Nature Trail another place of botanical wonder is the old Bagdad Cemetery. A sandhill woods west of Blackwater Bay, it has not been manicured into a golf-course green. The fact that old uncut cemeteries make great places to hunt for rare plants and good birding spots should be a lesson. The lesson might be: "the less we impose our sense of order on a place, the more ecologically sound the place will be." We were in search of orchids, more specifically one orchid, the threatened small ladies' tresses (*Spiranthes tuberosa*). The smallest of southeastern U.S. orchids, it blooms in summer. About the size of rice grains, its flowers are arranged in a spiral pattern along the tip of a slender stem. It reaches a foot tall. We would never have found it if it weren't for James Burkhalter, who told us all about the orchid. After flowering, its tiny capsules spew seeds the size of dust grains and then it dies back. In December it forms a rosette of small leaves that hug the ground and then it withers away in March. From its tuberous root, the plant sends up a flower stem, blooms, and the cycle begins again. As we walked around the cemetery spotting the needle-thin stalks with the tiny white spiral, I hoped from my grave such rare and delicate orchids might some day bloom.

In *The Orchid Thief*, Susan Orlean (1998) writes of her adventure into the wacky world of orchids and those who collect them. Her eccentric characters whose obsessions with orchids lead to crimes and other acts of desperation are among the strangest to emerge from the soggy South. From wealthy plant collectors to art smugglers to a Seminole Indian chief to conventional nursery owners, characters drift in and out of her tale. While the story line involves John Laroche's attempts to steal ghost orchids from the Fakahatchee Swamp, woven into the fabric of her tale is the history of orchid collecting, orchid growing, and orchid exhibiting. That Susan Orlean manages to transform Laroche, an arrogant foul-mouthed con man who ends up selling pornography on the Internet into a sort of Huck Finn character, speaks to the wizardry of her writing. Her trek through the Big Cypress swamp with two giant ex-cons carrying machetes and then getting lost with Laroche in Fakahatchee Swamp hint at her own obsession with the ghost orchid. Well-crafted diversions such as the land scams of the 1950s and 1960s by Julius and Leonard Rosen of the Gulf American Corporation, the development of Disney World, the Indian casinos, and places like Gatorama present the bizarre world of south Florida in all its insanity. It is a zany read.

Orchids certainly abound in Florida and not just the showy cultivars described in *The Orchid Thief*. Many are so small and nondescript they might be mistaken for weeds. And many people care about the survival of these plants. The Florida Native Plant Society is one organization that provides a forum for these concerns. One morning on another Florida Native Plant Society–Long Leaf Pine Chapter field trip, James Burkhalter told us of the rare crestless plume orchid (*Pteroglossas-*

pis ecristata). As we slogged through a low flatwoods near Tarkiln Bayou looking for white-top pitcher plants (*Sarracenia leucophylla*) and purple pitcher plants (*Sarracenia purpurea*), he described the unthinking and accidental destruction of the only known colony of this orchid in Alabama. Just north of Loxley, in the roadside pinewood prairie that contained the inconspicuous orchid, is precisely where Ace Hardware wanted to construct its huge warehouse complex. When James visited the site during construction to see if the orchid and its habitat might be spared, a security guard made him leave under threat of summoning the police to evict him for trespassing. The prairie was bulldozed and graded, a warehouse was built, and the bulldozed acres were landscaped with imported plants. Ace Hardware destroyed the only known Alabama colony of this rare orchid. James said, "How sad, how absurd, how ridiculous! Couldn't they just have built the warehouse a half mile up the road?" But that didn't happen. The story, however, had a happy ending. A couple of local botanists visited the site a few years later, and after much searching found three individuals of *P. ecristata* in a pine forest remnant just north of the warehouse complex. Even more fortunately, James also discovered the orchid in Blakeley State Park. Since this is state land, its habitat will be protected forever and Alabama will remain a home for this imperiled native orchid.

One dreadfully hot August, James Burkhalter led us on yet another field trip to see the rare crane-fly orchid (*Tipularia discolor*). The largest colony in the county, it bloomed like a tiny weed beneath a beech tree. As we stood dripping with sweat in that mosquito-infested underbrush, trying to get a good look at the nondescript, green-brown flower, listening to James's tale of how he discovered the plant and his county record, I felt such joy that there were people (twenty-two, in fact) who could be awed by the wonder of such a modest plant.

Another old cemetery, St. Johns, in Pensacola is home to one of the largest known colonies in the world of the unusual and rare winter grape fern (*Botrychium lunarioides*). One windy February morning, we gathered at the cemetery to help James and the Native Plant Society survey this endangered fern. Given a handful of marking flags, we were instructed to place a flag next to each plant. "Don't step on the graves!" James shouted, as we moved from one plot to the next marking the inconspicuous plants. Known as moonwort, the leaf of the winter grape fern is a tiny ground hugger, and the stem rarely taller than four inches. More the shape of a small dandelion than a fern, its half-moon-shaped subleaflets look like maidenhair fern leaflets. The leaflets merge from the ground in fall like a weed and grow throughout the winter. In January through April, it sends up a fertile frond bearing clusters of grapelike structures. This sporangiophyte contains sporangia that contain spores (remember, ferns produce spores instead of seeds). As we marked each plant and moved from plot to plot, another group removed the flags and counted them. After several hours, I paused from the back-bending task and looked out over the cemetery. The gravestones were beautiful; the family plots, probably more colorful than they had ever been before. The red, blue, yellow, and pink flags snapped in the wind like prayer flags. The blue sky, the stately old live oaks, and the crisp sparkling pines provided a lovely canopy for the ferns. It was a glorious morning to be alive. In that moment of joy, I imagined the winter grape fern taking over the cemetery, then the city, the county, the state, the nation, the world. And as Sylvia Plath (1981) writes in the voice of mushrooms, I imagined the winter grape ferns singing, "Our kind multiplies / We shall by morning / inherit the earth / Our foot's in the door."

Louisiana: Marshes and Swamps

West of the Mississippi River, Cameron and Calcasieu Parishes in Louisiana are very different habitats from the piney woods of the coastal plain. The coastal lands in this region are also disappearing but from a different sort of development. At an alarming rate of twenty-five acres per day, the land is eroding because of the loss of alluvial deposits. Where the Gulf Coastal prairie meets the Mississippi River flood plain, the land is sinking and eroding because the levees that were built to prevent floods no longer allow the river to overflow and deposit sediments. Mike Tidwell (2003) in *Bayou Farewell: The Rich Life and Tragic Death of Louisiana's Cajun Coast* describes this in a very readable fashion but as Louisiana wetland researchers, we had long understood and been concerned about this since the early 1970s. The truth is that politicians and policymakers rarely listen to scientists. But then, maybe it's the language of science that is difficult to listen to. As a graduate student, I had worked in the Louisiana salt marshes and had taken field trips into the Atchafalaya Basin and into the marshes west of Bayou Lafouche. So a trip along the Creole Nature Trail National Scenic Byway in the spring of 2002 was a sentimental journey. I was surprised to learn how changed these wetlands were.

From Interstate 10, Highway 27 leaves the smoke and smog of the oil refineries and industrial complex of (so aptly named) Sulfur, Louisiana, and runs south through a small fishing village called Hackberry. On through Sabine NWR, past the visitor center, the road moves along an impoundment called the Marsh Trail. This trail provides one of the easiest ways to get right out into the marsh. The mile-and-a-half trail bordered by big cordgrass (*S. cynosuroides*) encircles meadows of other cordgrasses (*Spartina alterniflora* and *S. patens*), bulrush (*Scirpus* sp.), rushes (*Juncus* sp.), cattails (*Typha latifolia*) and roseau cane (*Phragmites* sp.). Shrubs like wax myrtle (*Myrica cerifera*), marsh elder (*Iva frutescens*), elderberry (*Sambucus canadensis*), and groundsel bush (*Baccharis halimifolia*), plus woody emergents like hackberry (*Celtis laevigata*), willow (*Salix* sp.), maple (*Acer* sp.), oaks (*Quercus* sp.), and cypress (*Taxodium ascendens*) create a low canopy with a dense understory and make the place a mosaic of open marsh and thicket.

The western loop of the trail was lined with mulberry trees (*Morus rubra*) and plump ripe mulberries hung from the low branches. We picked handfuls and popped them into our mouths like popcorn. What sweet delight. White and glossy ibises with their long downward-curved beaks, purple gallinules with their candy-corn beaks and blue head shields, snowy and great egrets, and a sora rail waded at the water's edge. In the oaks and cypress, orchard orioles, eastern kingbirds, and common yellow throats flitted in the branches. The trail branched off toward an observation tower, and we were about to take it when a black plastic garbage bag in the middle of a trail blinked and moved. We were inches from it before we recognized that the bag was an enormous alligator. Luckily, he was not hungry or annoyed, and we changed our minds about taking that trail. Following the main trail, we vowed to watch the path a little more cautiously.

Nutria and marsh rabbits grazed along the grassy sides of the trail, and I thought how well some animals can adapt to new environments. Nutria are not native to Louisiana. Kim Todd (2001) in *Tinkering with Eden: A Natural History of Exotics in America* described how 150 nutria escaped in the 1930s from the Jungle Gardens of the wealthy, eccentric Edward Avery McIlhenny (of Tabasco Sauce fame) during a hurricane. From the salt dome of Avery Island, these bristly rodents made their way into the marshes and their populations rose to over a million by the 1960s. I remembered when they were all over south Louisiana as roadkill. Not quite as abundant today, they have heavily impacted the native marsh grasses. Biologists have long understood that when the population of one organism becomes too great, it can affect other organisms and the ecology of the entire system can be changed. My nonscientific self does not always make the distinction between invasive and native species, and my admiration for any creature that can make it in the Louisiana marshes had to be extended to this adaptable rodent. As we finished the last quarter-mile of trail, we were escorted back to the parking area by barn swallows, swooping and dipping, catching the sunlight and flashing it around. It was hard to leave this enchanting wetland.

A short drive from Sabine NWR, the Holleyman Sheeley Bird Sanctuary near Johnson Bayou was a typical oak hammock with dense thickets of oaks, shrubs, and vines—but it was so full of mosquitoes, we could not stay long. We had hoped to see migrating warblers, but the minute we stopped to scan the thickets, hordes of mosquitoes clustered around us like a dark mist. We remained long enough to watch a group of traveling birders persistently (of course) identify a Cape May warbler and a blackpoll in the live oaks at the entrance to the trails.

Leaving the sanctuary, we drove the deserted coastal road to the Texas border, stopping occasionally to take photographs of the spider lilies (*Hymenocallis crassifolia*), the white bracted sedge (*Dichromena latifolia*), and the wild irises (*Iris tridentata*), called purple flags, that painted the ditches. Crossing Sabine Pass we pulled into the boat launch park and watched laughing gulls swoop around the shrimp boats. As the gulls circled the boats, I thought of the long 350-mile coast of Texas curving down into Mexico. From the Louisiana border to Matagorda Bay, the Columbian bottomlands are similar to the Atchafalaya Swamp, river floodplains of hardwoods. Beyond that, huge spans of salt marsh and flats with many wildlife refuges and preserves make up coastal Texas. Broken by the urban sprawl of Corpus Christi, the marshes stretch down to Brownsville and the Rio Grande. I remembered the green jays, the great kiskadees, and the scissor-tail flycatchers I had seen at the Laguna Atascosa and Santa Ana NWRs in the Rio Grande Valley, one of the best birding spots in the United States.

Making our way back to Holly Beach and on to Cameron, Louisiana, we caught the ferry and crossed the intracoastal canal. The car bounced onto the ferry along with dozens of other cars and trucks. Only inches separated ours from the other vehicles, as the crew crammed as many vehicles as possible onto the small boat. The ferry sped across the narrow canal, docked, and everyone rolled off. It took only a few minutes to actually cross the canal and seemed a lot of work that a bridge might alleviate. But then a new bridge might be blown away in a hurricane or might open up the area to too many people, and, well, we all know that story. I applauded the citizens of Cameron for their wisdom.

The town of Cameron is mostly docks for seafood markets and offshore drilling operations. The highway curved through town and a sign pointed east to Chenier Isle. Cheniers are like barrier islands, but instead of being offshore sand bars, they are onshore remnant beach ridges. For about two hundred miles between East Bay, Texas (around Galveston), and Vermillion Bay, Louisiana, more than a hundred of these ridges mold the coastline into what is called the Chenier Plain. The long, narrow, forested ridges, some no more than fifteen hundred feet wide, some thirty miles long, rise only a few feet above the marshes. Their vegetation much like that of barrier islands, provides stopover habitats for neotropical migrants. We spotted some of the same birds we had seen earlier at the oak hammock, but the armies of mosquitoes made the stop a short one.

North of Cameron, the Cameron Prarie NWR was a wetlands of lakes. The water at road level reflected the afternoon sun. It was like driving along a mirror. I had not remembered such huge expanses of water. A driving loop called the Pintail Drive encircled a large freshwater impoundment. Feeding in the shallows a flock of a dozen roseate spoonbills sieved the brown water collecting small fish and invertebrates. Glossy ibis, egrets, and tricolored herons fed alongside the spoonbills. In the drainage ditch, purple gallinules appeared and disappeared in the grasses, and common yellow throats flittered in the hedges of wax myrtle and marsh elder.

As the day ended and we headed back to Sulphur, I was surprised at how easy it was to get into the marsh. What once took us (graduate students doing fieldwork) hours by boat, took no more than a few minutes by car. That these wetlands were so accessible to the public was both wonderful and, at the same time, troublesome. To be able to get into the marsh so easily was convenient, but I wondered if such accessibility would lead to development. Roads almost always lead to development. Perhaps, with those awful mosquitoes, biting flies, the southern heat, and humidity, marshes would never be great tourist attractions. Most people think of marshes as places in need of drainage, and even avid nature lovers are sometimes reluctant to enter them. So maybe the road and the land's increasing accessibility would not lead to the inevitable habitat destruction by development. Yet the land is eroding because its soils are not being replenished. Someday these spectacular wetlands may be gone unless ways are found to recapture the river deposits.

The next spring another sentimental journey took me to the Cypress Island Preserve of Lake Martin. Between Lafayette and Breaux Bridge, the Nature Conservancy preserve is located in the largest bottomland hardwood forest in the country, the Atchafalaya Basin. It is probably the largest wading bird rookery in North America. The backwater swamp hosts twenty to thirty thousand pairs of breeding birds annually from February to July. Among the low leafless button bush and the bald cypress the birds were in their breeding plumage. It was an Easter parade of egrets, spoonbills, and herons. The great egrets were adorned with long plumes and green eye patches that looked like theatrical eyeliner. Their plumes draped down like lace shawls and when they posed, they transformed the branches into lace figurines. The cattle egrets with purple-rouge beaks, the little blue herons with fluorescent blue bills, and the anhingas with patches of sky on their bills were courting or building nests. It was bird biology like nothing I had ever seen.

Florida: The Coastal Bend

The Florida landscape takes on a drier appearance as it curves down towards the urban sprawls of Tampa, St. Petersburg, and Ft. Myers. This part of the coast, the forgotten coast, is known as the Big Bend and is still relatively pristine (but not for long). From St. Marks to north of Tampa, the coastline is essentially salt marshes, comprised of great spans of needle rush (*Juncus roemarianus*) and several species of *Spartina*. The uplands are pinelands. Unlike the Everglades, whose past history and place in American literature have made it a national landmark, the north and central regions of Florida are less well known. Almost everyone has heard of the Everglades and has read Marjory Stoneman Douglas's *The Everglades: River of Grass* (1947), but there are great writings about central and north Florida as well. Marjorie Kinnan Rawlings (1938) set her story *The Yearling* in the region and Edwin Way Teale (1963) in his first of the American Seasons series, *North with the Spring*, described his travels in the 1950s in this part of Florida. Another naturalist, Archie Carr, who spent his life studying the region, also wrote of its great beauty in *A Naturalist in Florida: A Celebration of Eden* (1994). Published in the 1990s, it is a natural history of the forgotten part of Florida. That he chose to write not just another bitter vanishing Eden treatise but to remember the world before the wild lands were transformed, has great nostalgic appeal.

A trip to St. Marks NWR, the small fishing village of Steinhatchee, and Cedar Key reminded me that there are places in Florida still untouched by the Disneyworld mentality. What makes the marshes of the Big Bend coast different from the marshes of Louisiana is that they are not alluvial soils. Rather than thick layers of sediment from river deposition, these marshes are thin layers of sediment overlaying limestone bedrock. Limestone dissolves easily and when the water table falls, sinkholes result. Hence, the region is also known as sinkhole country. Springs are common in the area and millions of gallons of freshwater flow through the limestone. Unlike the water of the Everglades that moves like a sheet over the surface of a limestone basin, in this region, surface water seeps down into the aquifer and moves through a complex lattice of underground caverns. When it surfaces from the labyrinth of limestone caves, springs result. Hundreds of springs dot the landscape and cave divers come from all over the world to explore these watery worlds.

A single road runs through St. Marks NWR, transects seven miles of wetlands, and ends at an old lighthouse. We spent the afternoon making our slow way to the end of the road. Water lily pads floated at the edges of the roadside ponds and a few white blossoms appeared. By May the entire surface of the ponds would be a meadow of spiky, white flowers. Beyond the water lilies and above the distant pines, two bald eagles made synchronized circles. Moore hens pecked at the pond edge inches away from still alligators. Any minute we expected to see one of them get swallowed whole. But no one got eaten and we moved on to the marshes near the lighthouse. While some of our birding group identified the multitude of shore birds feeding on the flats, I sat on a bench overlooking the *Spartina* meadow. The sun glared down and the smell of the warm marsh grew stronger. It smelled a little yeasty. I thought, how like the aroma of baking bread; from the dough of *Spartina* grass and the thick organic detritus, the marsh makes bread and there is always enough to eat. As a biologist, I know the food chain is a complex web and all the marsh creatures—the crabs, larval fishes, and a host of other vertebrates, invertebrates, and microorganisms—are all interconnected. Just as the creatures of the marsh, we are also involved with one another in such complex ways.

Leaving the refuge we reached Steinhatchee around dinnertime. Except for one convenience store, everything in town was locally owned. There were no McDonald's, no Holiday Inns, no BP gas stations. What a joy to eat in a restaurant that looked like no other restaurant in the world. What a pleasure to stay overnight in a place where the pictures on the walls were the drawings of the owner's cousin. What a treat to watch the lady who lived down the road clip the azalea bushes in the early morning light with a hedger that made no noise.

The next morning a walk through the salt marsh at the end of the road-that-goes-nowhere gave us seaside sparrows. Highway 361 out of Steinhatchee once connected Jena to Horseshoe Point, but a hurricane washed most of it away some years ago and now its remnant simply ends in the middle of the marsh. The marsh vegetation was similar to other salt marshes, but scattered among the *Juncus* and *Spartina* weathered limestone rocks emerged from the ground. They looked like gnomes awakening from an uncomfortable bed. How odd to walk on such solid ground through salt marsh grasses. A sparrow rose from the grass and lit on top of a thin reed. Swaying in the breeze, he threw back his head and belted out a song. With the accompaniment of the wind in the dry grass, the sparrow's song became an exquisite clarinet concerto and the marsh, a glorious symphony hall.

Cedar Key is the northernmost range of the tropical black mangrove (*Avicennia germinans*), and we drove all over the island looking for tropical birds. The island's vegetation reminded me of the Yucatan landscape. Someone else in the group was reminded of Key West in the 1950s, with its old buildings and tropical ambience, before it became too trendy. As the sun beat down and we sipped cold drinks under a shaded picnic table, I wondered if all the Gulf Coast shoreline would disappear into an urban mess. I knew this coastline was under siege and the sprawl of Tampa-St. Petersburg and Ft. Myers would soon reach here. The fact that the St. Joe Company had sold thousands of its timberlands to developers meant the eventual transformation of this sleepy coast into the homogenized plasticity of south Florida. The wildlife refuges and preserves would keep some of the coastline pristine, but much of it would disappear into houses, hotels, condos, Wal-Marts, McDonald's restaurants, golf courses, and car lots—all the stuff people wrongly refer to as development. Just as it had happened on the coast from Pensacola to Panama City, it would happen here. As I thought about the future, a huge lump formed in my throat and I felt a terrible sadness descend over me.

As I write about places on the Gulf Coast where I have hiked, birded, or simply retreated to in order to reclaim some sense of serenity, I realize they have one thing in common. They are mostly public lands, part of the great American public domain. Free of buildings and excessive roads, they are natural places of refuge and sanctuary. When I watch the nightly news and see the angst on the faces of the world's refugees, the traditional peoples of Peru and Bolivia, the peoples of Afghanistan and the Middle East, and all the many African tribes, I also see the faces of the Henslow's sparrow, the manatee, the whooping crane, the red-cockaded woodpecker, so many homeless species. In this context, the issue of the public domain becomes more than my personal needs for recreation or my spiritual renewal. It becomes a larger issue of a place for every creature. There must never be "no room at the inn" for any species. Unlike the human refugee camps, which are often places of severe deprivation to be left behind as soon as possible, wildlife refuges and preserves may be the only home left for some plants and animals. We must recognize this and expand our public lands for the purpose of preserving all species. I am most patriotic when I think of what the United States has done to create such refuges, preserves, and sanctuaries.

The arguments that we need to preserve biodiversity because we may find medicines in rain forest plants to cure cancer or valuable commercial products, or any of the many other reasons put forth by scientists that make our human economic future brighter, are relevant ones. But these egocentric arguments may not be the most important. How often in our history have such products been the driving force behind cruel exploitation and acts resulting in terrible pain and suffering? If we move ourselves out of the center and consider a broader perspective, we might understand that we must preserve the species of the world because we are all part of a common connection. We share a common origin; we share a common biochemical makeup; we have the same genes. That humans have some of the same genes as the bacteria *E. coli,* and use the same biochemistry to sustain life is a fact. That *E. coli* and humans are related may be harder to visualize, but it is not so hard to imagine this connection to other animals and plants. As the most able creature on Earth, we may have the responsibility to protect our more vulnerable relatives. Ensuring a place, a home, the right habitat for every creature may be our responsibility. Some would say, it is, perhaps, our redemption.

Home as Personal:
The Home Place, Florida

20

M Y HOUSE IS ALIVE WITH LIFE. From the gray fuzzy fungi on the shower door and the pink ring yeast that inhabit my toilets, to the window sills where doves construct fiddle-stick nests, to the algae on the brick walls that looks like the greening of old tree trunks, to the spiderwebs that tangle in the corners like string gone astray, to the occasional honeybee that appears mysteriously with its buzzy dance of obsession, to the doodle bugs that roll in, die, and dry up like tiny screws, to the occasional tree roach that dies with its boots on, feet straight up in the air, to the ants that bring in soil and build tunnels in my air conditioner, to the flies that pester no end with their in-your-face attitude, to the squirrels that scamper some nights in the attic as if they were ghosts of Christmas past, to the woodbine that climbs like a green ladder to the roof, to the wisteria that has taken over one side of the house and would dominate the world if it could. In truth, I love each one of them like selfish children and usually let them be until they cross the boundaries of civilized discourse. Only then do I take defensive action. It is a conversation that never ends, an argument that is never resolved.

My yard is a miniature botanical garden, a tiny preserve, a sanctuary, and a place of discovery. A rectangle, 65 by 135 feet, I think of it as a southern microcosm, and I have observed it like a field biologist. Although my management approach is minimalism, in my obsession with measurement, I have counted some of the species. Like an ecosystem succession, the species (some native, some international guests) keep changing over the years. My most recent inventory includes 1) trees: twenty water oaks of varying ages (plus hundreds of seedlings that sprout from acorns the squirrels bury), three cherry laurel, two red cedars, a dogwood, a camphor, two choke cherries, four ginkgos, thirteen red maples, a Satsuma, a

173

plum, and two southern magnolias (plus the occasional popcorn tree that gets removed because my fellow Florida Native Plant Society members consider it an invasive; 2) shrubs: fourteen camellias, ten junipers, five (nonnative) azaleas, three wax myrtles, three leatherleaf mahonia, two St. John's wort, five low bush blueberries, five Turk's cap mallow, and ten wax mallows, a colony of oak leaf hydrangea, four sweet olives, a wild and crazy wisteria, four American hollies, seventeen Florida anises, numerous blue daze, and a papyrus; 3) vines: wild grape, sweet briar, woodbine, ivy, and smilax, all too numerous to count; and 4) grasses that I can't even begin to count or identify but the shade keeps them sparse. I don't count the annuals because they change from year to year like classroom students.

I have watched them in the changing seasons. The maples and the woodbine turn the yard into New England in fall. Winter brings the camellia blooms with their red perfection. At the end of winter beneath the bushes, the red rings of petals brown and blend with the oak leaves, reminding me that perfection and order are temporary states. In March the oak trees lose their leaves and for about two weeks, it rains spoon leaves. The oak limbs are nearly bare for a couple weeks. Then almost overnight they leaf out in a meek green and then turn a solid, more confident green. With full spring the parade of southern flowers moves by with its marching bands of splashy white dogwood, frilly azaleas, buttermilk-white magnolias, and plumed oak leaf hydrangeas. By summer, the hot, humid, and buggy weather descends like a curse, and I retreat into the house until September.

The birds know my home. One spring a flock of cedar waxwings arrived mid-morning and rested the day beneath the leathery magnolia leaves. Another spring, hundreds of robins discovered the choke cherries and in a single afternoon stripped every black berry from the trees in a food frenzy. The driveway was spotted with quarter-size black grainy polka dots, the remains of undigested choke cherries. For years, the irascible wrens have wintered in the backyard. A pair of cardinals raised three chicks in the cedar, and the Carolina chickadees have evolved a feeding ritual that pops them in and out of the feeder like the firing of spark plugs. Last winter two hermit thrushes wintered at the back fence. Towhees and brown thrashers keep the oak leaves well tilled. Passerines have been a great crested flycatcher, red starts, indigo buntings, gold finches, a prothonotary warbler and a hooded warbler.

Not for me, the manicured monocultured green lawn, trimmed as a golf course, sterile as a swimming pool. I need real life around me and lots of it. I need to live with some understanding of the shortness of life, to be reminded of the small truths and the great truth of life, that death catches us all. Not for me, the plastic flowers on my grave. Give me the infinite variety of life-forms while I am alive and let me be part of them in death.

When I think of my worst fear, it is to be homeless. I have seen homeless women in the cities and feel a despair that almost immobilizes me. To live without a home is beyond comprehension. I have read that the homeless do have nests. They are just not like mine. And I imagine, what harsh boundaries their poverty imposes. That I might lose the capability to carry out the actions it takes to have a home frightens me more than just about anything. Yet I understand that a large number of the world's people live without homes and that many elderly people in the richest country on Earth live in spaces not even remotely like home called nursing homes. I know that a large number of the world's species have lost their homes (their habitats) and because of that, they have vanished. The reality of homelessness is beyond grief.

The tiny lot where I have lived for the last decade has given me such joy and such a sense of place. Perhaps it is always out of home that we grow into a broader sense of place. I remember those years long ago when I stood watching my mother cleaning up after the hunters wondering if I would travel, if I would have adventures, if I would be able to write stories other than those from the kitchen sink. The answer has been yes. Yet my stories come as much as from the kitchen sink and a sense of home as from the world beyond. Perhaps our best stories come from both places. How fortunate I am to have both a home and the means to move about in a broader world, to be developing a broader sense of place.

Bibliography

Abram, David. 1996. *The Spell of the Sensuous: Perception and Language in a More-Than-Human World*. New York: Random House.

Ackerman, Diane. 1991. *The Moon by Whale Light: And Other Adventures among Bats, Penguins, Crocodilians, and Whales*. New York: Random House.

———. 1995. *The Rarest of the Rare: Vanishing Animals, Timeless Worlds*. New York: Random House.

Alabama Coastal Birding Trail. n.d. www.alabamacoastalbirdingtrail.com (accessed March 26, 2004).

Alcock, John. 1985. *Sonoran Desert Spring*. Chicago: University of Chicago Press.

———. 1990. *Sonoran Desert Summer*. Tucson: University of Arizona Press.

Aston, John, and Edgar Sneed. 2004. King Ranch. *The Handbook of Texas Online* at www.tsha.utexas.edu/handbook/online/articles/view/KK/apk1.html (accessed March 30, 2004).

Benzing, David. 1990. *Vascular Epiphytes: General Biology and Related Biota*. Cambridge: Cambridge University Press.

Berry, Wendell. 2002. A Native Hill. In *The Art of the Common Place: The Agrarian Essays of Wendell Berry*, ed. Norman Wirzba, 3–31. Washington, D.C.: Counterpoint.

Bishop, Elizabeth. 1983. The Moose. In *The Complete Poems: 1927–1979*, 169–73. New York: Noonday Press.

Bowden, J. Earl. 1994. *Gulf Islands: The Sands of All Time: Preserving America's Largest National Seashore*. Washington, D.C.: Eastern National Park and Monument Association.

Brief History of the Hudson Bay Company. n.d. www.gov.mb.ca/chc/archives/hbca/about/the_bay.html (accessed March 30, 2004).

Carr, Archie. 1994. *A Naturalist in Florida: A Celebration of Eden*. New Haven, Conn.: Yale University Press.

Canopy Database Project. n.d. http://canopy.evergreen.edu (accessed March 30, 2004).

Canopy Tower. n.d. http://canopytower.com (accessed March 30, 2004).

Carroll, David. 2001. *Swampwalker's Journal: A Wetlands Year*. Boston: Houghton Mifflin.

Champion Trees. n.d. http://championtrees.org (accessed March 30, 2004).

Chatwin, Bruce. 1977. *In Patagonia*. New York: Summit Books.

Chester, Sharon R. 1995. *The Birds of Chile: A Field Guide*. San Mateo, Calif.: Wandering Albatross.

Clough, Marshall. 1998. *Mau Mau Memories: History, Memory and Politics*. Boulder, Colo.: Lynne Rienner.

Cokinos, Christopher. 2000. *Hope Is the Thing with Feathers: A Personal Chronicle of Vanished Birds*. New York: Tarcher/Putnam.

Deming, Alison Hawthorne. 1994. *Temporary Homelands: Essays on Nature, Spirit and Place*. New York: Picador.

Diaz-Bolio, Jose. 1971. *Guide to the Ruins of Chichen Itza*. Merida, Mexico: Maya Area.

Dietrich, William. 1992. *The Final Forest: The Battle for the Last Great Trees of the Pacific Northwest*. New York: Simon and Schuster.

Dinesen, Isak. 1952. *Out of Africa*. New York: Modern Library.

Dolin, Eric Jay, with photographers Karen and John Holllingsworth. 2003. *Smithsonian Book of National Wildlife Refuges*. Washington, D.C.: Smithsonian Institution Press.

Douglas, Marjory Stoneman. 1947. *The Everglades: River of Grass*. New York: Rinehart.

Duany, Andres, Elizabeth Plater-Zyberk, and Jeff Speck. 2000. *Suburban Nation: The Rise of Sprawl and the Decline of the American Dream*. New York: North Point Press.

Englebert, Victor. 2000. Last of the Llama Treks. *International Wildlife* 30 (3): 40–47.

Ewing, Reid, R. Pendall, and Dan Chen. 2002. *Measuring Sprawl and Its Impact: The Character and Consequences of Metropolitan Expansion*. Washington, D.C.: Smart Growth America.

Finkel, Mike. 1998. Queen of the Canopy. *Audubon* 100 (5): 32–34.

Florida Native Plant Society. n.d. www.fnps.org (accessed March 28, 2004).

Forsyth, Adrian. 1984. *Tropical Nature*. New York: Scribners.

Fossey, Diane. 1983. *Gorillas in the Mist*. New York: Houghton Mifflin.

Frost, Robert. 1969. *The Poetry of Robert Frost*. Ed. by E. C. Latham. New York: Holt, Rinehart, Winston.

Garay, Glades, and Oscar Guineo. 1997. *Torres del Paine: Flora and Mountains*. Punta Arenas, Chile: Don Bosco Institute Labs.

Goodall, Jane. 1971. *In the Shadow of Man*. Boston: Houghton Mifflin.

Gordon, Deborah. 1999. *Ants at Work: How an Insect Society Is Organized*. New York: Free Press.

Halpern, Sue. 2001. *Four Wings and a Prayer: Caught in the Mystery of the Monarch Butterfly*. New York: Pantheon Books.

Hanify, Mary L., and Craig Blencowe. 1977. *Guide to the Hoh Rain Forest*. Seattle: Pacific Northwest National Parks Association and Superior Publishing.

Hemingway, Ernest. 1936. *The Snows of Kilimanjaro; and Other Stories*. New York: Scribners.

Hogan, Linda. 1995. *Dwellings: A Spiritual History of the Living World*. New York: Simon and Schuster.

House, Adrian. 1993. *The Great Safari: The Life of George and Joy Adamson, Famous for Born Free*. New York: William Morris.

Hoyt, Erich. 1996. *The Earth Dwellers: Adventures in the Land of Ants*. New York: Simon and Schuster.

Hurd, Barbara. 2001. *Stirring the Mud: On Swamps, Bogs, and Human Imagination*. Boston: Beacon Press.

———. 2002. An Appetite for Blueberries. *Nature Conservancy* 52 (3): 48–49.

Hutten, Martin, Karen Hutten, and Andrea Woodward. n.d. *101 Common Mosses, Liverworts and Lichens of the Olympic Peninsula*. Washington, D.C.: National Parks Foundation.

Huxley, Elspeth. 1959. *The Flame Tree of Thika: Memories of an African Childhood*. New York: W. Morrow.

Jordan, William R., III. 2003. *The Sunflower Forest: Ecological Restoration and the New Communion with Nature*. Berkeley: University California Press.

Kaufman, Kenn. 2000. *Kingbird Highway: The Story of a Natural Obsession That Got a Little Out of Hand*. Boston: Houghton Mifflin.

Kimmerer, Robin Wall. 2003. *Gathering Moss: A Natural and Cultural History of Mosses*. Corvallis, Wash.: Oregon State University Press.

Kingsolver, Barbara. 1998. *The Poisonwood Bible*. New York: Harper Collins.

———. 2002. *Small Wonder*. New York: Harper Collins.

Leakey, Mary. 1984. *Disclosing the Past*. Garden City, N.Y.: Doubleday.

Leopold, Aldo. 2002. *A Sand County Almanac: With Essays on Conservation*. Reprint ed. Cambridge: Oxford University Press.

Lowman, Margaret. 1999. *Life in the Treetops: Adventures of a Woman in Field Biology*. New Haven, Conn.: Yale University Press.

Lyons, Betsy, Nalini Nadkarni, and Malcolm North. 2000. Spatial Distribution and Succession of Epiphytes on *Tsuga heterophylla* (Western Hemlock) in an Old-Growth Douglas Fir Forest. *Canadian Journal of Botany* 78 (7): 957–68.

Madson, John. 1995. *Where the Sky Began: Land of the Tallgrass Prairie*. Rev. ed. Ames: Iowa State University Press.

Manning, Richard. 1995. *Grassland: The History, Biology, Politics and Promise of the American Prairie*. New York: Viking Press.

Mansfield, Howard. 1993. *In the Memory House*. Golden, Colo.: Fulcrum Publishing.

Matthiessen, Peter. 2001. *The Birds of Heaven: Travels with Cranes*. New York: North Point Press.

Markham, Beryl. 1983. *West of the Night*. New York: North Point Press.

McEwan, Colin, Luis A. Borrero, and Alfred Prieto, eds. 1997. *Patagonia: Natural History, Prehistory, and Ethnography at the Uttermost End of the Earth*. Princeton, N.J.: Princeton University Press.

Miles, Rosalind. 1989. *The Women's History of the World*. New York: Harper and Row.

Minter, D. W., P. F. Cannon, and H. L. Peredo. 1987. South American Species of Cyttaria: A Remarkable and Beautiful Group of Edible Ascomyetes. *Mycologist* 21:7–11.

Mitchell, John G. 2001. The American Dream: Urban Sprawl. *National Geographic* (July): 48–73.

Moon, William Least Heat. 1991. *Prairyearth: A Deep Map*. Boston: Houghton Mifflin.

Morrisson, Reg. 1999. *The Spirit in the Gene: Humanity's Proud Illusion and the Laws of Nature*. Ithaca, N.Y.: Cornell University Press.

Moore, Kathleen Dean. 1995. *Riverwalking: Reflections on Moving Waters*. New York: Harcourt Brace.

Nabhan, Gary Paul. 2002. *The Desert Smells Like Rain: A Naturalist in O'odham Country*. Reprint ed. Tucson: University of Arizona Press.

Nadkarni, Nalini, and Nathaniel Wheelwright, eds. 2000. *Monteverde: Ecology and Conservation of a Tropical Cloud Forest*. London: Oxford University Press.

Nelson, Reed. 1964. *The Caste War of Yucatan*. Stanford, Calif.: Stanford University Press.

Neruda, Pablo. 1991. *The Book of Questions*. Port Townsend, Wash.: Copper Canyon Press.

———. 1998. Solitudes. *Neruda at Isla Negra*. Fredonia, N.Y.: White Pine Press.

O'Connor, Irene. 1962. *An Introduction to Quinalt Valley Rain Forest*. Published by author.

Orlean, Susan. 1998. *The Orchid Thief*. New York: Ballantine Books.

Peterson, Brenda. 2001. Killing Our Elders. In *The Sweet Breathing of Plants*, ed. Linda Hogan and Brenda Peterson, 238–43. New York: North Point Press.

Plath, Sylvia. 1981. Mushrooms. In *The Collected Poems*, 139–40. New York: Harper and Row.

Pollan, Michael. 2001. *The Botany of Desire: A Plant's-Eye View of the World*. New York: Random House.

Pyle, Robert. 1999. *Chasing Monarchs: Migrating with the Butterflies of Passage*. Boston: Houghton Mifflin.

Ray, Jannise. 1999. *Ecology of a Cracker Childhood*. Minneapolis, Minn.: Milkweed Editions.

Rawlings, Marjorie Kinnan. 1938. *The Yearling*. New York: Scribners.

Record Trees in Olympic National Park. n.d. *National Park Service*. www.nps.gov/olym/edtrees.htm (accessed April 2, 2004).

Reinking, Dan. 2002. A Closer Look: Henslow's Sparrow. *Birding* 34 (1): 147–53.

Riley, Laura, and William Riley. 1992. *Guide to the National Wildlife Refuges*. New York: Colliers.

Roach, Mary. 2001. Tuxedo Junction. *Discover* 22 (7): 54–62.

Roads, Michael. 2002. The Spirit of the Forest. In *The Soul Unearthed: Celebrating Wilderness and Spiritual Renewal through Nature*. Rev. ed., ed. Cass Adams, 19–23. Boulder, Colo.: Sentient Publications.

Rundel, P. W., M. O. Dillion, B. Palma, H. A. Mooney, S. L. Gulmon, and J. R. Ehleringer. 1991. The Phytogeography and Ecology of the Coastal Atacama and Peruvian Deserts. *Aliso* 13 (1): 1–49.

Russell, Sharman Apt. 2003. *An Obsession with Butterflies: Our Long Love Affair with a Singular Insect*. Cambridge, Mass.: Perseus Publishing.

Sagaris, Lake. 2000. *Bone and Dream: Into the World's Driest Desert*. New York: Alfred A. Knopf.

Safe Harbor. n.d. http//northflorida.fws.gov/safeharbor.htm (accessed March 30, 2004).

Schueler, Don. 1996. *A Handmade Wilderness: How an Unlikely Pair Saved the Least Worst Land in Mississippi*. Boston: Houghton Mifflin.

Shoumatoff, Alex. 1978. *The Rivers Amazon*. San Francisco: Sierra Club Books.

Skutch, Alexander. 1971. *A Naturalist in Costa Rica*. Gainesville: University of Florida Press.

Southern Pines Ecosystem Projects. n.d. www.sagecouncil.com/safeharbor.html (accessed March 30, 2004).

Sternberg, Guy, and Jim Wilson. 1995. *Landscaping with Native Trees: Northeast, Midwest, and Southeast Edition*. Shelburne, Vt.: Chapters Publishing.

Stevens, William K. 1995. *Miracle under the Oaks: The Revival of Nature in America*. New York: Simon and Schuster.

Teal, John, and Mildred Teal. 1969. *Life and Death of the Salt Marsh*. New York: Ballantine.

Teale, Edwin Way. 1963. *North with the Spring: A Naturalist's Record of a 17,000-Mile Journey with the North American Spring*. New York: Dodd, Mead.

Theroux, Paul. 1979. *The Old Patagonia Express: By Train through the Americas*. Boston: Houghton Mifflin.

Tibbetts, John. 2002. The Freeway City. *Coastal Heritage* 17 (3): 3–13.

Tidwell, Mike. 2003. *Bayou Farewell: The Rich Life and Tragic Death of Louisiana's Cajun Coast*. New York: Pantheon Books.

Todd, Kim. 2001. *Tinkering with Eden: A Natural History of Exotics in America*. New York: Norton.

Wallace, Marianne. 2001. *America's Prairies and Grasslands: Guide to Plants and Animals*. New York: Fulcrum Resources.

Wallis, Velma. 1993. *Two Old Women: An Alaska Legend of Betrayal, Courage and Survival*. Fairbanks, Alaska: Epicenter Press.

Weidensaul, Scott. 1999. *Living on the Wind: Across the Hemisphere with Migratory Birds*. New York: North Point Press.

———. 2002. *The Ghost with Trembling Wings: Science, Wishful Thinking, and the Search for Lost Species*. New York: North Point Press.

Welty, Eudora. 1979. Some Notes on River Country. In *The Eye of the Story: Selected Essays and Reviews*, 286–99. New York: Random House.

Whitten, T., R. E. Soeriaatmadja, and S. A. Afiff. 1997. *The Ecology of Java and Bali*. Vol. 2 of *The Ecology of Indonesia Series*. Berkley: University of California.

Willard, Nancy. 1989. The Hardware Store as Proof of the Existence of God. In *Water Walker*, 16. New York: Alfred A. Knopf.

Willock, Colin. 1974. *Africa's Rift Valley*. Amsterdam: Time Life International.

Wilcove, David. 2002. The Price of an Owl. *Living Bird* 21 (4): 6–7.

Wilson, E. O. 2002. *The Future of Life*. New York: Alfred A. Knopf.

WWF. 2001. *A Biodiversity Vision for the Valdivian Temperate Rain Forest Ecosystem*. Washington, D.C.: World Wildlife Fund. Available at www.worldwildlife.org/wildworld/profiles/terrestrial/nt/nt0404_full.html (accessed March 30, 2004).

Ziewitz, Kathryn, and Jane Wiaz. 2004. *Green Empire: The St. Joe Company and the Remaking of Florida*. Gainesville: University Press of Florida.

General Travel Guides

Bernhardson, Wayne. 1999. *Lonely Planet: Argentina, Uruguay, and Paraguay*. Oakland, Calif.: Lonely Planet.

Bernhrardson, Wayne, and Alan Samagalski. 2000. *Lonely Planet: Chile and Easter Island*. Oakland, Calif.: Lonely Planet.

Doggett, Scott. 2001. *Lonely Planet: Panama*. 2nd ed. Oakland, Calif.: Lonely Planet.

Fodor's 96 Mexico. 1995. New York: Fodor's Travel Publications.

Fodor's Kenya and Tanzania. 1992. New York: Fodor's Travel Publications.

Indonesia, Malaysia and Singapore Handbook. 1994. Chicago: Passport Books.

Insight Guide: Chile. 1999. New York: Langenscheidt Publishers.

Rachowiecki, Rob. 1994. *Lonely Planet: Costa Rica*. Oakland, Calif.: Lonely Planet.

Williams, J. G. 1967. *A Field Guide to the National Parks of East Africa*. London: Collins.

Index

About the Author

Mary A. Hood taught microbiology and conducted research in microbial ecology at the University of West Florida in Pensacola. She served as poet laureate for the West Florida–Pensacola region. She has authored numerous scientific and technical articles, and published a number of poems as well as a collection of poems.